DANCES with WAVES

Around Ireland by Kayak

To Horst with Best wishes

Brian Wilson

1999

'Paddle well, Paddle far'

BRIAN WILSON is a well-known and respected member of the British canoeing scene, specialising in extended sea-kayaking expeditions and adventure travel. He graduated from Edinburgh University with a degree in philosophy in 1984, and won the Scottish Superstars competition in the same year, as well as twice becoming British Universities Judo Champion.

Having worked with many of the major Scottish conservation and environmental organisations, Brian is now a freelance environmental contractor specialising in traditional stonework, thatching and vernacular building conservation.

Brian lives by the sea in Ullapool in northwest Scotland with his French partner Marie-Pierre and daughters Malin — named after the stormy but beautiful seas of Malin off the northern coast of Ireland — and Manon. Among his greatest pleasures are unspoilt coastlines, blazing driftwood fires and good books; and among his ambitions are paddling, burning and reading — and perhaps writing — his way along many more of the world's finest shores, not necessarily alone. His previous book, *Blazing Paddles*, is an account of his 1,800 mile journey around the coast of Scotland.

What they said about *Blazing Paddles*,
Brian Wilson's account of his 1,800 mile
journey along the Scottish coast.

'... As good a maritime saga as has come out of the Scottish seas ...
There is a hilarious account of a sojurn on Soay; and of a play
session with a killer whale! ... He makes diversions into history and
myths; navigational and environmental matters; fine descriptions of
seabirds and animals, and the incomparable coasts ... He has been
touched with the splendour of a great idea carried out.

Sir Alastair Dunnet, SCOTSMAN

'... Without doubt the best sea canoeing travel book
I have ever read.'

CANOEIST Magazine

'A quite exceptionally gifted writer ... A sense of humour and a
strong dash of poetry and romanticism ... This is an outstanding
travel book, right outside the run of ordinary sports writing.'

JERSEY EVENING POST

'Much bigger than a story of adventure, and streaks ahead
of a nautical log.'

Richard Crane, Traveller and Adventurer

'I don't know whether the adventure itself or the story of it deserves
the greater admiration; the combination strikes me as a triumph –
which I hope will have many successors.'

BBC RADIO 4 (on which *Blazing Paddles* was
serialised for 'A Book at Bedtime')

DANCES *with* WAVES

Around Ireland by Kayak

Brian Wilson

THE O'BRIEN PRESS
DUBLIN
IRISH AMERICAN BOOK COMPANY (IABC)
BOULDER, COLORADO

First published 1998 by The O'Brien Press Ltd.,
20 Victoria Road, Rathgar, Dublin 6, Ireland.
Tel. +353 1 4923333; Fax, +353 1 4922777
email: books@obrien.ie
website: http://www.obrien.ie

Published in the US and Canada by the
Irish American Book Company (IABC)
6309 Monarch Park Place, Suite 101,
Niwot, Colorado 80503
Office: Tel. 303-652-2710; Fax. 303-652-2689
Orders: Tel. 800-452-7115; Fax. 800-401-9705

ISBN: 0-86278-551-0

British Library Cataloguing-in-Publication Data

1 2 3 4 5 6 7 8 9 10
98 99 00 01 02 03 04 05 06 07

The O'Brien Press receives
assistance from

The Arts Council
An Chomhairle Ealaíon

Typesetting, layout, design: The O'Brien Press Ltd.
Cover photograph: Woody Woodworth, supplied by SuperStock
Maps: David Langworth
Cover separations: Lithoset Ltd.
Printing: Guernsey Press Co. Ltd.

~ CONTENTS ~

~ ACKNOWLEDGEMENTS ~

I could have completed neither the Irish journey nor this book were it not for the love, support and freedom provided by my partner Marie-Pierre. Thanks M-P!

With special thanks to:
Barbara Wallace, Barbara Nolan, Jack O'Sullivan, Deirdre O'Sullivan, Don and Anne Curtin, Gerry Sheridan, Jackie Keogh, Vince MacDowell, Brian and Maureen Fryer-Kelsey, Maura and Ronan Grady, Douglas MacDonald, Iain MacAulay, Richard Crane, Kenneth White, Mary Wilson, Edinburgh University, Department of Celtic Studies, Dublin University, Department of Irish Folklore, Howth Yacht Club, Royal Yacht Club, Dunmore East Yacht Club.

Also for sponsorship support:
Sola Lenses, McNulty Seaglass, WildWater Equipment, Lendal Paddles, Damart Clothing, North Cape, The Ordnance Survey Office of Ireland.

The publisher wishes to thank the following for permission to reproduce photographs in this book: Pierre Claret – Seven Heads Bay and Sherkin Island; John White – underwater shot of Fungie the Dolphin. For permission to quote the following song and verse extracts: page 175 'St Brendan's Voyage' by Christy Moore/Bal Music; page 217 'Song for Ireland' by Phil Colclough/Bucks Music; and a special thanks to Kenneth White for permission to use so many extracts from his work.

For Malin and Manon
May the waves dance gently with you

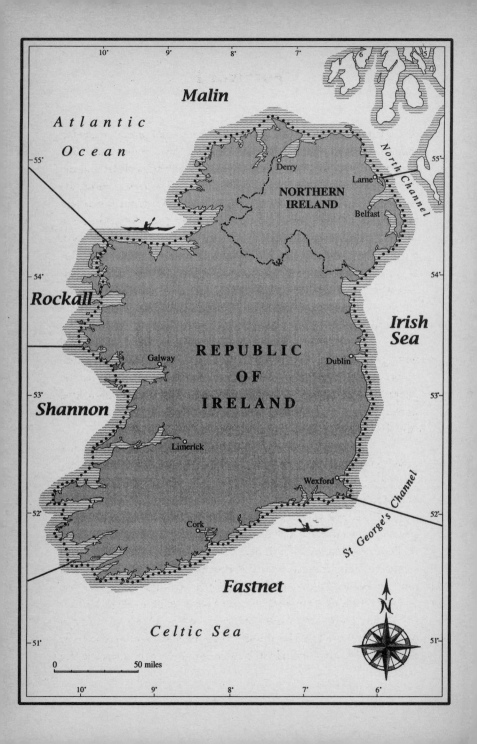

Foreword

A sea kayak can offer a special view of the ocean and its changing moods. No other vessel brings the sea-going traveller into quite such intimate contact with the saltwater; it nuzzles or slaps all around the needle hull in which the occupant sits, only head and torso above the level of the surrounding water, while the messages of the waves and currents are constantly transmitted through the shivering and flexing of the vessel's skin. The kayaker's viewpoint, I have always thought, must be somewhat similar to that of an inquisitive seal as he lifts his slick head above the water and gazes at the shore. The horizon, so low that it is frequently blotted out by the gentlest wave, sinks into the intervening trough until the next wave or swell lifts the viewpoint – and suddenly the coastline spreads out again before the view.

By paddling round the coast of Ireland in his kayak, and writing about what he saw over the backs of the waves or as he comes ashore to rest or re-supply, Brian Wilson gives us a glimpse of what the people and places are like, and how they reacted to this salt-stained nomad who comes sluicing up out of the sea, or is discovered stretched out and exhausted in the lee of a harbour slipway.

This is a surprisingly varied tale. After all the Irish coast is a fairly well-charted and often-photographed repetition of cliffs, rocks, headlands, beaches, strands, bays, all subject to that quirky mixture of rain, sunshine, calms and gales which characterises the North Atlantic summer. Yet when seen from a kayak, bobbing among the waves, and given a perspective that includes the additional contours of history and tradition, all manner of fresh detail emerges. In some places the sea wanderer finds an intriguing overlap between Celtic mythology and modern oceanographic science. In other localities he has close encounters with maritime wildlife. Excited and incontinent gannets of the Skelligs splatter him with excrement, and off Dingle his meeting with Fungie the dolphin is a delight. The exuberant dolphin repeatedly pays him the acrobatic compliments due from one energetic sea mammal to another, and the lone kayaker feels very privileged.

Brian Wilson deserves our respect as well as Fungie's, because his long and often arduous solo journey, undertaken in 1990, was neither a stunt nor a self-imposed ordeal of the sort which has later to be justified by a book. His story is a record of observation, not self justification; the difficulties and discomforts are kept in the background, and the sights and human incidents are what matter. In his great circuit, which took him through the entire litany of the Shipping Forecast – Irish Sea, Fastnet, Shannon, Rockall and Malin – Brian Wilson met kindly, helpful and supportive men and women. His favourable reception tells us something about Wilson himself: the determined, persevering and modest Scotsman brought out the best in his Irish hosts.

Occasionally there are warnings. The kayaker must dip his paddle blades in the floating sewage which fouls several parts of the Irish Sea coast; and off Mizen Head the physical strain and strange light combine to create the image of a ghost galleon sailing out of history. But in general this is a book as down-to-earth as any can be that is essentially sea-borne, and many readers will recognise their favourite stretch of shoreline, from Dublin Bay to Dingle and beyond, and want to compare it with their own experience. With humour and a sense of humanity Brian Wilson escorts his reader into the nooks and crannies of the Irish coast, and he succeeds in giving an entirely new meaning to the phrase 'peripheral vision'.

Tim Severin
Co Cork

IRISH SEA

~ *Larne to Carnsore Point* ~

202 miles

NORTHERN
IRELAND

ANTRIM

Larne

Island Magee

North Channel

Belfast Lough

Belfast

Ards Peninsula

DOWN

Strangford Lough

Portaferry

Mourne Mountains

Ardglass

Killard Point

Newcastle

St John's Point

Slieve Gullion

Shieve Donard

Dundrum Bay

Kilkeel

Annalong

Dundalk

Carlingford Lough

LOUTH

Dundalk Bay

Dunany Point

Clogher Head

Drogheda

Laytown

MEATH

Skerries

R. Boyne

Lambay I.

Ireland's Eye

Howth

R. Liffey

Dublin

Dalkey

WICKLOW

Bray

The Wicklow Hills

Wicklow

Wicklow Head

R. Avoca

WEXFORD

Arklow

Courtown

R. Slaney

Cahore Point

The Raven Point

Wexford

Wexford Harbour

Rosslare

Greenore Point

Tuskar Rock

Carnsore Point

tonn Rudhraighe

Irish
Sea

N

0   5   10 15 20   25 miles

7'   6'   5'

54'   54'

53'   53'

CHAPTER 1

Rising Damp

Now I shall take my boat again
and row out through the grey rain
to the cold salt blaze of the sun
I shall rock out there in the loneliness
the silence that is no man's business
Till the winds open and let me pass
to the sudden crying of a hundred gulls.

'At the Great Gate', Kenneth White

Never fall asleep below the high-water mark. It ought to be the first rule of the coastal traveller; yet I watched drowsily, dispassionately, from my tent on the saltmarsh, as the wind-driven surges of a spring tide reached the ragged line of debris that marked its previous limit. It paused only briefly to collect its strength, then swelled even higher, blackening the lichens and leaving the exposed stone looking like wet denim. Soon the rain was falling so hard, and the tide rising so fast, that it seemed I was in at least as much danger of drowning tonight on the Irish coast as I had been during a full day at sea.

For three days the kayak had struggled southwards against winds verging on gale force. From the port of Larne in county Antrim, down the coast of Island Magee, across Belfast Lough and round the crooked arm of the Ards peninsula, the wind and rain had hardly let up for a moment. The Irish Sea, a shallow grey basin, wide-filled with wind-whipped waves, had protested against every paddle stroke of southward progress, sending backward tides, gusty headwinds and great green waves of drenching water to trouble my route.

Earlier that evening I had splashed ashore at Tara Bay, north of Portaferry, wet through, and chilled to the bone. My skin felt like congealed lard, and my feet, wet since morning, squelched soggily in my sea-shoes when I moved. From my sodden hair, and the strained skin of my brow, salty water ran down over my eyes and lips, stinging like neat iodine. Glad at least to be on land, I had quickly pitched the little tent well above the high-water mark of the day before, and slumped into my sleeping bag. But with over an hour still to go before full tide, the sea had already reached a rock just three feet in front of the tent, and a briny saltmarsh dampness was seeping in through the groundsheet. Backed by the strengthening gale, the rowdy tideline continued to advance, brim-full of organic wreckage, broken seaweed and driftwood.

Heavy with fatigue, I watched lazily as the sea inched closer and closer. Finally my nerves got the better of my lethargy, and an action threshold was reached. In bare feet and shorts, I scrambled onto the spongy grass, bundled my camp into a dripping portable mass, and waddled inland in search of a higher, drier patch. By the time I had slipped twice, hopped over a barbed-wire fence and re-pitched the tent in the rain and darkness in a field generously littered with cowpats, I was just as wet and filthy as if the tide had come right in the front door.

It was a long, miserable, fourth-of-July night: huddled damp and shivering in the tent while the rain rattled over in noisy assaults. Beyond the saltmarsh the sea roared ominously on the skerries, and a mist of grey pessimism filled my sleepless mind. I was in fact due to paddle nonchalantly up the Liffey into a press and sponsorship conference in Dublin – a full hundred miles away across the Irish border – by noon the next day. But in three exhausting days I'd done a mere forty-two miles, along what I'd hoped would be the easiest section of the Irish coast. That hundred miles might just as well have been a thousand! And how long was it going to take to paddle *twelve* hundred miles round the entire coast of Ireland, with all the tide races, exposed capes and Atlantic swells I'd meet along the way? At that moment the whole project seemed like a crazy

fantasy: too long, too dangerous and too wet; and the very purpose
of it all began to seem rather obscure. I had only two hopes. The
first, for a break in the weather – perhaps even the briefest
appearance of the elusive Irish summer – was quickly dashed as the
midnight shipping forecast reeled off a clockwise rosary of gale
warnings for the Irish coast – Fastnet, Shannon Rockall, Malin –
and added the qualification 'imminent' to the gloomy prediction for
Irish Sea.

The second hope was simply that my present run of negative
feelings would turn out to be a temporary dip, rather than a steady
downward spiral. There was a large element of *déjà vu* in lying
frustrated and despondent in a tent, hostage to weather and mood,
with depressions dominating both. These very same emotions had
surfaced during a previous solo kayak journey round Scotland five
years earlier, when I had been gale-bait for four months on end, and
I remembered them well; they were as predictable, or as changeable,
as the weather itself. Most importantly I knew that a break from a
period of foul weather would almost always be accompanied by a
lighter, more positive mood, which in turn would be reinforced by
the chance to re-establish the natural rhythms of travel, discovery
and all the aspirations of the journey. It was stagnation, more than
just the weather itself, which tended to bring my spirits down.

There is nothing quite like a cold sodden night in a squalid
tent for encouraging a thorough critical appraisal of one's place in
the universal scheme of things. Inevitably it starts off with an
anti-philosophical meditation along the lines of 'What in the name
of Larry have I done to deserve this?' But eventually, as the mind
wanders back along the familiar pathways of plans, aspirations,
motivations and past experiences, you find yourself rediscovering
the very reasons why that soggy tent on that particular waterlogged
patch of the earth's surface, however perverse it may seem at the
time, is perhaps exactly where you needed to be, had planned to be,
and even, in some strange way, enjoyed being. As the night drizzled
on the same patterns of thought which had led me to give up a

full-time job and take temporary leave of my home in Scotland and my girlfriend Marie-Pierre in an attempt to paddle a kayak around the coast of Ireland, began to replay themselves like a long-lost familiar music tape.

'My name is Brian, and I am a shoreaholic.' I think perhaps I have always loved coastlines more than any other single manifestation of the earth's physiognomy, and when it comes to matters littoral, all thoughts of profit, career or conformity desert me entirely. By my reckoning, to be by the shore is to be near some of the richest concentrations of wildlife, the most generous sources of free food – and driftwood on which to cook it – and the most practical travel options which this planet has to offer. It is not by coincidence alone that our ancestors colonised these northern lands by way of water; for wind, wave and current offer a free ride to the canny wanderer; and coastlines tend to lure the eye, and eventually the boat, always over the next horizon. To me the coast holds all the magic and more that others may find in a cathedral, a rainbow, a tranquil lake or a mountain skyline; piers, harbours and lighthouses are among my favourite forms of human architecture, and scenery always seems somehow incomplete without an element of seascape in it. My idea of luxury is a driftwood fire on a sheltered beach; and to paddle a kayak along an unfamiliar coastline, exploring, spacing out the days, beaching in the brine, is as compulsive an activity as I ever came across.

Perhaps it is simply that I grew up in Scotland, some of whose western seascapes are the equal of any in the world, but I fear that even the most objective review of my life and interests would reveal an abnormal fascination, almost an obsession, with the sea and coast. As a part-time postal worker at the age of twenty, for instance, I would drive like a maniac round the streets of Aberdeen, collecting parcels at breakneck speed and emptying mailboxes in record times, just to be able to spend ten minutes of each collection-round parked on the Aberdeen seafront, dreaming of coastal journeys and gazing out across the North Sea towards

Norway like a love-struck teenager. Even as a student I was always immeasurably happier on sea-kayak trips around the Scottish Hebridean islands than at any pub gathering, dinner party or night-club, and the first thing I did after graduating was to disappear for four months on a mammoth journey eighteen hundred miles around the coast of Scotland. That trip at the age of twenty-two had been a real in-at-the-deep-end experience, from which I learned many of the practical realities of extended coastal travel: not only the subtle patterns of danger that lurk among swell and tide, and the incredible beauty of the shore in all her moods, but also the addictive, bittersweet experience of travelling alone.

After the Scottish journey, and the writing of *Blazing Paddles* – my account of the adventures of a wandering kayak – I settled into the first of a series of challenging and very enjoyable jobs in conservation and environmental protection which fully occupied my time and energy over the next five years. Perhaps it was because much of my work – as a countryside ranger on the Aberdeenshire coast, a wildlife warden on the western seaboard of Argyll, and a conservation field officer ranging widely throughout the whole of Scotland – kept me in regular contact with the coast and islands, that I was able to ignore for a time my obsession with coastal travel. But, like any other addiction, it was always there, lurking and simmering only inches beneath an otherwise calm and rational outward appearance, and I knew that one day I would have to indulge it again.

It almost got the upperhand one year when I travelled to the Irish National Coastal Communities Conference in the idyllic village of Allihies, West Cork. There I met a range of fascinating characters, including Mary Robinson who went on to become Ireland's first woman president; and I sat outside drinking Murphy's Stout, listening to fiddlers play, talking about the coast with fish farmers and lobster ranchers as the sun sank beyond the Skellig Rocks and the Atlantic horizon. On that occasion, with the smell of salt air still in my nostrils I returned dutifully to Edinburgh.

But several months later, when the organisation for which I worked began to devote more energy to developing team-building exercises, time-management courses and mission statements than to practical conservation, I decided it was time for me to get back in touch with the strongest currents in my life, and to renew acquaintance with the shore. I wanted to be able to plan my days in accordance with tide and weather instead of corporate ideals and productivity targets. What I needed more than anything in the world was a decent fix: nothing less than a continuous, self-contained voyage round a small country with a fascinating coastline; above all I longed to push off from an unfamiliar beach with an empty diary and a fully laden kayak. I handed in my notice at work, and immediately began to make serious preparation; the physical training, equipment gathering, sponsorship hunting and route research that are the precursors of a long journey.

But *where* to go? Despite occasional forays into warmer climes such as Morocco, Sardinia or the Greek islands, I have always been strongly drawn back to the northern and western corners of Europe, those boreal and Atlantic regions where the vagaries of the climate, the unpredictability of the seasons and the occasionally frightening manifestations of wind, wave and tide are (in most cases) more than compensated for by the variety of Atlantic seascapes, the magic of the northern light, long stretches of pristine coastline, and colourful pockets of hospitable humankind who still manage to coax a living from the uncompromising sea. If you go far enough north and west in Europe, you come upon one final shore before the great Atlantic: one last frontier between the continental landmass and the mighty ocean. Here two thousand miles of rugged coastline, great bays and a scattering of offshore islands rub up against some of the most active tidal streams and the most powerful ocean swells in the northern hemisphere, creating a convoluted, mountainous perimeter which ranks among the world's most superlative seascapes. That shore is Ireland; and it was to Ireland, I realised, more than anywhere else in the world, that I wanted to take my coast-hungry kayak.

One important plus of a circumnavigation is that it is much easier to describe to the layman than nebulous ideas about the esoteric appeal of extended coastal wanderings. It is every bit as concise and pictorial a concept as an attempt to scale a mountain or cross an ocean. It is easy to explain, simple to summarise, and yet can be made to sound sufficiently heroic and daring when the need arises. A circumnavigation is therefore the type of journey which lends itself perfectly to the unholy trinity so revered by penniless expeditioners: sponsorship, publicity and fundraising.

I began in the usual way by writing with glowing details of my circumnavigation plans to all the large companies that one would associate immediately with Ireland. Then, as I waited for a tide of cheque-filled envelopes and encouraging replies, I concentrated on gradually increasing my training in fitness and technique, running and kayaking for several hours most days along Edinburgh's Union Canal. Weeks passed, but although there was a steady improvement in my fitness level there was nothing, not a nibble, from any of the big fish in the sponsorship pond. With a second draft and mailshot I cast my net a little wider, contacting any and every company I could think of with even the most tenuous of links with Ireland. Another couple of weeks went by in which I continued to get stronger and faster on the canal, and to run gradually out of postage stamps and sponsorship ideas. Several equipment manufacturers sent me essential kayaking gear, including paddles, spraydecks, waterproof storage bags and so on, simultaneously boosting my confidence and relieving expeditions funds a little; but summer was almost upon me, and as yet I still had no major sponsor.

Knowing that it is sometimes the vaguest and least likely of connections that proves most fruitful, I tried a little desperate lateral thinking: I'd be travelling by kayak; the kayak was made of glass reinforced plastic or fibreglass; fibreglass is one of the most ubiquitous construction materials in the modern world; why not look into some of the multinational companies with interests in the international fibreglass market? Even after the briefest research many leads seemed to point to the Pilkington group of companies. Working backwards then led me to Pilkington Visioncare, one of the world's leading optical equipment businesses, and eventually to one of its subsidiaries, Sola Lenses in county Wexford in Ireland.

It was the very epitome of a long shot, I thought as I wrote to Sola outlining my proposal to paddle the Irish coast, but through a stroke of sheer luck and timing it paid off. At that very same time they were looking for a novel, high profile means to promote the newly established Eyebank Ireland charity, and it was an opportunity that we could all relate to. They saw in my journey both a mobile publicity vehicle and an ongoing event which could be twinned with a land-based fundraising campaign; and in one fell swoop I had adopted both a major sponsor who would underwrite the costs of the journey, and an innovative charitable cause with which I could fully sympathise. A promotional partnership was formed, agreements signed and meetings swiftly arranged.

It seemed hard to believe that within one month of joining forces with Sola I had taken my first tentative paddle strokes into the gale-lashed Irish Sea and now, only three nights later, I was lying alone in a dripping tent trying to remember exactly how it had all come about. At last, with the sudden feeling that in fact I'd travelled a route far longer and more convoluted than those forty-odd Irish Sea miles would suggest and, with the renewed conviction that this was indeed where I wanted to be, I listened more tolerantly to the ranting breakers on the shore and fell eventually into a deep sleep.

~ ~ ~

Next morning, with a severe gale – force nine – forecast, there was no choice but to stay firmly on land. I walked over the steep lanes of lovely county Down until I came to the village of Portaferry on the tidal narrows of Strangford Lough and phoned Dublin to warn them that I was running well behind schedule.

'Sure that's no problem at all,' said the reassuring voice of Carmel from the public relations company. 'Where are you now anyway? *Port-a-ferry*? Well, that's not on our map here, but just stay put and we'll arrange a van to pick you up at five o'clock.'

That left enough time for a quick pint, and the *craic* at the little pub was enough to restore anyone's flagging spirits.

'Goin' round the country in a canoe, eh? Well, amn't I just after reading something about that in the paper!' said Bertie Bailey, a small, stocky, bristly man; a voluble badger, talking so thick and fast that it was difficult for anybody else to squeeze a word in. 'Oh surely, if you're havin' another pint I'll join you ... Guinness, if you please.

'Now, tides, tides is the thing. You'd have to know all about the tides round here I'd say. *Fierce* tides we have in the narrows there; worst waters in the British Isles, some say. Aye, they fairly tear into the lough – many a boat's gone down into that and never came up again! Ye know, they were after thinkin' of puttin' in a sort of a power-station thing to use up the tides there, so they were. Fuckin' stupid idea! Sure, haven't we got enough bloody electricity without we go fishin' more of it up out of the sea?

'By the way, 'twas the tide itself that washed ould Saint Patrick in here in his little boat, and dumped him at the mouth of the river. That would be in the year of *four hundred and thirty-two*.' He spoke as though he remembered it personally. Somehow Bertie had managed to drain his pint without compromising his monologue; so I bought him another, and used it as a foot in the door to ask him about the wildlife of the lough.

'Oh the *cratures*!' he said. 'Jeez, you'd see some sights from that canoe of yours. Oh aye, you can't beat the Strangford Lough for the ould sea cratures. All kinds of strange beasts there are. Some of them friendly enough, and others – well, you'd have to know about them. There's the flatty-fish, the plaice, for instance. It has two eyes on the same side of its head! D'you know how that happened? Well, it was Saint Columba – yer man that went to Scotland yonder; ye'll know the one – he stepped on a plaice as he was coming ashore from his currach, so he did; slipped an' fell an' got an almighty soaking. So he puts a curse on the fish, for to have both eyes on the top of its head so's it could avoid getting in the way in future! Some boy, that Columba. Your good health, brave man!'

He drained his second pint, and began to look towards another. Passing him a third black pint, I asked if there were any sharks around these parts.

'Oh aye; plenty, so there are,' piped up another man, nodding over at Bertie and his three empty glasses and laughing. 'And some of them are on land.'

'This is a brave man, but,' said Bertie, slapping my back. 'A brave man, for wasn't he in the papers with his canoe?' Warming to his new theme he continued, 'Aye, brave man. Goin' right roun' the country. So brave that if ye roasted him to dust – ye'd have *brave* dust, so ye would!'

~   ~   ~

At half-past five in the evening a large white Securicor van pulled up at the slipway at Tara Bay. I quickly emptied the kayak and strapped it to the roof rack, and we headed southward, across by the Strangford ferry, towards the Republic. The driver, a solemn, stony-faced Ulsterman, broke his silence only to point out the sites of various infamous bombings, shootings and burnings, increasingly frequent as we approached the guarded frontier posts of the border. I broke into a sudden cold sweat as I realised I had no passport or proof of identity. The kayak on the roof was painted in bright republican green and gold; all my personal kit was carried in an ex-army ammunition canister; and I had two-thirds of a gallon of stove petrol in a bomb-shaped metal flask at my feet. Would the guards shoot first, or wait to ask awkward questions in a Belfast cell? Never mind the *Guildford Four*: what about the *Aberdeen One*! But minutes later we had cruised unchallenged through both the customs and military checkpoints, and were safely in the Republic. Just south of the border at Dundalk, the van pulled in at the huge Ballymascanlon House Hotel and leisure complex.

'Right. That's as far as I go,' said the Ulsterman. 'Somebody else is to pick you up here in the morning.' He unstrapped the kayak brusquely, dumped it on the lawn, and drove off north again as though it pained him to be on the south side of the border.

'You must be the canoeist,' said the friendly hotel receptionist. 'Now, you're not to worry about anything, sir; your canoe will be locked safely in the stables, and your account is being looked after. There's a meal ready for you, and the residents' bar is just through there. There'll be nothing to pay; enjoy your stay.' It was like having a fairy godmother. Somewhere behind the scenes, perhaps aware of the inconvenience of the Dublin press launch, my sponsors, in the sensitive, unobtrusive way in which they were to support the whole kayak journey, were doing a grand job of oiling the cogs and smoothing my path to the capital.

Having been virtually whisked away from the damp and cramp of a one-man tent where I couldn't even sit upright, the hotel was a complete culture shock. After a fine meal, I relaxed and washed my clothes in a deep, hot en-suite bath, then stretched out in a double bed with clean sheets, feeling like a piece of flotsam which had just washed up in the Sea of Tranquillity.

I met Pat Gabbott and his pretty wife Carol at an early breakfast. He had already unlocked the kayak from the Ballymascanlon stables and strapped her to a makeshift wooden frame on top of his van; he seemed as keen to head south as the previous driver had been desperate to return north. Pat and Carol had a big, ramshackle panel van, with a broken roof rack, a holey exhaust and a side-door held on with a nail; but the stereo was excellent, the chat was lively and humorous, and Carol rolled us endless cigarettes while the van whisked noisily south. On the outskirts of Dublin Pat swerved to avoid the tail end of a dramatic *gardaí* car chase. Gunshots rang out and the grid of interlocking streets briefly resembled 'Hill Street Blues' as cars screeched round corners and hurtled airborne over road bumps. We heard later that two men in the leading car had been shot dead after robbing a bank.

From the moment Pat Gabbott's van pulled up outside Dublin's famous Point Depot concert venue next to a spotless limousine belonging to the Lord Mayor of Dublin, it was obvious that my sponsors had laid on something much bigger than a quick 'photos and sandwiches' launch. Paddling the kayak around on the slow, glassy waters of the Liffey by the Grand Canal Docks, combined photo opportunities for the press with a chance for me to unwind from the van journey. But then the kayak was dried, polished and laid in the centre of the Point Depot's reception area, where the show began in earnest.

Following an opening speech from the Irish government's then Minister for Health, Rory O'Hanlon, I explained the various features of the kayak: its foot-operated bilge pump, waterproof storage hatches, deck-mounted compass and spare paddles. I demonstrated how I would be sealed into the cockpit so that waves couldn't enter the boat, and how it could be 'eskimo rolled' upright in the event of a capsize. Then I described how I would be self-sufficient for the journey, carrying a tent, sleeping bag, food and a cookstove, tightly packed inside the kayak, and would need no back-up team or land support. Finally I wished Eyebank Ireland every success with the fundraising campaign which was to be run in parallel with my journey. Ever since I'd first heard the name 'Eyebank', I'd found it difficult to dispel the mental image of a row of glass jars full of staring eyeballs floating in clear liquid, like pickled eggs on a chip shop shelf. But I had to admit that, even if only for that reason, the name had the all-important ability to lodge in the mind.

Eyebank president Michael Collins gave a captivating speech on the work of the charity. He hoped that something in the region of £30,000 would be raised through Sola Lenses' support of the Round Ireland Kayak expedition and that as a direct result sight could be restored to at least five people that same year. With a completely straight face, he went on to say: 'It is my sincere hope, Mr Minister, ladies and gentlemen, that one fine day in the not too distant future the people of Cork could be supplied with corneas which have come, for instance, from county Kerry, thereby vastly improving the prowess of that city on the fields of football and hurling!'

There followed press and radio interviews, more photographs, and a fine lunch, all of which passed smoothly and painlessly with the warmth and humour that seemed to characterise even the most official of functions in Ireland. Within three hours of arriving I was ready to head back north with what the next day's newspapers would be calling 'The *Sola* Kayak'. The Gabbott van journey back was like the fast rewinding of a short film. We bumped and wove through the grid of hilly streets, past the bullet-ridden shells of the bank-raid getaway cars; sailed unchallenged again across the border into Northern Ireland, and arrived once more in the squally rain of coastal county Down. I had declined the offer of a second night at the hotel, in order to prepare the kayak for an early morning start. After a couple of days lost to weather, road travel and publicity, I was itching to get back on the water as soon as possible. There was a heck of a long way to go.

~ ~ ~

Gales buffeting the little tent ensured that I was awake for both the midnight and early morning shipping forecasts, although neither announced anything more encouraging than force seven southwesterlies. By seven o'clock I was carving an extremely ragged kayak route south past treacherous reefs and inshore skerries, to the final fingers of the Ards peninsula at Ballyquintin Point. Beyond Ballyquintin stretched the wide mouth of Strangford Lough, the first open-water crossing of my journey.

The Vikings, who had names for all the important harbours and headlands of south and east Ireland, such as *Wex-fjord* and *Carling-fjord*, left the name *Strang-fjord*, 'the fjord of violent tides', with good reason. Twice daily half a billion gallons of tidewater rush in and out through Strangford's narrow bottleneck, creating swirls and eddies, and making it impossible for a small boat to travel against the flow. Planning for exactly this kind of water, I had packed *Sola* extra carefully, with the heaviest equipment close to me in the centre of the kayak; leaving the stern light enough to lift in a following sea, yet not too light for the rudder to get a grip, and the bow buoyant enough to rise up over the waves in front. The tide was already beginning to strengthen as I started the two mile crossing, folding itself into angry lumps, restrained only slightly by the opposing wind and narrowing shores of the lough.

One of the most basic of boating techniques is the *ferry-glide*, often used to cross rivers without losing way downstream. Strangford was flowing like a respectable river rapid as I angled my bows into the current and began a controlled, sideways glide across its rushing waters. It seemed strange to see breakers foaming white on the downwind side of islets and skerries as the effects of the inrushing tide over-ruled the more usually dominant wind; and it was easy to believe the legend that it was the tide which caused Saint Patrick to land and settle at Strangford. Journeying from the south by skin-boat, he'd been bound for the Antrim coast, where he had tended goat flocks as a boy slave, when irresistible currents, like the hand of God itself, swept his boat in through the narrows, and onto the Strangford shore.

Aye, the tide flushed through the narrows like a mill race; and I knew that if I capsized here I'd be washed in, within minutes, back to Portaferry and Bertie Bailey again. I put an extra push behind each paddle stroke and battled into the centre of the troubled channel. Beneath me *Sola* rose and sank on each wave crest with a motion that managed to be both frisky and biddable at the same time, like a young horse, full of energy yet eager to please. Very slightly I tilted her angle seaward to make the best of each wave's energy, and the rudder cocked in harmony behind me. Eight feet forward of me, her pointed bow occasionally dipped into the flesh of the wave in front before springing loose in a confetti of sparkling spray and, for the first time in the journey, I felt sparks of exhilaration beginning to kindle. Every now and then the entire front half would lift and crash downward as the kayak regained full contact with the water, and a quivering thump would run through my whole body. The surface of the sea was level with my hips, while the whole length of my legs, encased within the kayak bow, lay below water level. The result, part of the unique experience of the kayak, was to feel curiously part of the ceaseless motion of the sea's surface.

It took just over an hour, with both wind and tide strengthening all the while, to reach Strangford's far shore at Killard Point, and a further hour, against a headwind, to the fishing harbour of Ardglass. The headwind continued to rise, steadily approaching the forecast force seven, and by the time I reached St John's Point at the rocky northeastern edge of Dundrum Bay my progress had slowed to a crawl. Whenever I stopped paddling to check the map or wipe a wave-splash from my eyes, I would drift backwards at a speed far greater than I had been achieving forwards. From beneath the lighthouse at St John's Point the tide pouring, wind-driven, out from Dundrum Bay looked every bit as powerful as the Strangford current, and I was wary of leaving the last slight shelter provided by the rocks of the point; doubtful whether I could ever hope to stem such a mass of moving water.

'She'll swamp ye, swamp ye, so she will! I was nearly swamped meself!' shouted a yellow-oilskinned fisherman in a wildly tossing boat. His outboard motor was screaming with the strain of battling against wind and tide, whining periodically like a dentist's drill as the boat rose and fell in the mounded water; but so loud was the roaring of the waves that I had heard nothing of his approach until he was right alongside. Unlike his open boat, my sealed kayak was unlikely to be 'swamped'; it was entirely watertight and seaworthy, even if capsized, for as long as I had the energy left to roll it back upright, and to continue to power it forward. Nevertheless, the prospect of taking some of those steel-cold grey waves over the head and being driven ashore in small pieces was not a welcome one. I could already imagine the coroner's report on my misfortune:

> *... snuffed it due to a combination of rheumatism, chronic pleurisy and hypothermia, complicated by a massive intake of assorted seaweeds.*

I decided to stay at the point, bobbing in the slight shelter provided by a gap in the skerries, until conditions looked better. The fisherman too decided against heading into Dundrum Bay. 'Wait till the turn of the tide!' he shouted. 'The wind will drop then, so she will.' He turned his boat and headed away for a gentler harbour.

CHAPTER 2

The Three Waves of Erin

There shall come a wave whose crest shall sparkle
and whelm thy home in thine island.

Tonn Chlíodhna, translation by Edward Gwynn

The mariners of ancient Ireland knew well that sea conditions in the vicinity of Dundrum Bay were not to be treated lightly. Many, many years ago, before the advent of cartography; before seismology and the systematic study of the ways of the earth; and long before the infant sciences of hydrography and oceanography, three great 'waves', or *tonnta,* were known to the people of Erin. That is to say, according to the ancient topographical system of old Ireland, there were three major centres of flood tide and wave generation affecting the Irish coast. The first of these, the 'Wave of Ruairí', was in the east, in what we call today the Irish Sea. The second, the 'Wave of Clíodhna', was located in the southwest, off the coast of county Cork, in the region known today as Fastnet. And the third, *Tonn Luim,* was to be found off the wild country of Donegal, in the Atlantic northwest, in the sea area we now call Malin. Collectively these were known as *Trí Príomh-thonnta na hÉireann,* the 'Three Waves of Erin'.

Several minor centres of wave and tidal activity were also recorded by the ancient Irish, especially where these were important as marker waves, indicating the locations of famous events or occasions, or marking important boundaries. In the southeast, for example, there were *Tonn Inbhir* (or *Tonn Tuaithe*) at the mouth of the Bann, *Tonn Bhinne Eadair* and *Tonn Diune Mic Fanad* near the old port of Howth, and *Tonn Duibhlinne* in Dublin Bay. The southern half of

Erin was said to extend from the Boyne river to the marker wave *Tonn Inghíona Gheanainn* in the far southeast, off the headland now called Carnsore Point, in county Wexford. Similarly, the province of Connaught in the west was supposed to extend from *Tonn Inse Caerach* (Kerry) in the south, to *Tonn Inse Glóire* off the Mayo coast. Other waves were named, such as *Tonn Tuaithe* near Ballintoy, county Antrim; but of all these minor waves, the traditions of only one were kept alive into the present century. Local lore locates *Tonn Toime* in county Kerry, either near Glenbeigh, between Ros Beith and Inis in Dingle Bay, or at the head of Dingle Bay just off the Rosbehy peninsula. Like many notorious areas of turbulent water in Scotland and Ireland, this wave was said to be guarded by a mysterious old hag known as the *Cailleach Toime*, and was thought to be the entrance through which Oisin accessed *Tír na nÓg*, the 'Land of Eternal Youth'.

The three main 'Waves of Erin' were thought to embody considerable powers: not just the power to move the sea and the weather, and power over those who would sail through their dominion; but also the ability to influence tragedy and disaster, justice, revenge and national interest. They were even thought to possess the 'power of lamentation' during a national crisis, and it was believed that this power would return at any time in the future when disaster should threaten the island of Erin. Through the ages the 'Three Waves' have become linked or associated with various mythological or heroic figures, an expression of the belief that many Irish deities and supernatural beings either resided in, or were closely associated with the sea. Legends and folk tales have grown up around the waves and been passed down through generations in ballad, poem and story. In most of these tales it is far from clear whether the great 'Waves of Erin' referred to individual apocalyptic events, to entities such as single, overpowering tidal waves, or to recurring stormy or difficult tidal conditions. It is, however, interesting that all three of the main waves – and many of the minor *tonnta* also – coincide fairly closely with areas where significant tidal movements can still be traced today using modern methods, and where contemporary mariners, navigating the Irish coast, must still exercise caution and respect. A diagrammatic representation of the 'Three Waves of Erin', according to ancient folklore, would overlap significantly with the symbols and arrows on a modern tidal stream atlas or Admiralty Chart for the Irish coast.

Tonn Rudhraighe, the 'Wave of Ruairí', one of the notorious 'Three Waves' of ancient lore, was located in the Irish Sea off Dundrum Bay, significantly placed between the Irish coast and the Isle of Man. Manannan Mac Lír, after whom the Isle of Man is named, and from whom derives its famous three-legged symbol, was said to have some control over the sea in general, and over the 'Three Waves of Erin' in particular. Manannan was the son of Lír, the Irish sea god – also called Llyr in the Welsh pantheon – a sort of Irish Neptune whom some scholars consider to have been the prototype for Shakespeare's *King Lear.* Tradition places Lír's kingdom in the north of Ireland, probably off the northwest coast, where the third of the great waves is located; but Manannan, his warlike son, was closely associated with activities in the Irish Sea. He is supposed to have used the mystical 'Waves of Erin' to drown or shipwreck many of the enemies of the legendary race of the *Tuatha de Danann*; and in order to defeat their enemies, the *Firbolgs,* at the Battle of Moytura, he is said to have ridden from the Isle of Man to Ireland on the 'white horses' of the sea.

~ ~ ~

On the turn of the tide I picked my way carefully through narrow passages where the waves of the Irish Sea broke their anger on a maze of reefs and skerries, rather than directly across my boat. It was a risky, shallow passage, calling for caution and unhurried judgement as the sea sluiced through to offer a route between two rocks, or withdrew just as quickly to reveal jagged bare fangs; and perhaps a kayak is the only boat that could have negotiated it in those conditions. Eventually it came to an end. I broke at last, on an impatient wave surge, right over the final skerry and into Dundrum

Bay itself, where lay a vast basin of white-capped frenzy.

In that strong southwesterly wind, there was no hope of crossing twelve miles of Dundrum Bay to Annalong and the Mourne shore. My only option was to go round the long way: to skirt the rim of the bay like a nervous dog with its back to the wall. I crossed one very small bay towards the village of Minerstown, then bore west; but constant wind and spray, and the morning's battles with headwinds, had left me with very little strength, and there was nothing I could do to prevent being blown roughly ashore on a wide, windswept beach of shallow surf and low, eroded sand-dunes. I rested there for a while; tried to keep warm with gentle exercises, and replaced lost energy with a snack; then I decided that I might as well be cold and wet *on* the water as off it. I'd give it another go. Out across elongated southwesterly ranks of shallow, powerful surf, I forced the kayak. Waves broke on the bows and blew into my face, or occasionally broke directly over my head, and gradually I became wetter and wetter; but with inordinate effort I clawed my way back into Dundrum Bay. Progress was very marginal, and not at all economical; enormous physical effort was spent in gaining mere yards. But those yards became miles, and those miles took me eventually to Newcastle town, where I stood, bent over on the slipway, hands on knees supporting tired shoulders, as the rain poured down over my face. I wept tears of exhaustion and frustration, having covered only twenty miles in twelve full hours.

~ ~ ~

The Irish Sea is a narrow, shallow trough – almost landlocked – running a distance of some two hundred and forty miles, north to south, between Scotland, England, Wales and the east coast of Ireland. At its widest point, between Ireland's Dundalk Bay and the English resort of Morecambe Bay, along a line just south of the Isle of Man, the Irish Sea measures only about one hundred and twenty miles; and in several places, in clear weather, one can quite easily see right across it with the naked eye. At both its northern and southern ends the Irish Sea forms narrow funnels through which, twice daily, it empties and refills, the tidewater streaming through at strengths reaching eight knots at times, depending on the phase of the moon. One of the most interesting of the Admiralty sea charts of the British Isles is the one that covers the North Channel of the Irish Sea, and illustrates the overfalls, races and tidal whirlpools formed along the coasts of both Antrim and Scotland as a result of the activity of the Irish Sea. At the narrowest point there are only twelve miles between the Antrim coast and Scotland's Mull of Kintyre. Within the basin of the Irish Sea there is little scope for a serious build-up of swell, such as one finds in the wide Atlantic, or even in the Celtic Sea off the south coast; nor is there a great fetch across which the wind can cultivate large wave patterns. It can, however, be an extremely stormy and tempestuous sea, subject to the rapid build-up of short, steep wave patterns, and all the problems associated with the tidal activity at its two ends. 'Irish Sea' is a distinct forecast area in the shipping bulletin, mainly because it plays by its own rules. Its weather is governed largely by the land masses that surround it; and its mercurial changes of wind strength and direction are as likely to be due to changing land temperatures as to oceanic weather fronts.

The Irish Sea forecast next day threw me back into the realm of southwesterly gales, and it looked like being yet another day heavy in effort, and light on progress. But if there was to be a sheltered area anywhere, it would be in the lee of the Mourne mountains. Between Dundrum Bay and Dundalk Bay lies the Kingdom of Mourne, one of the most compact mountain areas in the entire British Isles. Within a thirty mile circle no fewer than fifteen summits rise to over two thousand feet. Most of the massif is over fifteen hundred feet; and Slieve Donard, peaking at 2,796 feet, 'sweeps down to the sea' just south of Newcastle town.

It was, at least, a bright day. Out in the Irish Sea, beyond the wind shadow of Slieve Donard, a big, angry sea-pattern was running, stirred by the strong southwesterlies; but very few clouds were managing to climb over the Mourne massif, and the sea and sky over the Irish Sea were as full of colour as I'd seen them since leaving Larne. In Newcastle harbour the yacht masts clanged and tinkled in the breeze like the neck-bells of Alpine cattle; *Sola* lay in the sun, patiently waiting to be packed and harnessed for the day. I sat on the sheltered slipway, beneath the great sweeping flank of Slieve Donard, with my head resting against warm concrete; and when I closed my eyes I could almost imagine I was in an Alpine meadow.

My Alpine daydream faded all too quickly as I moved the kayak, at a snail's pace, round the Mourne coast against a stiff breeze. Here, where the mountains of Mourne really did sweep down to the sea, were all the details that never got into the Percy French song: caves, skerries, small cliffs and cascading streams. Gulls soared easily on the hillside winds, and solemn groups of prehistoric-looking black shags made a brave show of trying to dry their open wings in the sun and breeze. I once read and memorised a quaint little rhyme which made the life of a shag seem idyllic. It went:

> *... and would, like thee, I were all these things,*
> *Could sit out there where the white rock gleams,*
> *With the bright sun warming my outstretched wings,*
> *Digesting herrings and dreaming dreams.*

But, on reflection, I can't imagine that many creatures on earth have a more miserable time than the shag. Slow, clumsy and easy to catch, the Scottish islanders used to export them by the hundred to London, plucked and beheaded, under the label 'Hebridean chickens'. No great shakes in the flying stakes, they are condemned to doing most of their own food-gathering underwater, where their bottle shape and rear flippers are at least of some use. This means that they are regularly soaked, and have to spend inordinate amounts of time standing on cold, damp, stony ledges trying to dry their feathers. Even if they weren't continually splashed with sea-spray, don't they realise that they need to rinse the salt off? That salt water will never fully dry in a sea breeze? The whole process is quite futile. I have even seen shags in winter frozen to the rocks by their wet feet, waiting for the next salt tide to loosen the frost. The rusty, throaty cackle that is the shag's equivalent of birdsong seems in a sad way to sum up its whole life story.

Unlike sheer cliffs or rocky headlands, where a landfall is often dangerous or even impossible, the Mournes sweep gently, rather than steeply, down to the sea, leaving at least some vestige of safety and security to the coastal traveller. But the further I crept round the Mourne coast, the more I began to feel the direct strength of the headwind, and the going became increasingly difficult. Squalls tumbled down the mountainside, giving little warning before rattling my balance and trying to pluck the paddle from my hands. The kayak's rudder was useful for holding a course head-on to the worst squalls, but as the coast became more exposed to the full gale I decided I couldn't go on for much longer. A steady force eight wind is just about manageable in a kayak, but I knew that as I became more tired a sharp gust or squall might easily succeed in stealing the paddle, or in tipping the kayak over, and in an offshore wind I could not afford the risk. Having come only five miles south of Newcastle I had to haul ashore.

How long could these blasted winds continue, I wondered. Statistically the Irish Sea gets an average of two to three gales each month during the summer; each lasts for approximately three days, often leaving the sea rough for a further two days afterwards. Well, perhaps there had been some mistake: the entire summer's quota seemed to have arrived during the first half of July, and showed little sign of letting up yet!

Out of the wind, the sunshine was pleasant enough. Fast, scudding cloud patterns and brief showers of rain alternated with longer periods of bright blue sky. During the brighter spells the shore was a riot of colour. It was a speckled coastline of pastel-coloured boulders smoothed by the sea, and wet shingle which shone and reflected in the sun. *Sola* sat contented on a long curving ridge of tide-stacked seaweed, backed by white surf on blue water, and rejoiced in her own bright shades of gold and green. I stripped off in the shelter of a large rock, built a woodfire, basked in its smoke with coffee and a book, then dozed off and waited for a lull in the wind. If only I could keep my mind from dwelling on the lack of progress, this was perhaps as fine a pattern for existence as I could imagine: punching my way through a lively sea, in a boat containing a kettle and a bag of good books, was as near to an image of heaven as I'd ever been able to form.

Towards evening the wind dropped just low enough and long enough for me to struggle round to Annalong, a timeless little fishing harbour tucked beneath a dramatic mountain backdrop. I'd done only eight miles, but there was little point in going any further as the wind was already strengthening again, and I pulled the kayak out at a steep slipway with the help of three young boys who seemed to appear from nowhere. Anyone looking for solitude on the coast of the Irish Sea had better travel outside of the school holiday season. No matter how late the hour, how foul the weather or how quiet your arrival, the holiday kids of the coastal villages, desperate for some novelty to liven the long summer days, are sure to find you out. Within minutes of getting the kayak onto land there were kids and small dogs all around it, over it and in it, fascinated by this odd colourful object and its occupant which had been washed up on their patch. In the broad, melodic accent of county Down, they fired endless questions at me during the entire time I was getting dried and changed.

'What kind of a boat is it?'
'What does that bit do?'
'Will it hold my weight?'
'And his too?'
'Which is the front?'
'Where does the petrol go?'
'Where do you sleep?'
'Do you want to sleep at my house? Sure I'll ask me ma.'
But these kids were great. There was absolutely no question of them

stealing or breaking anything; at least not deliberately! It was as if, just by landing at their village, I'd already become their property. They were determined to look after both *Sola* and me, and their cheerful energy was a tonic at the end of a day alone. I left two tough-looking boys as a guard of honour for *Sola*, while two little girls went to collect water for me, and one toothless little ragamuffin took me by the hand to show me where the chip shop was. I felt a little like Gulliver landing in a friendly Lilliput.

They found me again next morning, sitting with a soda bread breakfast in the lee of the slipway, procrastinating about setting off. The forecast was for yet another southwesterly gale; but my little friends helped me launch, and waved goodbye, and I bounced from wave to wave, determined at least to improve on the previous day's mileage. That wasn't to be. Within an hour the wind just became too strong, whipping the paddles away from my hands on almost every stroke, and causing the blades to miss their purchase on the water more than once. It was no good. My target would have to be Kilkeel, ancient capital of the Kingdom of Mourne, and harbour for the main east coast fishing fleet. At the end of a second hour I fought my way round the big waves slopping over the Kilkeel breakwater, and watched seaward as the larger, more powerful fishing boats linked up with the smaller ones to tow them homeward against the growing gale.

There was a tremendous relief in reaching the sanctuary of the inner harbour. After the continuous melée of the open coast it was like stepping inside a double-glazed house and closing a heavy door against the storm. '*Department of Transport SPEED LIMIT 4 knots*' read a notice at the harbour entrance. Chance would be a fine thing, I thought. At least I was in little danger of being fined for speeding; even on a good day, with a favourable tide, I would be hard pushed to top four knots.

At last I had peace to think again. As I drifted towards the main dock I passed a floating, broken fishbox which had also struggled down from Ardglass, and mused on whether I'd now be able to find some shelter from the gale for the night. 'KILKEEL SAYS NO!' announced a brash slogan, freshly painted in huge capitals on the harbour wall. At first I took it for a football team motto, but then I remembered: Kilkeel, and most of the North, were saying 'No' to Dublin involvement in Northern Ireland's government, and to the initiative known as the Anglo-Irish Agreement. It was a firm negative which had been reverberating through Northern Irish politics for almost a century.

Today was the ninth of July, already high season for the marches of the Protestant Orange Order, building up to the climax of the unionist year on the Twelfth. In several coastal towns and villages I'd already seen red, white and blue bunting flying above the streets. Orange banners and murals portrayed King Billy on horseback, or demanded deliverance from Papism; and the Union Jack stripes painted on kerbstones were the ritual markings of the traditional loyalist territories and marching routes. On the twelfth of July up to twenty thousand people throughout the North would turn out on marches held to commemorate the anniversary of the Battle of the Boyne in 1690, where the Catholic King James II was defeated by the Protestant King William of Orange. They would be wearing orange sashes in honour of King Billy, and bowler hats in memory of their bowler-hatted grandfathers who opposed the British government's attempts to incorporate Ulster into a united Ireland in 1912. On bonfires all over the North, effigies of the Pope, or Irish tricolor flags, would be burned. The marches themselves would be colourful lively affairs, with flute players, baton twisters, banner wavers and stomping drummers fuelled by a blend of virtuosity and fanaticism which occasionally went out of control.

A Northern friend, with strong unionist connections, had once shown me his prized possession, a bloodstained Lambeg drum which he kept under lock and key. Up to three feet in diameter, goatskin on an oak frame, strapped vertically onto the drummer's chest, the Lambeg is known as the 'Heartbeat of Ulster'.

My friend described how the marching drummers demonstrated their commitment to King Billy by crossing and re-crossing their hands as they beat the drums, and said it was not unusual for them to finish the march with their wrists bleeding profusely over the drums. It was all very difficult for an outsider to understand. As far as I could gather from the history books, the real King William had been a hunchbacked Dutchman with no real interest in Ulster apart from its Protestantism; what's more, the Battle of the Boyne seemed a heck of a long time ago. But memories are long, and tend to distort sentiments. And, as has become evident also in Bosnia and Beirut, the hatred of neighbours and brothers occasionally runs even deeper than that of strangers and aliens. The archaic structures of the Orange Order and masonic lodges still seemed to run the twelfth of July show; and the omnipresent threat of paramilitarism cast a sinister shadow over the whole pageant. 'UVF' read another slogan in six foot lettering on the harbour wall next to an unequivocal-looking 'NO SURRENDER!' in blood-red paint. Whoever wrote those had not done it in furtive secrecy. I hoped that by the twelfth of July the winds would ease, and I would be well south of marching country.

Ashore, I was investigating the burnt-out shell of a beachside house as a possible shelter from the gale when yet another gang of beach urchins arrived. One girl told me that the house was haunted by the ghost of a farmer's wife who had been cut up and fed to the cows. So I decided the tent might make a cheerier shelter after all.

At times a horde of a dozen beach kids might seem like a real nuisance, but when you have a long afternoon ahead, and a lot of camp chores to do, their cheeky enthusiasm and limitless energy can be a real asset. Delegation is the key. Soon they were gathering driftwood for a fire, picking winkles from the rock pools, and mussels from the shore; filling my waterbottles, and begging potatoes, cheese and beans from parents and shopkeepers in the village, while I relaxed in the tent and read my book. We sat that evening in a huddle round a big fire and cooked baked potatoes with assorted fillings, coffee, chocolate and marshmallows. The crazy, giggling chatter that buzzed around those kids as they stoked the fire and tried to prise winkles from their shells with safety pins, was almost as warming and lively as the fire itself; and I'm sure I laughed more that evening than I had on the whole of the trip so far. It didn't seem to matter any more that I'd only come six miles; and besides, the forecast was looking slightly better for tomorrow. When I packed to leave next morning I found, carefully tucked in my lifejacket pocket, a little note wishing me 'Good Luck Brain', and a 'save jerony'. It asked that I 'Say Hi to everyone in Scotland for us' and demanded 'Send us a pota of you and your conoo, OK,' and was signed Amanda, Bobbie-Jo, and Lindsay Tannahill.

CHAPTER 3

FLOTSAM

There does be a power of young men floating around in the sea,
and ... when a man is nine days in the sea and the wind blowin', it's
hard set his own mother would be to say what man was in it.

Riders to the Sea, JM Synge

With six o'clock came the early morning imperative – almost as
inflexible as a train timetable – to haul myself out of the warm
sleeping bag into damp, salty clothes, to pack the kayak and catch
the southbound tide, the Carlingford Express. There was no time
for another snooze; it is the ebbs and flows which call the shots for
inshore travellers. To disregard them would be not only to miss the
offer of a free lift, but to court potential disaster at some of the
major channels and headlands.

The morning breeze was light and accompanied by a lovely
sunrise as I pulled away from the Mourne skyline and over the
imaginary sea border at Carlingford Lough into the Irish Republic.
There were no checkpoints, no border security, and no dotted
white lines; and if there was any borderline out there in mid-lough, it
was a rough and choppy one; a line created by a stiffening breeze
against an inrushing spring tide. But the gales and gusts of county
Down had retreated, and within a half-hour I had crossed the lough.
My first footfall in the Republic was a breakfast stop on a black
beach near Cooley Point at the wide mouth of Dundalk Bay.
Dundalk Bay was going to be a ten mile crossing, my longest yet. It
would require a good fill of chocolate, an empty bladder, three or
perhaps four waterproof song sheets – and perhaps a compass
bearing! Cooley Point was a good place to arrange all that.

I'm certain that we have innate rhythms; they reside in the head, the heart, in the ears, in the loins, and even in the paddle. Paddling like music, or dance, or sex, is polyrhythmic; it taps into deep-set internal banks of rhythm which are sometimes constant, sometimes changing. Sometimes the beat itself is strong, self-sufficient, self-perpetuating like an infallible metronome. At other times the internal rhythm needs a little help; you can reinforce it with a rap or a mantra, mouth some lyrics, or even belt out a song at full volume. And the canoeist, alone at sea, can get away with this better than most folk. All he needs is a selection of song sheets, waterproofed and strapped to the kayak's deck.

'Give me those ho-o-o-nky-tonk women!' I sang as I struck steadily away from Cooley Point, firing the kayak forward to a livening blues rhythm. An hour passed, and in mid-bay I hit choppy water where medium strength offshore winds were pushing mighty lumps of Dundalk Bay water out into the Irish Sea. When at last the target shore seemed equidistant with the 'old' shore, I took a brief break from paddling and stretched my back as best I could. Conditions were still reasonably stable. There were no breaking waves, and only small white-caps; but I was still over an hour from the nearest land, and keen to get right across in case the rapid increases in wind speed – which had been the pattern of recent days in this squally area beneath the hills – were to reassert themselves. So I changed the song sheet for a quicker tune, sang louder and faster, stepped up the paddling rhythm, and fixed my bows on Dunany Point.

> From Bantry Bay up to Derry quay,
> and from Galway to Dublin town,
> No maid I've seen like the brown colleen
> that I met in the county Down.

It was high tide as I reached Dunany, and a cushion of soft, dried carrageen seaweed welcomed the tired kayak. For the first time in the journey I felt the satisfaction of having gained some distance. I stripped off my damp clothes, gathered driftwood, brewed coffee on a little fire, dried myself and snoozed in the sun. There were fresh views, across the next wide bay to Clogher Head, and back north to the increasingly hazy and indistinct forms of the Mourne mountains; and new views, like tired arms, were marks of progress. For a couple of balmy hours I slept in the afternoon sun, then covered the final four mile crossing to Clogherhead in a further hour of sunshine. Of east coast locations, the hamlet of Clogherhead is one of the most spectacular in setting. On a clear day the whole blue range of the Mournes across Dundalk Bay can be seen, sweeping in an arc of shore and mountain, from Slieve Gullion, home of the ancient Celtic heroes, to St John's Point on the northeastern edge of Dundrum Bay. The winds which had dogged my passage around those distant points already seemed to belong to another world and another time.

Closing in on Clogherhead, I was looking forward to just sitting on the little harbour wall and watching the evening sun at the end of a twenty-six mile day; but the sun itself had betrayed me. Several people had noticed the strange rhythmical flashing of my wet paddle-blades in the low rays of the late afternoon sun, and had trained curious binoculars towards the kayak as I crossed the bay. So by the time I was identifiable by the naked eye, a veritable reception committee was already waiting. Paddy Hodgins, harbourmaster for over forty years, stepped forward from the crowd and directed me to the best slipway.

'Welcome to Clogherhead!' he roared. He very kindly drove me into the village's Lobster Cafe, where I demolished a huge portion of fish, chips and beans, and a deep pot of tea. And when I'd finished, there was Paddy again, waiting to give me a lift back to the harbour.

At the inner harbour I got into conversation with Aidan Sharkey, owner of the *Seaquester*, a quite beautiful little wooden yacht with larch planking and mahogany fittings, like a miniature floating log cabin. Aidan spent an hour explaining the intricacies of maintaining and caring for his pride and joy, then announced with a shrug that it was time he was off home for his tea and, quite unexpectedly, offered me the use of *Seaquester* for the night.

'Sure, just pull the hatch shut when you leave in the morning,' he said, as though he'd known me all his life. So I paddled *Sola* round from the slipway, tied her bow-line to the little yacht, climbed aboard with a bag of food, and a book and spent the evening alone below decks, feeling like Captain Cook planning his next voyage of discovery. I slept early, rocked by the gentle swaying motion of a moored boat on a rising tide. Soon after midnight the mahogany creaked, my bed suddenly adopted a less acute angle, and the sounds of water lapped at a level above my head; *Seaquester* was afloat at high tide. I was sorry to leave the peace and tranquillity of Clogherhead but, in order to avoid the oozing sludge of diesel and mud which the harbour would become at low tide, I had to jump ship on a fast ebb at five-thirty in the morning.

~ ~ ~

From Clogherhead to Skerries, fifteen miles south, the coast is one wide, gently curving bay. I passed well to seaward of Drogheda, where the infamous Boyne river meets the sea between counties Louth and Meath. After paddling eight miles in about three hours against a headwind, hunger, bladder and sheer exhaustion forced me inshore on a broad, shallow, sandy beach at the quiet seaside resort of Laytown. I slumped into a plastic seat at a small café, just in time to hear the end of a pre-recorded interview about my kayak journey being broadcast by the 'Gerry Ryan Show' on one of the national radio stations, Radio 1.

'That was the courageous, and frequently very wet, Brian Wilson, who is at this very moment rowing his canoe somewhere round our coast,' said Ryan. 'If you see him, be sure to give him a wave – as if he hadn't enough already, ha-ha! – or better still, phone and tell us where he is!'

'But – that was *me*!' I gasped to the waitress who was trying to take my order for breakfast. Either touched by the notion that she was serving a star, or more likely frightened that this might be my last meal, she smiled sympathetically and began to dole out some special charitable treatment. Without the manager noticing, she took my jacket away to dry above the stove, sneaked me double rations of fried egg (one hidden beneath the other), and slipped me an extra coffee. When I got my jacket back it had a small bottle of fresh milk and two bacon sandwiches, still warm, in the pocket. I even got a quick hug 'for good luck' as I slipped out the door; and set off with new enthusiasm, out through low, wind-driven breakers, past Balbriggan and the remains of the bay.

Two hours later as I passed Skerries village, the warmth of the bacon sandwiches in my breast pocket had died away, but their gorgeous aroma had strengthened. Despite the strong headwind, incoming tide and massive energy burn-off, I was now sure that the kayak was moving at a fairly steady four knots, and I rewarded myself with a stop for those teasing sandwiches on Inis Phádraig, or St Patrick's Island. St Patrick himself is supposed to have stopped on this little island on his way from Wicklow to Ulster, but I'll bet his bacon sandwiches tasted no better than those from the Laytown café.

One thing is certain: the shores of the island would have been a great deal tidier in St Patrick's day, and I wondered what the saint would have thought of the unsightly mounds of garbage which had built up on his tidelines over the years. The multiple strand-lines of St Patrick's Island were a colourful amalgam of seaweed and driftwood with aluminium and tin cans, bottles, tangled fragments of rope and fishing nets, and a hundred types of brightly coloured plastic containers – from oil drums and industrial detergent bottles down to tiny cotton buds and tampon applicators.

Any one beach or bay facing a certain wind or tide acts as a random sample, a checkpoint, and a rough gauge of the amount of such garbage which must be at large in the surrounding sea. At any given moment, hundreds of thousands of tons of human-generated rubbish must be either afloat in the Irish Sea, lodged on the sea bed, or temporarily resting on a beach somewhere. It is not only unsightly, but is a problem for wildlife, for human communities, and even more so for future generations. Unlike the flotsam of last century, most of today's sea-borne garbage is virtually indestructible, and therefore steadily accumulating. Painted wood endures on average for thirteen years in the sea. Tin cans will last for about one hundred years; aluminium cans for more like three hundred years. But plastic bottles, and most other plastic items, will endure in the sea for almost *five hundred* years. Plastics are by far the worst variety, and the greatest by volume, of modern flotsam, and one of the biggest problems for our seas. The very properties that make plastics so useful as a material in modern life – lightness, buoyancy, durability, bright colours and resistance to decay – also make them a nightmare as litter in the oceans and along our shores.

A recent British scientific report showed that almost one-third of all fish taken from the Atlantic had ingested plastics. Thousands of birds, fish and sea-mammals are lost each year, tangled and drowned in discarded lengths of plastic netting, rope and packaging materials adrift in the sea. That spring, as I was beginning to plan and prepare for the Irish journey, no fewer than eight whales had been washed up dead on the shores of Donegal. The exact cause of death was unknown, but was widely thought to have been due to ingestion of, or choking on, plastics. One of the difficulties facing the sea is that the macropollution, or sea garbage, is so diverse in its origins, and so awkward to quantify scientifically, that it is difficult to initiate effective steps to reduce it. Present legislation focuses mainly on dumping at sea by ships. But little has been done as yet to decrease the amount of waste being introduced to the sea from coastal sources (factories, farms, fish-farms, domestic, dumps, etc). Because the amount of litter introduced annually is still increasing, and because the items themselves are virtually indestructible, the well-equipped beachcomber of the future is likely to need a JCB just to progress along the tideline, and a skip-lorry to carry off his finds.

A long afternoon took me on south, with a brief offshore detour to the rugged bird sanctuary of Lambay Island, and eventually to Howth on the northern edge of Dublin Bay. It was a fast crossing from Lambay to Ireland's Eye island and the ancient port of Howth. At long last the wind had stepped out of my way; it swung round behind me, and was to stay in the eastern sector for most of the next fortnight.

It was at Howth that the Vikings used to gather their longship fleets before the raids, up the east coast and even across to Wales, which so terrorised the medieval monks that they began to prefer rough weather to calm:

> Bitter is the wind tonight;
> It tosses the sea's white hair.
> I do not fear the wild warriors from Norway –
> who course on a quiet sea

Howth today is a smart fishing and yachting harbour; a popular suburban resort; a fashionable area of nightclubs, restaurants and upmarket marinas, where Vikings are an endangered species; and on that bright July evening, in the middle of the regatta season, the bay was full of activity. Crossing warily in the wake of four classes of yacht and dinghy races, I rounded the 'Eye', and then piled strongly and very quickly into the harbour, grounding at sunset with a full thirty miles under the belt.

Howth Yacht Club had a spacious new marina, and a towering, futuristic-looking clubhouse full of bars, lounges and shower-rooms, to which I hoped I might be allowed brief access. Passing several exclusive-looking 'Members Only' notices, I eventually came up against a locked and guarded security door. Salty, sweaty and weary, I knocked on the big door, determined at least to ask for a shower. 'Out of the question,' thought the security guard; but in the face of my persistence he agreed to ask the club secretary.

'Is that the canoe man? Of course he can come in!' said the secretary. Quite by chance, he had seen my approach from Ireland's Eye, on the tail end of the final yacht race, through binoculars, from the elevated eyrie of the club's upper lounge. 'Sure, I was listening to you on RTE only this morning.'

The great ball of Irish hospitality was about to roll yet again. Down in the shower-room I met Pat Murphy, fresh in from winning a yacht race, who offered me a room with his family for the night; another helpful club member had quickly arranged for a local fibreglass worker to put a reinforcing strip onto *Sola*'s hull where she showed signs of wearing thin; then I was invited to the Vice-Commodore's table for a three-course meal, including strawberries and cream. Perhaps the most amazing thing was that all this had happened within two hours of touching down on Howth slipway.

Hospitality at the Yacht Club continued next morning when I was given a stream of free coffee and a comfortable office from which to make phonecalls and to link-up with national radio. I had a wonderful view over the harbour, and could even see *Sola*, far below, belly-up in the hands of the fibreglass repair man. Despite its plush interior and exclusive membership rules, the Yacht Club couldn't have been more helpful to me. Any sense of the class-orientated snobbishness sometimes associated with similar establishments was kept firmly at bay by Irish humour. The club secretary handed me the Visitor's Book to sign, saying, 'By the way, Hamlet's in town.' I signed my name below the flamboyant signature of the Prince of Denmark himself, who was here for a dragon-class yacht race, and pursuing some business interests. Perhaps the Vikings were planning a comeback after all?

~ ~ ~

A long day of superb weather and mileage began with an early crossing of Dublin Bay, which was thick and turgid with the copious products of the city's untreated sewage outfalls. Mats of brown sludge and accumulated scum swirled in the eddies of my paddle blades, and rafts of sea birds gathered, feeding noisily on the discarded waste products of Dublin. The smell was horrific, and only began to ease as I drew nearer to Dalkey, shining Dalkey, ten miles south of Dublin itself.

The Irish Sea has, over recent years, been steadily gaining a reputation as a sea with a pollution problem. I had seen little evidence of this until I reached Dublin Bay; then suddenly, courtesy of one bay where untreated sewage spewed visibly from antiquated and insufficiently long outfall pipes, it became much easier to believe that reputation.

The discharge of sewage into the sea is not always necessarily harmful; its effects on the natural environment vary according to the nature of the sewage itself, the amount, time and position of the dumping, and the general health of the sea. But, apart from the obvious risks of disease, sanitation, and the unsightly fouling of holiday beaches, the main problem is that untreated sewage eventually begins to decompose 'naturally'. As it breaks down in the sea, it uses up the dissolved oxygen which is so necessary for the respiration of fish, animals, plants and micro-organisms in the sea itself, and thereby begins to influence the natural balance and food chains. In extreme cases high nutrient levels can lead to algal blooms, the so-called 'red-tides', which can poison fish and cause shellfish to become toxic to humans and other animals, including birds.

One marine authority revealed that in the late 1980s the Irish Sea was receiving over 1,570 million cubic yards of sewage each year – sufficient to cover the Isle of Man to a depth of six feet! In addition to straight sewage disposal, we know that about 100,000 tons of industrial spoil, and chemicals such as DDT-based pesticides, PCBs (polychlorinated biphenyl) and heavy metal compounds, were being dumped into the Irish Sea annually. And, just as worrying as a bay full of stinking turds is an entire sea which is increasingly absorbing radioactive waste, pumped or leaked, as is so often reported in the media, from sources such as the Sellafield plant in England, the Hunterston station in southwest Scotland, and the nuclear submarines which patrol the region. There is already evidence of an increase in fish diseases related to radioactive pollution in parts of the Irish Sea. Being relatively shallow, and largely enclosed, the Irish Sea is unsuited and unable to deal with high levels of pollution. The high levels which have been indicated in several surveys must therefore be taken very seriously as a warning that the capacity of the Irish Sea to absorb and dispose of our waste has already been exceeded. Although levels of radioactivity have been falling and some significant actions have recently been taken to clean up Irish beaches and inshore waters, continued reduction of this pollution is urgently needed, along with remedial action, if the Irish Sea is not to become synonymous with pollution.

Ireland's image as a healthy, fresh country with a pristine environment is crucial to the prosperity of its agriculture, fisheries and tourist industries within the European market. And, reputation and image aside, as an island nation Ireland cannot afford to neglect its relationship with the sea – for its *own* sake. The sea has a profound effect on who we are, what we are, and how we live; and, given that nowhere in Ireland is more than seventy miles from the sea, the shoreline is a definitive feature of the Irish psyche. I couldn't imagine many people wishing who they are and how they live to be defined by the state of Dublin Bay, or of the Irish Sea itself as I passed through it on that muggy summer morning.

~   ~   ~

Dalkey, in the bright, shifting skies of early morning, looked like a seaside village in Moorish Spain. White-painted *casa*-style houses lined the sea-points; three fortified houses still survived from the middle ages; and the famous Martello round tower added very convincingly to the illusion. I had missed the tide running through Dalkey Sound, and let myself in for a hard slog through that narrow passage. But the going felt far stiffer than I'd expected. No matter how hard I paddled, I just couldn't seem to make much progress. It was quite a mystery until I heard a shout from the cliffs above and behind me, 'Come back! Hold on – you've been caught!'

It was a frantic cliff-fisherman whose hook had become lodged in my rudder. Neither of us had noticed until, convinced he had caught something very large, he had run out of line and began to panic. I reversed back with the tide, unhooked his line and waved to tell him it was free. 'Jaysus!' he shouted down laughing, 'I just hope I don't catch anything bigger!'

Off the hook, though still against the tide, I moved much more quickly for the next eight miles before stopping for a very quick snack at the little town of Bray, tucked neatly into the shore near where Bray Head rises steeply from the sea. The Dublin Bay DART train rumbled around the bluff headland, diving in and out of tunnels like a clockwork model; and behind Bray rose the elegant quartzite peaks of the Sugarloaf mountain. There would be a mountain backdrop for the next twenty miles, with Djouce Mountain, Kippure and the Wicklow mountains exchanging attractive profiles behind the wide sweep of Broad Lough. The uplands of eastern Ireland lie almost parallel to the coast itself, so projections into the sea to form headlands, cliffs and peninsulas are much less common than in the west. High rocky headlands such as at Howth, Dalkey, Bray and Arklow are exceptions to the rule. Generally this is a coast of low-lying, modestly contoured, gently shelving seascapes.

Just off Wicklow Head I picked up the second ebb of the day. The speed and set of the tide carried me quickly towards the lighthouse-crowned headland itself, and into the wild frenzy of the Wicklow tide race. A fringe of crazy popping water was stirred into a lively line-dance by the light easterly breeze. Just offshore from the race I spun southwards on a wide bracket of rushing water, a cool aquamarine spruced up with white foam, watching the cliff and skyline buck and duck, rotate and recede. South of the headland I pulled out of the tide race, towards the shore, to watch a tribe of grey seals playing and fishing in the eddy stream. Some of them, hauled out high on vertical rock-stacks which they could never have climbed, and on which they were now stranded until the next high tide, looked distinctly embarrassed as I approached. But I kept my distance, not wishing to frighten them into doing themselves any damage.

South of Wicklow Head were a series of small headlands, low cliffs, sheltered coves and lovely sandy beaches. Being so close to Wicklow town, and on a sunny July day, almost every beach was filled with holidaymakers to the extent that very few areas of sand were left unclaimed. I cruised along, just a half-mile offshore, from which vantage point the busy beaches bore a close resemblance to successful pieces of fly paper. To have stopped on any of these would have meant an inevitable crowd gathering round the kayak within minutes, with the usual questions. I paddled on. Eventually I found one very quiet beach and hauled up to brew a cup of coffee. The only other people on the beach were a lovely Spanish girl of about eighteen, in a fairly frugal swimsuit, and two extremely well-spoken young Dublin kids to whom she was an *au pair*. Though I'd have rather chatted to the pretty *senorita*, the kids were obviously bubbling over with excitement about the kayak.

Very politely the little boy, about seven years old, asked beautifully phrased questions in a carefully refined accent. 'Do you often go far from the beach? Can you stop whenever you wish to? How many miles can you travel in a day?'

But when I told him about two basking sharks I'd seen earlier that day, his eyes opened wide. '*Aw, holy shit!*' he shouted in a broad Dublin brogue, and his little hand shot up to his mouth, just too late to stifle a second expression which was probably quite comprehensible, even in Spanish.

By the time I reached Arklow town I'd already gained a full forty miles from Dublin. However it was ten o'clock; darkness had fallen surprisingly quickly, and I realised suddenly how tired and hungry I'd become. The ubiquitous group was there, fishing from the harbour wall as I turned from the open sea, in between the twin breakwaters of the industrial harbour entrance. They were quite surprised to see a lone kayak come out of the semi-darkness, and I thought I'd have a little mischievous fun by adding to the confusion as I passed by. First I made a great show of checking my compass; licked my finger and held it up to the breeze; then in my weariest, corniest, mock-American accent I shouted up: 'Hey buddy, is this *Ireland*?'

Under cover of increasing darkness I forged up the river Avoca to where the lights of cars showed the first bridge crossing, and the river became too shallow to paddle any further. I tethered *Sola* to the bank, and stepped onto land beside the spot where a small huddle of old men leaned patiently on a riverside railing, just waiting and watching me arrive. Suddenly, like a scene from 'Last of the Summer Wine' or 'Dad's Army', the pensioners burst into action. They had read all about this Round Ireland Kayak caper, and now it had landed out of the darkness, right at their feet. In their own quaint, semi-military style, they were determined to find a way to be of service. From among the ranks someone was delegated to guard the boat, while another volunteered to find somewhere that I could go to eat.

In Arklow town the dreaded closing-time, like a food and drink curfew, had already fallen, and I assured them that I had some food in the boat anyway. But the cronies touched gnarled fingers to wrinkled noses, and folded flapping ears in consultative thought; then in a sudden conspiratorial rush they bundled me off to the rear entrance of Charlie's Bar where, sat down between crates of empty beer bottles, I was able to get an illicit hot meal. When I came out again, one old fellow was waiting like a sentry at the exit. He patted my back like a secret sign, glanced left and right for an imaginary enemy, and waved me on my way. As I fumbled my darkened way back into the kayak my hand felt an odd arrangement of small pebbles on the riverbank. I shone my headtorch to find a secret message reading 'GOOD LUCK' formed from little white stones; but the little old men – leprechauns probably – had disappeared into the night.

Floating down the silent midnight river towards the sea, the quiet darkness broken only by the lights of tankers and trawlers at the docks, and the belly-rumbling of the Arklow fertiliser plant, was an eerie experience. I had decided to try to reach Wexford, a further forty-five miles, by the following evening. Sola Lenses, whose factory is in Wexford town, were planning a small party for my arrival. The wind was low, the tide was favourable and the coast south of Arklow looked, on the map, to be relatively uncluttered by islands, reefs or skerries. Everything seemed just right for a night paddle. Besides, it would probably have been just as difficult to make camp as to paddle in that darkness. All the same my nerves were on edge as I paddled into a narrow pool of brightness thrown by a harbour floodlight. Suddenly I jumped as a hand reached towards me from the black water: an industrial fisherman's rubber glove, buoyed up by air in the fingers, forever grabbing skyward as though for Excalibur. It bobbed off into the night, but my heartbeat didn't settle until I was well beyond the harbour and among the purer, cleaner, darker waves of the open sea.

Blindly, but on a compass bearing, I rounded Arklow Head with its confused tidal rush. The noise of the waves, magnified in the darkness, made it sound like a major tide race, but I knew from the steady motion of the kayak that there was no real threat in those waters. I ploughed on, into and through the night, enjoying the novelty of paddling without scenery, without light; of travelling with one of the major senses entirely absent, and the others heightened.

~ ~ ~

At about four the pure night began to fade. A hint of orange appeared on the eastern horizon and began to glow, develop and spread over the edge of the world. An hour later the sun rose as a great sizzling orange orb. It seemed to have a little difficulty in finally pulling its lower quarter from the sea, but then floated happily just above the horizon, spilling citrous light across rippling waters, on a widening highway which seemed to centre on, and move south with me. With the sun came a brief warmth, then a rapidly strengthening wind. As the tide turned against me and the swell built up, I began to realise just how tired I had become, and that the night's paddle was now over. I'd covered fifty-seven miles since leaving Dublin, and needed a proper break. I pulled ashore at Courtown harbour, ready to sleep just as the town itself was waking up. The forecast was for gales throughout the day, and a team of local lifeboatmen, gathered for a morning training session, decided to don dry-suits and go fishing in the harbour instead. It was clear now that I wouldn't be able to reach Wexford in time for the party unless I could arrange to go by road.

At midday Joe Gabbott, brother of Pat, arrived to collect me and the kayak in yet another big old van. After travelling for so long at four knots at sea level, the van seat seemed incredibly high up, and forty miles per hour now felt like rallying speed. After two days without a decent sleep, and with the sun streaming through the van window, I nodded off almost instantly in the passenger seat. My head swung to and fro, banged against the windows and bounced off my chest as Joe negotiated the bumpy pot-holed minor roads of county Wexford. Just before stopping we hit a huge rut and my whole neck whiplashed forward with an ominous cracking sound; and by the time we had reached the river I was certain that I'd pulled several muscles as well as dislodged the vertebrae in my neck. A nagging pain had begun, but it was nothing compared to what was to develop over the next week as a result.

I woke with a jolt as the van ground to a halt on the north bank of the river Slaney, and opened my eyes to the bizarre, dreamlike sight of twenty kayaks, decorated with coloured balloons, and occupied by canoeists wearing Round Ireland Kayak T-shirts. Apparently the Barrow canoe club had agreed to escort my kayak across to Wexford town for the reception and to make sure I didn't go astray. Already Joe Gabbott, like a man with a mission, was filling helium balloons and tying them onto my kayak until it looked quite capable of *flying* across to Wexford on its own.

We began to cross the bay, a surreal-looking motley flotilla of colourful, helium-assisted canoes. Halfway across we were joined by two boatloads of Wexford sea-scouts in the flat-bottomed 'pram' boats which traditionally negotiate the shallow sandbanked waters of the bay, and by another boat with a four-pair team of oarsmen. Together we pulled onwards, joking and capering, towards Wexford town. At first it seemed simply coincidental to me that the strains of a brass band floated over the quay and down river. There's obviously something important on in town today, I thought. But, as we approached the quay, the other boats began to fall back, pushing me forward on my own. It was only then that the brass band really piped up, and a great cheer rose from a crowd of hundreds of balloon-waving people lining the Wexford seafront. I was appalled. Stunned. *All this was for me!* I wished the sea could just open and swallow me up, but there was nothing I could do to escape. It was all meant in the best spirit of Irish fun, and I'd just have to swallow my modesty and try to enjoy being the star attraction for as long as it would last. I bit my lip, waved up to the crowd of onlookers, and paddled to the quay. Hitching *Sola* onto my shoulder, I hauled her up thirty feet of steep steps to the street above, pretending that it wasn't excruciatingly painful on my damaged neck to do so.

Up on the Wexford seafront a full-scale carnival was underway. There were literally hundreds of people, adults and children, there to see the kayak arrive, support the cause, and above all to enjoy themselves. Cameras were flashing, kids wanted autographs, and the kayak – looking quite the star of the show – shone beautifully in the Wexford sunshine. While the band struck up the 'Boys of Wexford' under the canopy of the Allied Irish Bank, I was offered an introduction to the Mayor of the town, an opportunity which I would normally have embraced with as much enthusiasm as a dental appointment. But Wexford's lady mayor was no red-faced overweight civic dignitary. Helen Corish wore her chain of office, obviously designed with far more bullish necks in mind, like a fairy would wear a suit of armour; and yet managed to move among the crowds with a cheery smile or a witty remark to anyone who caught her eye. A sparkling young woman from an old and respected Wexford family, she bore office in an unassuming and natural way, destroying in one fell swoop all my stereotyped prejudices of mayordom. It was a pleasure to meet her. Helen Corish and I were whisked away by car to the Ferrycarrig Hotel, up river from Wexford, where the Slaney flows through a deep narrow gorge, and where the tranquillity of rural Wexford, which hung in the air, was about to be challenged. The next round of formalities and festivities was about to begin.

What a peculiarly schizophrenic existence, I thought. At midnight I'm alone in the open sea, paddling a kayak through the darkness; then by mid-afternoon I'm nibbling sandwiches at a classy country hotel with the lady mayor! As far as I knew, the kayak was still on the quayside in Wexford, and by now I felt that I had lost any slight control that I ever had over events. Like a piece of flotsam I seemed to have become caught up in a rip-tide of episodes which had little in common with my original concept of the kayak journey. And yet there seemed no point in clinging too tightly onto fixed goals and self-imposed targets. I had recently given up a job that had become too narrowly focused on aims and objectives, time-management and mission statements; and it was important that this Irish journey didn't get caught up along those same blinkered tram lines. There are times when a single-minded attitude and determination of purpose are entirely inappropriate, when the currents of vibrant opportunity that sweep through even the most tightly-planned schedules become so insistent that to resist them in favour of some inflexible vision would be a denial of all that makes life colourful and enriching. The currents of Irish wilfulness and enthusiasm, which were to sweep me along through the entire trip, had become very strong; and I felt that it made no more sense to resist them than it would to attempt to paddle the kayak against a strong sea-tide. I could only hope to lighten the floating load, to surf along on top of events, enjoy the ride, and hope for a gentle landing at the end of it all.

From one day's dawn to a second day's dusk can seem like a very long time. A hotel receptionist kindly showed me the room which had been booked for me and I decided to have a relaxing bath. By then I'd slept only two hours in the last two days, and so as soon as I lay in the warm water my systems closed down, and I slept like a baby for three hours. I woke to the sound of Irish music and the excited laughing and talking of many voices coming from a large, brightly coloured marquee by the river. There was a buzz from the hotel intercom, and then the cheery, teasing voice of Sola Lenses' business manager, the inimitable Deirdre O'Sullivan, suggesting that it was about time I showed up at my own party!

Oh God! I thought, as I quickly dressed and trotted downstairs, I'd forgotten about the party! I had no idea what time it was, and only a vague idea of what day. The sounds of revelry continued to strengthen as I crossed the lawn. Sola's entire staff, plus friends and spouses were already gathered in the marquee; I was about to be guest of honour at the biggest party I'd ever attended. All went quiet as I entered the tent, and I'd no idea what I was expected to do. Suddenly everyone stood up, singing and cheering, while the live band played me in with the battle-chant of the Irish football team at the Italian World Cup finals: 'OLÉ! OLÉ! OLÉ! OLÉE! OLÉ! O-OLÉ!'

I then had to make a quick 'welcome' speech and to start the dancing. God! I thought again, this is worse than getting married! But beneath the bewilderment I was aware of a growing feeling of being deeply touched by all this, and by the whole Irish spirit. Think *flotsam,* I told myself. The party was about to begin, and no-one in the world has a talent for enjoying a party like the Irish.

What a night! Two live bands played tremendous, continuous music; there was free food and subsidised drink for everyone; and of Sola's three hundred employees, at least three-quarters seemed to be under thirty, female, very pretty, and quite uninhibited about enjoying themselves. As guest of honour – this peculiar phenomenon which had grabbed all the press attention, and provided an excuse for a big work's night out – I proved quite a curiosity among them. I hardly had a chance to sit down all night. And in the middle of a swirling, flowing process of hugging, laughing, dancing and photo-taking, I decided it was kind of fun being flotsam in an Irish whirlpool. After two weeks of sea air and sea-kayak solitude, it all seemed quite unreal. As the night wore into morning the party just got hotter and wilder, and I realised that I was enjoying every minute of it. I danced a waltz with the Mayor of Wexford; was close to tears as I listened for the first time to the words of the 'Fields of Athenry'; and stood entranced as Helen Corish sang a soft, haunting version of 'I Want to be Seduced'. At one in the morning the *gardaí* tried to close the party. But their wrath was defused with a diplomatic explanation of the kayak journey and its charity connections, and the party continued for several more hours. At about four o'clock a marquee full of glowing revellers joined together in a massive Conga dance which would have made the *Mardi Gras* seem tame, then slowed gradually down and stood quietly as the band moved into a more solemn tune.

'Would you all please be upstanding for the National Anthem,' requested the band leader. The entire crowd of dishevelled, bleary-eyed Irish party-animals prised themselves upright, and tried to look as serious as possible. Whereupon the band burst suddenly and enthusiastically, for one last time, into a wild and raucous round of 'OLÉ! OLÉ! OLÉ! OLÉ!' which, still ringing in my ears, seemed to bear me up the Ferrycarrig stairs to bed.

FASTNET

Carnsore Point to Dursey Island

269 miles

FASTNET

WEXFORD

WATERFORD

CORK

Cork

Celtic Sea

toNN chLíodhna

Carnsore Point
Saltee Islands
Ballyteige Bay
Hook Head
Waterford Harb.
Brownstone Head
Dunmore S. East
Tramore
Waterford
R. Suir
Dungarvan Bay
Helvic Head
Mine Head
R. Blackwater
Ardmore
Youghal
Ballycotton Island
Ballycotton
Cobh
Passage West
Cork Harbour
Crosshaven
Kinsale
Old Head of Kinsale
Courtmacsherry Bay
Seven Heads
Dunworly Bay
Galley Head
R. Lee
Skibbereen
Toe Head
Baltimore
Sherkin Island
Clear Island
Cape Clear
Fastnet
Crookhaven
Roaringwater Bay
Mizen Head
Three Castle Head
Sheep's Head
Dunmanus Bay
Crow Head
Bear I.
Bantry Bay
Dursey Island
Slieve Miskish Mts
Caha Mts
Derrynasaggart Mts

0 5 10 15 20 25 miles

52°
51°
52°
10°
9°
8°
7°

CHAPTER FOUR

Prince of the Saltees

*The faces of old seamen have always an expression of severity left
upon them by the vexation of perpetually looking out for changes.*

The Toilers of the Sea, Victor Hugo

The southern fringe of Ireland, from Carnsore Point to the Fastnet
Rock, where counties Wexford, Waterford and Cork meet the
Celtic Sea, is a spectacular coast, textured with havens and
headlands, and haunted by echoes of bygone eras of ocean
voyaging. This is Fastnet, a coast whose carbuncles and belly-rolls
conceal, amongst other surprises, Europe's first lighthouse,
civilisation's oldest yacht club, and a legacy of voyages, invasions,
piracy and smuggling that seems at the same time ancient and yet
strangely tangible – both picturesque and sinister. Over this whole
coast hangs the kind of salty haze under whose influence *Treasure
Island* and *Lloyds Register of Shipping* no longer seem poles apart;
where fiction and geography fuse, and where every seaman's story
seems to have a foothold in reality.

Fastnet is a coast of wrecks and wreckers. The jagged,
reef-fringed shores of south Wexford have, over the centuries,
proved among the most treacherous for shipping in the whole of
Europe. Great, broad tides swing towards Carnsore Point and the
Tuskar Rock, heaving along like rivers, pouring over the shallow
reefs and swirling round the rocks and islands. It was not without
good reason that Ballyteige Bay became known as 'the graveyard of
a thousand ships' during the days of sail. Any sailing ship driven by
an onshore gale between Hook Head and the rocky islands which
fringe Ballyteige Bay, would have had little chance of survival.

Among the frequent wrecks of centuries past were many who, after making the long Atlantic crossing, mistook the Hook Head lighthouse for the Eddystone light off the Cornwall coast. In fog or storm, through simple navigational error, or occasionally following the false luring lights of wreckers, many ships steered due north into the jaws of Ballyteige under full sail, believing they were running safely up Plymouth Sound. In 1803 – a year of severe storms – no fewer than eleven large sailing vessels were wrecked at Ballyteige, and local chronicles refer to 'the quantity of masts, spars and dead bodies that were driven ashore'.

~ ~ ~

As the kayak closed south towards Carnsore Point in a dense sea fog, visibility was limited to about twenty-two yards, and the approach had all the tension of a nautical game of blindman's buff. 'Bumsore Point' might have been a better label. Prolonged dampness, salt water and paddling movements had begun to cause pressure sores right where my pelvic bones were in constant contact with the hard seat of the kayak. 'Necksore' would have been even more appropriate, as my damaged neck had now completely seized. I could move freely below the shoulders, but any jerky movements sent excruciating spasms of pain up through my neck, as though there was no longer a joint between my head and body. Turning my head had become impossible, meaning that I had to rotate at the waist and roll my eyeballs in order to look anywhere other than directly ahead. Luckily the sea state, even near Carnsore Point, was relatively calm so far, and I paddled steadily onward in the blinkered style of an android mime-artiste with a chronic rust problem.

Sub-sea geologists, surveying this area for the proposed siting of a nuclear power station, recorded tidal streams of up to eight knots round Carnsore, and already I could feel a power implicit in the water. It was a steady, pouring sort of power, an insistent, unstoppable sluicing around the right-angled granite headland, emptying the great basin of the Irish Sea. It was obvious that, at times, the wind and ground swell must stir and ruffle that tide to a hell-wash of white foam and breakers as it stumbles over the submerged banks and counter currents of Carnsore. But, contrary to what one might expect, the worst turbulence of the Carnsore race occurs around times of high and low water. I'd planned my passage for around half-tide, and for the moment the ebb current was strong but benign. Through the fog I could already sense the banks and cliffs rushing past on my right and I watched as the compass began to register southwest around the point itself. Increasingly I could feel beneath the kayak a long, smooth sea swell which I hadn't met with in two hundred miles of the Irish Sea and, despite the foggy screen all around, I knew that I'd entered the wider nautical arena of Fastnet: a new sea county, subject to a new area forecast, governed by different rules, stronger prevailing winds, and new ocean games.

~ ~ ~

Thick mists, like sea-borne pollution, it seemed, pay little heed to borders drawn for human convenience; and so my crossing into Fastnet brought no immediate improvement in visibility. On a three knot tide and a bearing of west-southwest, I was heading blindly seaward, five miles into the fog of the Celtic Sea in search of the briny-sounding Saltee islands. Dewy swirls of mist parted across my bows, and seemed to close again as the rudder ploughed its shallow furrow behind the kayak. All was hushed and heavy, muffled and moist. Then from the gloom ahead came the unmistakeable low growling of waves breaking on rock. Before I could puzzle out its source I was being drawn rapidly towards a great jagged reef whose torn, winged profile seemed to stretch far into the murky distance on both sides.

Fiercely, and with a roaring din, the tidal river flooded over the long shallow barrier in a sucking series of standing waves. Instinctively I hesitated, back-paddling to tread water, gaining the time needed to consider a safe passage. Then, quickly selecting a sluice where there was sufficient water between the kayak and the fangs of rock which poked out from the reef, I put the paddle back in gear and shot forward over turbulent water. As I surfed the broad reef-waves, leaning and ruddering to avoid the last few toothy rocks, a brief but splendid shaft of sunlight suddenly split the fog. Two stiff-winged fulmars glided over the kayak and, above the wavetops, I had my first view of the Saltee islands, lying now only about two miles to the south.

By the time I had cleared the great reef and reached the Saltees, Fastnet had shed her gloomy grey shawl. The afternoon sun had boiled off the last of the sea fog and the islands glowed balmy and still like illustrations from a children's picture book, or stepping stones into the colourful history of the Celtic Sea. Down the centuries the Saltees have been home to Celtic monks, Viking raiders, smugglers and pirates, fugitive political leaders, farmers and fishermen, and sea birds by the thousand. The landbound cynic's sneer that an island is 'just a piece of sea with no water in it' is perhaps nowhere more mistaken than among the Saltee islands, where every paddle stroke unfurls yet more of a coast rich in the lore of loot-laden sea-reivers, and every step ashore reveals another legend or curiosity.

The southern coast of the Great Saltee, the larger of the two islands, is a sea-shattered, rock-girt maze of caves, tunnels, geos and stacks whose names, such as the Cat-Cliff, the Giant's Chair and the Labour-in-Vain rock arch, have the salty tang of a treasure map or story book. Natural features on the island bear a mixture of names from Norse, Irish, English and the local Yola dialect. And caverns called Devil's Den, Hell Hole, Happy Hole and the China Shop recall previous service as the caches, dens and glory holes of smugglers from a bygone era. Several have entrances submerged at high tide, yet with internal chambers that remain dry, providing ideal secret vaults for jewels, brandy, spices, and other sea-borne wealth smuggled from the Continent or plundered from the merchant ships of the Celtic Sea. So easily, these caves could have been the perfect templates for Matthew Arnold's:

> *Sand-strewn caverns, cool and deep,*
> *Where the winds are all asleep:*
> *Where the spent lights quiver and gleam;*
> *Where the salt-weed sways in the stream.*

The rocks and caves were brightly, but subtly, colour banded, with each band demarcating a degree of exposure or salinity like a laboratory litmus test. Just above the waves the rocks were dark. Blackzone lichens gave the appearance of tar smeared on the rocks, and along this band pink sea-urchins clung like carefully placed ornaments. Immediately above the blackzone was a bright orange band where several species of orange and yellow lichens seemed to thrive in a rich mixture of salt spray and sunlight. This band in turn gave way to the greenish-grey, tuftier *Ramalina* lichens, safe from all but the stormiest of seas and the highest of tides.

In an evening sun as bright as Spanish gold, I paddled on round the island, by Lady Walker's Cave, past Molly Hoy, Celbooly and Dead Man's Cliff, until I came full circle, to a boulder-cleared landing which faced north towards the Irish coast. Here, spreading my damp gear on large sun-warmed stones to dry, I headed ashore to explore the interior of the Great Saltee. Almost immediately the tropical *Treasure Island* image, which the Great Saltee had exuded at sea level, had its counterpart on land. Avenues of palm trees, twenty feet high and swaying in the evening breeze like a scene from the Cayman islands, led on past an old well and a derelict house, to the lush, tussocky summit of the island. On a knoll called Tomeen I lay down among cushions of thrift, campion and deep shrubbery, fertilised by a thousand sea birds, and gazed out over three hundred and sixty degrees of glorious Fastnet seascape. Shining lazily in the south and east lay wide open sea; westward into lingering haze faded the recurring headlands of counties Waterford and Cork; to the north were Little Saltee Island and, curving away towards the Irish shore, the tidal reef known as St Patrick's Bridge.

This was the reef I'd encountered in the afternoon mist, and I wouldn't have been the first vessel to come to grief on it. Above half-tide it is at its most dangerous to boats. Its rocks are hidden, and treacherous currents boil over them like a weir. Local fishermen will most often detour round Little Saltee Island to avoid the reef; but to unsuspecting mariners from other parts it has long been a hazard. So much rock is exposed at low tide that, until this century, local farmers driving cattle to Little Saltee were able to use it as a causeway. And they did so with every confidence, as it was commonly believed to have been built by that very best of marine engineers, St Patrick himself.

Legend has it that the Saltee islands only appeared after St Patrick's epic routing of the Devil, who had been lurking in the Galtee Mountains of county Tipperary. To speed his escape the Devil chewed a huge lump out of a mountain – known today as Devil's Bit Gap – and ran with it towards the coast. The bold St Patrick grabbed up a boulder to fling at the Devil as he swam out from the Wexford coast. That boulder landed half-a-mile offshore and can still be seen today. But the Devil swam on undeterred. In saintly fervour, Patrick continued to catapult hundreds of rocks in an attempt to sink the swimming Devil, and it was these which formed St Patrick's Bridge as they fell. But still the Devil swam on, until after two-and-a-half miles a portion of the bite of rock fell from his mouth and formed Little Saltee. A half-mile further south he lost the bigger bit, which of course became the Great Saltee. What became of the Devil himself is not recorded locally, but there are still those who claim that the Saltee islands are really the *Galtee* islands, and by rights belong to county Tipperary!

From the grassy heights it was easy to see that the mischievous role played by the Saltees in the briny annals of the Celtic Sea owed as much to their actual position as to their secret dens and booty holes. The Saltee islands dominate the busy sea lanes off the south coast of Ireland, on routes to and from St George's Channel, the Continent and the old Atlantic trade routes to the New World. Between the sixteenth and eighteenth centuries sea voyages of discovery, trade and piracy went through a massive expansion. Vast quantities of precious metals, alcohols, tobacco –

and even human slaves – were on the move by sea, and the ships of England, France, Spain, Ireland and America were battling for domination of these very waters. Stir the cocktail with some of the worst tide and shoal conditions in Europe, and spike it with pirates and sea-reivers with false luring lights, and corsairs from the Barbary coast preying like hyenas upon damaged and defenceless freighters, and it's little wonder that the Saltees became an infamous base-camp for smuggling and illicit trade.

Moonlighters and freebooters, well versed in local currents, tides, weather conditions and coastal hazards, would have been virtually invincible among the Saltee islands, the Fastnet equivalent of the Caribbean's Grand Tortuga; and many's the cache of rum or rifles, furs or fine wines that would have been trans-shipped in secrecy behind the cliffs of the Great Saltee before being rowed in to the Wexford coast under cover of darkness. From the Saltee clifftop it was not difficult to imagine the scene: the bump of wooden oars from the bouldered cove below; the shouts and curses as bales and barrels are stacked hastily above the tideline; dim, flickering shafts of torchlight, woodsmoke and rum-reek escaping from the cavern cracks; and rough laughter, lubricated with illicit spirits, mingling with the slap of waves and the shrieks of a thousand sea birds.

Coastal smuggling reached a peak in the seventeenth and eighteenth centuries as improved roads enabled smugglers to distribute contraband more easily and quickly to the growing markets of the big cities. Tobaccos, snuffs and illicit liquors – brandy and port for the gentry, gin for the poorer classes – were in great demand. All around the coasts of Britain and Ireland, in coves, inlets and on deserted beaches, barrels and boxes were being offloaded in the certain knowledge that, inland, huge profits were there for the taking. The risks were amply justified by the rewards.

In today's terms smuggling is often associated with the most sinister aspects of organised crime, and international cartels trading in drugs, arms, pornography or endangered species, and tends to meet with a fairly universal condemnation among ordinary folk. But two or three hundred years ago smuggling had a quite different image. It was far more mundane goods which were netting big profits for the smuggler; there was no automatic assumption among the common people that just because something was illegal it was also wrong; and smugglers were more often local rogues than faceless gangsters. Those engaged in 'the moonlit trade' could almost always rely on a certain degree of help, or at least complicity, from the public. The people of the coastal districts often saw the government of the day as something remote, oppressive and upper class. Its representatives, the customs and 'preventive' officers, frequently met with outright obstruction of a sort almost unimaginable today. Such anarchy among the local people was deep rooted. Many believed that the natural rights of men to free trade were being threatened by the customs officers. Smuggling could be seen as a social protest against the harshness of the laws, the iniquity of certain taxes, and the very unfair distribution of wealth. In this light smugglers were history's most popular criminals, Robin Hood characters, re-distributors of goods. They provided an outlet for the natural roguery of ordinary folk and, as Kipling's 'Smuggler's Song' records, many a blind eye was turned in the coastal villages.

> *If you wake at midnight, and hear a horse's feet,*
> *Don't go drawing back the blind, or looking in the street;*
> *Them that asks no questions, isn't told a lie,*
> *Watch the wall, my darling, while the gentlemen go by.*

Of course, ideologies aside, a small share of the goods or profits, would no doubt render local people all the more likely to take the side of the smuggler against the authorities. Hidey-holes, cellars and caves were carefully kept secrets; laden pack-ponies struggled up winding coastal paths; and hundreds of fit men along the coasts moonlighted for cash or kind, hefting contraband goods from the sea to safe houses inland.

> *Four and twenty ponies, trotting through the dark;*
> *Brandy for the parson, baccy for the clerk,*

Laces for a lady, letters for a spy,
Watch the wall, my darling, while the gentlemen go by.

~ ~ ~

The cries and calls of the seafowl have always been the dominant soundtrack of the Saltee islands, now a bird sanctuary of international importance, home to gulls, auks, gannets and cormorants and many more, as well as a staging post for seasonal migrants. Many of the island's features are named after their sea bird residents, such as Fulmar Bay, Makestone and Big Shag Rock, and the island air is charged with the reek and racket of their constant presence. From the great vaults of the smugglers' caverns shot colourful rock doves. So straight and fast was their flight, and so bright the pastel shades on their wings that it was hard to believe these were the wild cousins of the fluttering, limping, down-and-out fowl of our city squares and railway stations. Along the clifftops, fulmars soared on rigid pinions, like radio-controlled aeroplanes, approaching the cliff ledges as though preparing to land, but then banking off suddenly at the final moment. Fulmars spend three-quarters of their lives at sea, so perhaps they feel as distrustful of making a solid landing as I would about stepping off the cliff into thin air.

It is quite uncanny just how similar certain sea bird noises are to demented human laughter and, periodically, as a wave of manic shrieking and cackling would rise from the cliff-side bird colonies, I was reminded of the strange story of Paul Rasmussen.

Rasmussen was a clergyman in a small Icelandic village, many years ago. When English raiders landed from three ships, Rasmussen evacuated everyone from his village, then he too fled, carrying his seven-year-old son on his back. The weight of his son slowed him down, so he hid the boy in the mouth of a cave, warning him not to come out until he saw his father returning. Rasmussen then ran on, but was hampered by his long, heavy cassock, so he took it off and dropped it. The Englishmen could not catch him, but for a joke one of them put on the cassock. As they passed the cave, the little boy, thinking he recognised his father, came out, and so was carried off by the raiders.

Rasmussen saw them from the beach, and with a grim determination set about making black magic, using one cockle-shell to represent each of the English boats. He sang, drew signs in the sand, and set the three shells upon the water. One drifted towards the open sea; the other two turned over and sank. Sure enough two of the English ships also ran aground, broke up and sank. So Rasmussen had his revenge; but as he stood watching from the beach, the body of the boy washed up at his feet. People say that he looked for a moment at his son then let out a horrible shriek of grief, which turned slowly into an ugly, cackling laugh. He went on laughing hysterically as he stumbled blindly, nakedly down the coast, his laughter echoing from the cliffs and along the shores. Paul Rasmussen kept on walking, and kept on laughing, but was never seen again; and perhaps when you think you are hearing the raucous cries of the sea birds, it may be that crazy Paul Rasmussen is calling to you along the cliff.

~　~　~

One of the Saltees has gone missing! Early maps clearly showed a third island, which is now absent both from modern maps and from the Celtic Sea. One wonders, did it just sink? Were the early maps simply wrong? Or has St Patrick been rearranging the coastline yet again? Certainly the Saltees were a rich mixture, full of surprises. Perhaps the most unexpected of all, a truth as strange as any fiction, was the stone armchair at the island's summit – the *throne* of Prince Michael the First.

Michael Neill, who died in 1998, was the son of a Wexford farmer. After making some money in England, Neill set up a factory in Dublin making roof preservatives and cattle feed. In 1943 he bought Great Saltee Island, and took the title of Prince Michael of the Saltees, erecting the throne, an obelisk and a flagstaff for the occasion of his own coronation. The obelisk bears his profile, carved in stone along with various quaint inscriptions. The throne itself shows a coat of arms – a shield held by two buxom mermaids. Each quarter of the shield depicts a different bird, acknowledging the Saltees' rich wildlife heritage. The inscription on the throne reads:

> *This chair is erected in memory of my mother to whom I made a vow that one day I would own the Saltee islands and become the first Prince of the Saltees. Henceforth my heirs and successors can only proclaim themselves Prince of these islands by sitting in this chair fully garbed in the robes and crown of the islands and taking the oath of succession.*

Michael the First

Another edict declares that:

> *No man or assembly of men has any right whatsoever to interfere in the affairs of the Saltee Island ...*

At least there was nothing to the effect that visitors were prohibited, or that a fee was payable for landing; and had Prince Michael the First achieved any lasting benefit or improvement on the islands, it might have seemed fairly unobjectionable for his ownership to have been so eccentrically commemorated. But, as far as I could make out, nothing had been done in almost half a century to halt the islands' ecological decline. In the light of the condition of the Saltee islands – barren, unkept and infested with rats which will take their toll on the sea birds – he was just another absentee owner. The whole concept of obelisks and edicts, erected by Prince Michael in honour of himself, seemed incredibly egotistical, and I wondered what the smugglers of past centuries would have made of it all.

Today the Saltees lie uninhabited. Despite their ease of access, comparative fertility and gentle climate, they had been among the first of the Irish islands to be abandoned by their inhabitants – and the absence of a population where one could patently live quite well always adds a ghostly atmosphere to an island. Rats and rabbits scamper unchecked on turf that once might have known the play of children or the stroke of the spade, and the sea birds are undisturbed, save for the passing of small fishing boats and the summer tours from Kilmore Quay.

I returned from the rabbit-hopping island summit to my camp on the rocks just as a big red sun hovered low in the evening sky. From the black sky that succeeded the sunset, fell a heavy dew, soaking my bedroll and hair. But on that night I was Prince of the Saltees, and the rats – the *luch Francach* or 'French mice' that infest many similar islands as a result of innumerable shipwrecks – kept a respectable distance. The breeze was combing the palm leaves, and the dark tide was lapping on the boulder beach. I felt quite complete and content, and realised that very few people ever know quite such a magical solitude as this. Then I wondered why it was that I felt no need for company, and understood that the desocialising effect of even one day alone at sea is quite incredibly powerful.

There are moments in any solo journey when loneliness surfaces as the dominant emotion, but for me these had always been short-lived, bearable and counterbalanced by the joys of self-reliance and an uncompromised freedom. Travelling alone allows one to sprint ahead or to lag behind as the fancy takes you, to move at one's own pace, or at least to be moved the more easily by the other forces at play whether they be the tides and currents of the sea, the stubborn streaks of wind and weather, or the events and characters by which one is inevitably influenced along the way. Though not by nature a complete hermit, solo travel was a mode which I'd found suited me well.

Travelling, in itself, sets the mind in motion 'wherever it be ...' But a man alone in a kayak, dependent on neither a machine nor another person or animal, drops clean out of society and the concerns of normal daily life. Away from – perhaps even out of sight of – the land, he becomes the focus of an entirely different existence, where his concerns are not those of commerce or communication, rank, class, race, income or gender, but those of technique, skills, weather and seascapes. The cumulative effect of continuous or consecutive days at sea, then, might range from a slight re-shuffle of his life's priorities, to a paradigm shift, a 'sea-change' in his general consciousness.

For me, long periods of discomfort and monotony, strung out along the measured rhythm of paddle strokes, with the mind in neutral, emptied, were punctuated with occasional flashes of insight or inspiration, perceptions of beautiful events in the natural world, or (what seemed at least at the time to be) solutions to world problems! Some events happened in a flash: the riffle of a fish on the sea's surface; the rising, wheeling fin of a porpoise; or the whiplash death-strike of a heron in the shallows. Others unfolded slowly, gradually, perceptible only to someone obliged to sit at sea level for hours at a stretch, or days in a row: the cycle of tides in a moon's turn; weather fronts rolling like amoebae over an entire coastline; and the constant changing of light and colour on the sea.

Over the ten weeks of my Irish journey, there was not one single day in which I didn't hear the sound of the sea. I would rise with it in the morning, and fall asleep to it at night; sometimes cacophonous, sometimes melodic; an alarm call, a lullaby, a running commentary and a soundtrack. And decisions on what to do with the day could never be made without reference to the sea, the tide and the weather. For all these reasons, I reckoned that continuous travel round a coastline must be in many ways similar to living on a small island; and stories of the lives of Irish islands had captivated me for many years. (I did not know then just how literally I was soon to become captivated by an island at the far end of Fastnet.)

Against a backcloth of black velvet, shooting stars flashed across the Fastnet sky. I watched them, my back against a rounded rock, and a coffee in my hand, allowing a matching mental meteorology to continue unchecked in my head. Shooting thoughts, bright, fast-moving ideas with no apparent past or future, flashed into consciousness, then burned themselves out against a darkening backdrop of pleasant tiredness.

~ ~ ~

At the first movement of morning my neck gave a pained spasm, stiffened, and began to ache fiercely in the chilly air. But the sun rose quickly, warming the protesting muscles and drying my dew-soaked bedroll during the two hours it took to breakfast and pack. Quite apart from any fashionable notions of the harmful effects of the sun's rays, the deep healing effect of the sunlight on damaged muscle was quite tangible. It was ten when I left the Great Saltee, heading into a hazy sea that promised an ever-strengthening morning sun, on a bearing for Baginbun Head. The headland, for the moment invisible across eight miles of sea, was not a true destination, for I calculated that the west-going tide would carry me around the peninsula of Hook Head, the first of the great south coast headlands, long before I would regain the Irish coast.

Into the warm heart of the brightening morning I paddled, unfettered by lifejacket or shirt, feeling the salt breeze on my body, and the occasional cooling splash of blown spray; and enjoying the special mindset produced by being surrounded by shining sea in all directions, out of sight of land, just cruising. An hour passed in what Kipling called the sea's 'excellent loneliness', a magical solitude and silent motion, with the paddles rotating to the intoned rhythms of tunes in my head. But when the Saltees had all but faded I realised that I had company on the Celtic Sea. The distant purring of a fishing boat began to grow louder and closer; and from that hazy indistinct region that is not quite sea, but is certainly not sky, she materialised. Cutting back her engine she coasted in close, gently and carefully, a wooden deep-water lobsterboat in beautiful emerald green, with an old walrus of a fisherman grinning down at me from the gunwhale.

'Now whir have ye come from in that brave yoke?' he shouted, amused at the little kayak so far from shore. Hardly an inch of his face was free from the cracks and crevasses of a life at sea, where salting winds and soaking squalls alternate with blazing days of sea-reflected sunshine. Of all the moods of the sea's calendar, I thought, perhaps it is these sun-charged days which leave the deepest tracks on sea-faring faces. Eyes so often narrowed to form wrinkled glare-resistant slits are eventually tanned to rawhide, salt crusted and seasoned until they can no longer fully open again. Although I had been squinting into the morning sun for little more than an hour, the reflected glare from the sea's surface had been extremely powerful; the skin of my own face was already drum-tight, and the crow's feet around my eyes seemed as if chiselled in mahogany.

It was difficult to estimate the age of the lobsterman – anything betwen a battered forty and a sprightly seventy – and even harder to make sense of his strong accent; something I attributed to the influence of the ancient Yola dialect, a mixture of Somerset English and Flemish, spoken in parts of Wexford until the beginning of this century. But we exchanged nautical nods, agreed that the morning was fine, and nattered about lobsters and crabs, porpoises and petrels, cabbages and kings. I was curious to know how, in this featureless expanse of open water, he could find his way with confidence to the sites of his lobster creels, marked only by the tiniest of pink floats.

'Ah now, ye can do a lot at sea with "common sinse",' he said. 'And there's virry little ye can do withoot it!' he added with a wry glance at the kayak. 'And, of course, I have my *bearings*.'

'You do use a compass then?' I asked.

'Not at all! I have the bearings in *here*.' He tapped his forehead firmly.

When he talked of his 'bearings' he seemed to mean something neither magnetic nor digital, but more like runes, open sesames or way-words. He and other local fishermen apparently memorised rhymes and chants that referred to islands, skerries or onshore features such as prominent headlands, peaks or even buildings. By superimposing two features along one line of sight, then sailing on that transit until a further two were in alignment along a separate sightline, and perhaps confirming that with a third 'bearing', the fishermen locate precise, unique and perhaps secret points on the sea's featureless, heaving surface, and record those positions in mnemonic rhyme. It was an ancient system, he said, perhaps as old as the Vikings. The bearings were passed on in an oral tradition, rather than written down: it was more accurate, and more secure, he said. Rather than using the names on modern maps, some bearings referred to coastal features in traditional lore and dialect, often from such a unique sea-level perspective that they would probably be quite incomprehensible to land-based people.

He chanted examples of bearings used for pilotage directions such as entering safe harbours in rough conditions, and keeping clear of dangerous shoals. Yet others might describe locations the fisherman had never yet visited; so that when he reached them he would have the bearings to find his way safely. The notion reminded me of the Aboriginal songlines of Australia, whereby native tribesmen are taught songs that name key features of landscape along the lines of travel followed by their Dreamtime ancestors as they 'sang' the land into existence. These tribesmen need no maps to follow their Walkabout routes, only the songs that they have committed to memory; and here was a practical similarity in modern day Ireland.

'What would you do in fog or bad visibility?' I asked, thinking of my experiences of recent days.

'Oh well, then we do have the compass, and also a depth tester we can use at a pinch, but you can't *rely* on them,' he replied, as though dismissing such technology as, at best, rather bland gimmicks.

Despite our slightly divergent navigational techniques, it seemed we were heading in a roughly similar direction across the rolling, dazzling desert of blue, and so he offered me a tow. The thought of forsaking a further hour's slog at four knots across a featureless sea, in favour of an exhilarating tow of perhaps fifteen knots was certainly tempting. The problems were how to attach the tow rope, and how to steer the kayak to prevent it from broaching at speed. If the kayak's bow veered away from the fishing boat I'd broach and capsize; if it edged too close to the boat I'd be trapped against its hull. Even on such a fine day the thought of being minced by the propeller, or being hauled along upside-down at full tilt was not attractive. On the other hand the sea was indolent and glassy, stirred only by the slightest of swells, and I thought that the rudder might just manage to control the kayak even at speed. Besides, it was too good and too rare an offer to miss.

'Ha! We'll try it so,' said the fisherman. He tossed me down a thick hank of hairy coir rope. I looped it tightly round my wrist and leaned back. The paddle was fixed lengthways on deck, and I lashed my lifejacket to the foredeck ready for action if needed. The fisherman disappeared into the wheelhouse to rev the engine. With a cough of diesel fumes the rope tightened, and suddenly we were off! Five knots – ten knots – and climbing until the engine's rumble stabilised at *fifteen* knots, full power. I gripped tightly on the rope, pressed hard on the footrest, and the speed of the trawler translated itself through my body to the skidding, skiing hull of the slender kayak. Instantly a wake of fizzing white water appeared at my stern, and the rudder became ultra-responsive to the slightest foot pressure. A touch of the right toe, and the kayak swung wide away from the speeding boat, only to be brought back with equal ease by a pressure on the left.

'Yee-hah!' Like an olympic water-skier I wove to and fro, leaning in and out of carving turns, roaring with exhilaration. The kayak, reaching speeds far beyond those for which it was designed, shot welcome splinters of wave spray over my toasting torso, and a broad grin of adventure over my sun-warmed face. So much for 'common sinse', I thought, as the fisherman leaned on elbows over the gunwale, smoking, smiling and giving me thumbs-up signs. He seemed to have lost all interest in searching for creels, and looked as if he was considering whether or not to reel in this unusual catch instead. It was then that I realised that the rope to which I was attached disappeared up over the drum of the boat's creel-winch in a series of business-like coils; if he were to trip the gear for the

winch I'd be hauled unceremoniously into the air, kayak and all!

But what a way to travel! Scudding effortlessly through a morning of flashing blues like a marlin leaping after a flying fish. Of course, it was too good to last. Eventually the lobster-boatman, responding presumably to one of his mysterious bearings, began to slow the engines, and soon we had stopped among a flotilla of tiny pink buoys, the mark of a deepwater crustacean rendezvous. Try as I might, I couldn't persuade him to abandon the lobsters, bearings and the azure sheen of the Celtic Sea, in order to tow me round what remained of the Irish coast.

'Sure, I'm a terrible one for the women,' he said. 'I'd be stopping for those little dark ones in Kerry and Clare, trouble though they are, and I'd only be slowing ye down so. Besides, I'm happy these days between the Hook and Carnsore; off ye go now, and the good luck with ye!'

I was cast adrift and, after a last wave, set about returning to my own bearing towards the Irish coast. It wasn't entirely uncomplicated. From an initial four miles along a course of three hundred degrees, I calculated, I'd been hauled for twenty minutes at perhaps fifteen knots on an unspecified bearing back out seaward. The bright dome of the sky glared like the inside of a huge hundred watt lightbulb; the sea was vast, almost luminous, and the land so distant. Only Hook Head occasionally peered over the undulating horizon at two hundred and seventy degrees, and from the fact that it took me a further two hours to reach land, it seemed I'd gained more by way of a pleasant diversion than any genuine assistance from the morning's pot-haul tow.

CHAPTER 5

Stout and Swell

Write poetry?
rather follow the coast
fragment after fragment
going forward
breathing
spacing it out.

'Coastline', Kenneth White

By midday the morning's haze had become a blaze, and the sun, high in the southern sky, laid a molten highway right across to the Irish coast east of Hook Head. It singed the glassy surface until it seemed that the sea itself would bear its brand forever. It walloped fiercely on my bared back and shoulders, making it necessary to eskimo-roll the kayak several times just to keep cool. The contrast between the scorching, windless, dazzling day and the silent balm of the frigid dark water beneath was a delicious shock, fending off heatstroke and sunburn, and allowing me to keep up a steady paddling rhythm towards shore despite soaring temperatures. From five miles offshore, the coast of southern Ireland looked like an endless succession of promontories. The headlands of county Waterford – Hook Head, Brownstone Head, Helvick Head and Mine Head – faded westwards, giving way eventually to the buttresses, peninsulas and great capes of county Cork. Historically many of these promontories and headlands had fire-signal towers on their highest points. Each would be within sighting distance of at least two others; and an alarm signal, perhaps warning of an invasion from the west, could be flashed along the entire south coast almost as quickly in the fifteenth century as it could using the telephone and satellite systems of today.

As I approached the coast, more and more of the western headlands began to disappear from view, sliding politely into line, one behind the other until eventually the great fist of Hook Head entirely dominated the scene. It was a daunting sight; a prominent rocky outcrop with a reputation for a fearsome tide race, and a humbug-striped pepper-pot of a lighthouse standing broad and tall above surf-fringed skerries. The present light-tower, at a mere seven hundred and fifty years old, is a relative newcomer to this dangerous promontory. An ancestry of stone, timber and earth structures at Hook Head dates back to warning fires known to have been tended here by Christian monks in the fifth century, and it is reckoned that a coastal warning beacon has been maintained at Hook Head longer than any other in Europe. At its foot I could see why Hook Head was a point from which fifteen centuries of boats had been conscientiously shooed away. A churning tidal rip known as the Tower Race was roaring angrily over an uneven bottom, and a line of overfalls stretched southwards from the point, marking the area where the tide from Waterford Bay ebbed across the shallows and encountered the main west-flowing tide of the Celtic Sea. In foul weather this would have been a place to avoid. Any boat hijacked by those overfalls, or driven into the great bay between the Hook and Forlorn Point to the east, in an onshore gale, would be ground to fragments on the toothy rocks which bracket the sea here on all sides.

The tide race had to be tackled and crossed, but in the glorious stillness of the early afternoon, with no wind to complicate the sea conditions, I bounced onward lightly, and with unusual confidence. The little kayak seemed to pulse with energy, perhaps an extra charge absorbed from the morning's sun; and I was deep in a stuttering mental word-play on the *Sola* kayak, my *solo* journey and *solar* power as we crested the foaming, bucking waves and carved a tactical route between the spewing centres of bright mayhem that formed the centre of the tide race. But no sooner had I rounded Hook Head than a thick obscuring mist rolled in, enveloping all, including my intended landfall, three miles across Waterford Bay at Dunmore East. On yet another compass track I groped my way across the bay to the Dunmore slipway, finishing the day's journey with a narrow avoidance of a lethargic basking shark, and a total of twenty sun-bleached miles. Strangely the band of sea fog was confined to the bay, and the little harbour and pier at Dunmore East were hung about with listless bodies, heat-draped after a day of sapping sun, as though some plague or epidemic had hit the village. Once a port bustling with the seasonal activity of the herring fleets, Dunmore East is today a tranquil holiday village. Its main focus, the picturesque harbour and bay, now provide a safe and attractive venue for sailing and windsurfing summer schools, and angling charters.

The dense offshore fog, and the lack of wind, had meant that, for the would-be yachtsmen and sea-anglers of Dunmore, sunbathing had been the main activity of the day. The unexpected sight of a lone sea-kayak appearing from the wall of mist, disturbing a shark, and heading for the pier produced a flurry of activity on shore worthy of a marauding Viking longboat. After weaving briefly through the colourful yachts becalmed in the bay, I pulled into the pier to find an abundance of willing, welcoming hands to help with the haul ashore and usher me straight into the sailing clubhouse. Salt-rimed, dry roasted and slightly dazzled from a heady overdose of sun and sea, I was more than happy to accept the generous hospitality and facilities of the sailing school. The mirror in the club shower revealed a strange chimera, a briny, mahoganied beast with an urchin-stubbled chin, and a sharp sunline across the midriff where the kayak and spraydeck had shielded my white abdomen and legs from the sun. The shower itself, my first since Wexford town, was pure luxury. Anyone overhearing my groans and sighs of bliss might well have imagined that there were two, or perhaps more, of us in that cubicle, as the cool water slaked my skin and flushed away days of accumulated salt crust. A couple of pints of stout and a brace of cheeseburgers miraculously restored the inner man, and by early evening I was ready to seek out a suitable spot to bunk down for the night.

Try finding an inconspicuous place to lay out a bedroll in an Irish seaside village in July, where cheery holidaymakers and lively sailing-course teenagers throng the streets and harbour until the small hours of the morning! A steady procession of inquisitive mariners deterred me from lying down peacefully by the kayak on the pier; and every available corner of the village seemed either bathed in flashing light, or invaded by super-charged kids with holiday fever. But in one respect Dunmore East was unusual, for nesting on broad cliff-ledges just above the bustling harbour and streets – though normally quite shy of human presence – is a colony of kittiwakes. Despite being among the brightest and most vocal of gulls, the busy little kittiwake colony of Dunmore East seemed to be able to conduct its business with hardly a second glance from the bustle of fishermen and merrymakers below. What's more, they had the perfect vantage point for overlooking the harbour, the yacht club, and *Sola* where she lay at the pier. That clinched the decision. Quick as a flash I scrambled, bedroll in hand, up a series of footholds to a broad, cleanish cliff-ledge above the village, and settled down to roost in peace among the murmuring, chuckling kittiwakes of Dunmore East.

~ ~ ~

The warm morning breeze was full of the cries and smells of the little white gulls. But apart from waking at eye-level with a curious kittiwake, the morning of the nineteenth of July differed only in requiring a climb down to sea level, and in cleaning guano as well as dew from my sleeping bag. As at Howth, the early session brought myriads of kids to the sailing school, all suddenly fascinated by the weird species of vessel that had found its way to their slipway. Fielding questions, demonstrating gadgets and allowing a queue of inquisitive urchins to test the kayak seat meant that packing up took longer than usual, and it was high noon as well as high tide as ten pairs of hands launched *Sola* seaward once more.

Excitement had mounted as a grand sailing escort had been arranged for my departure. Coaches and group leaders had been making subtle enquiries as to what speed I could manage, whether I thought I could keep pace with the dinghies, and whether I could hold a straight course; and now a huge flotilla was assembled, waiting as I eased out from the slipway. Foghorns and hooters blasted, and suddenly the bay was a kaleidoscope of colour and fluttering activity. The weaving and tacking of the red-sailed, bright-hulled yachts and the sleek cruising green and gold of *Sola's* straight path were like an artistically choreographed opening scene from the *Pirates of Penzance*. Perhaps most dazzling of all was the fierce undiluted blue of the midday sky, faithfully reproduced in the unruffled water of the bay. The morning's offshore breeze was dying away to a sultry whisper, and as I paddled leisurely out through the fleet of dancing hulls, their dandy red sails had already begun to hang rather limply. Gradually *Sola* nosed forward as the little yachts began to lose windage, surrendering one by one to the irony of being unable to keep up with the humble arm-powered vessel they had set out to escort. As the last boat fell becalmed in the bay I held back briefly and twirled the paddle high above my head in thanks; then I turned and concentrated on increasing the gap between the kayak and the happy summer crowds of Dunmore East.

The sea curled over the edges of the kayak's bow, and fell away; curled and fell away; curled and fell away. It felt pure beneath me; its spray salting my cheeks, refreshing, astringent, a sea of glints and flashes, of bright curling waves half-hidden by the glare of the sun reflecting on their smooth backs; a sea to be lost on; a drifting unchanging highway of the sun on which *Sola* danced like a cork. An hour's paddling in sparkling warm Irish water took me westwards along a cliffy coastline past Swine's Head, Brazen Head and Brownstone Head. Fore-going a stop on the crowd-flecked sands of Tramore, I crossed the bay to beneath the famous 'Metal Man' statue on Great Newton Head, erected to warn nineteenth-century mariners away from the dangerous bay, and continued towards the alluring rock-loaf shapes of the Sheep islands. At the end of a second hour I shot through a natural archway near Garrarus, and began to turn gently towards a distant sandy bay for a rest and a snack. Suddenly, from the corner of my eye I became aware of a lone swimmer, about a mile from shore and still swimming strongly towards me. Surprised and intrigued, I stopped paddling, waved hello and allowed the swimmer to approach the kayak. Did he need help? Did he want to warn me about something? With a swift lunge he grabbed the kayak, hoisting himself aboard in one smooth movement, and sat there facing me, legs astride the front deck, grinning broadly and talking with the pace of a race commentator.

Even before he introduced himself, I realised that this was a character to be reckoned with. Despite being taken by surprise, and even slightly offended, by his unorthodox boarding tactics, I guessed that he was an athlete, and probably a canoeist; one had to understand the balance of a kayak in order to mount it from the water with such disconcerting ease. To cap it all he seemed to know all about me, my journey, and even my book, *Blazing Paddles*. This was Dermot Blount, the leader of a team of four kayakers who had circumnavigated Ireland. In almost perfect weather, and with a strong team, he had achieved a very fast and impressive journey, very different in style and objectives from my own, but not without its own share of adventures. In an article about their journey Dermot had written:

> *I would not recommend such a trip to anybody, or even any canoeist. It requires a lot of skill, strength, stamina and knowledge to accomplish such a feat. Other essentials are drive, and a touch of madness.*

Dermot certainly seemed to have the last two qualities in abundance, but then so, perhaps, did I, and soon we were heading shoreward to continue our chat. Perched on deck like a muscular leprechaun, Dermot neatly swung round to face forward and lifted his legs from the water, never for one moment interrupting his flow of banter.

'One thing is bothering me, you know – and now that I've met you I'll have to confess. That newspaper article that I wrote, well ... I pinched the title for it from that book of yours, *Blazing Paddles*. I should have cleared it with you, but it just slipped me mind.'

I quickly assured him that I had no problem with that, but he insisted that he at least owed me a pint of Murphys in atonement. 'Sure and, as luck would have it, I know just the place!' he added.

Having quickly disposed of the kayak above the tideline, at Garrarus, we made our way to the back kitchen of Rocket's Bar, Tramore, where the highlight of the evening was about to begin. On massive earthenware plates the size of truck hubcaps, we were served portions of spare-ribs which would have satisfied Desperate Dan. These were followed rather quickly by half a large chicken each, with stuffing, bread, and a huge communal pitcher of whole, boiled jacket potatoes – salted, buttered and sufficient to feed a family of six. Dermot, with hardly a second glance, tackled the feast as he seemed to handle most challenges: head on and without hesitation. I was hungry enough from paddling to make a pretty brave attempt, but when the final tattie was halved and dispatched, we both breathed deeply and reclined in replete satisfaction on the wooden bench. I was astounded as the kitchen door swung open again and a couple of great wedges of apple-pie and cream were brought in. These in turn were washed down with mugs of coffee, and several pints of stout. Dermot, finishing the last scrap on his plate and wiping it clean with a crust of bread, pointed out that a few stop-overs like this could make kayaking round Ireland an almost fattening proposition.

'*A pint of plain is yer only man!*' said Dermot, quoting Flann O'Brien. The evening continued with more beer, a few games of pool, and a compendium of advice on the dangers and delights of parts of the Irish coast. Later, one of Dermot's circumnavigation team came in. Mick O'Meara, a competitive whitewater racing canoeist with a weightlifter's hulking build, asked if he could paddle with me on the following day. And with an arrangement made for a morning rendezvous, I headed back through the night to my beach just as a red glow faded over the Sheep islands in the west. For the fifth night in succession I slept in the open, beneath a winking Fastnet sky, on warm sand which moulds to the contours of the back like an orthopaedic mattress. I lay there thinking over the events of the day. Despite the apparent repetition of the routine – get up, launch the kayak, paddle all day, stop, eat, camp – each day seemed to bring new surprises, and to unfold entirely differently from its predecessor. I fell asleep wondering what tomorrow would bring.

~ ~ ~

Waking in a dew-covered dawn, the views to the Sheep islands were as impressive at sunrise as they had been at the previous sunset. The two hours between waking and launching were always a magical time of day. My sleeping bag quickly dried in the strengthening sun, while I dressed and breakfasted. It looked like being another scorching day along the Irish coast. Laboriously, I rolled my cargo-tanker of a kayak, eighteen feet at a time, over forty-five yards of shingle beach to the water's edge. I was sitting there, slumped, sweating and panting, when Mick arrived in shorts and vest, jogging lightly down the beach carrying his sea-kayak in one hand like an empty briefcase. We set off first along the shore, then headed offshore, southwest into a thick sea fog, on a bearing for Helvick Head, beyond Dungarvan Bay. With Mick as pacemaker – a fresh, hard-punching, high-stroking paddler, marathon racer and Liffey Descent champion – and my neck now almost completely healed, our progress was excellent. After burning up fifteen open sea miles, we forfeited Helvick Head for the distant, but more prominent Mine Head, still five miles away. We were two bared bodies; half-man, half-kayak; like centaurs on watery horses, paddles flailing and powering the boats through the Celtic Sea on a rhythm set in perpetual motion, a matter for engineering rather than physiology. Having someone to talk and joke with on the water was such a novelty that the strain and the miles just slipped by unnoticed; by lunchtime we had covered twenty miles in well under four hours.

Lunch, at one of the countless, nameless, tiny boulder-fringed coves that punctuate the Irish south coast, was a chance to brew some tea, relieve the bladder and to swim among sea stacks draped with purple seaweeds like Hawaiian grass skirts. Thalassotherapy is the expensive name for it in the city pamperiums. The cold seawater first tensed, then totally relaxed the strained muscles of neck, shoulders and upper back, toning and rejuvenating the whole system like a therapeutic massage. And after a drying snooze on sun-warmed boulders we were virtually ready to repeat the morning's efforts afresh. Swapping kayaks with Mick reminded me of how buoyant and responsive the unloaded craft can be, but immediately I felt unsteady, uncomfortable, as though after three weeks my body had irreversibly, monogamously moulded itself to the shape and feel of *Sola*. Despite her heavy payload and suspiciously low plimsoll line I was quietly glad to exchange boats again at the next break. Past Ardmore, Ram Head and Whiting Bay, we reached at late afternoon the ancient walled sea town of Youghal. The last eight miles had been a slog against wind, tide and the outflow of the Blackwater estuary, and we were glad to beach the boats, change quickly and head into the village for a parting pint at the end of a respectable thirty-six mile day.

I spent the evening exploring Youghal (pronounced 'yawl') which, in a strange and amusing way seemed vaguely familiar. Squeezed between a cliff and the great bay, with the town wall running along the clifftop, at the mouth of a beautiful river, Youghal held resonances of village scenes from almost any old sea-faring or buccaneering movie I'd ever seen, with tall, irregular, stone buildings, narrow, cobbled streets and semi-enclosed stone-built docks. An eighteenth-century clocktower which straddles the main street, had previously been a prison from whose windows Irish prisoners were hanged as a warning to their countrymen of the folly of challenging the English colonists. Enamelled, swinging pub signs showed colourful images of square-riggers and spouting whales. It was here that the old Gregory Peck version of *Moby Dick* was filmed, and a few nips and tucks would have easily restored the town to its former salty image. To exchange the few cars for horse carts, pile the street corners with barrels of salt and rum, and add a few peg-legged extras, would have been to create an instant seventeenth-century set for a swashbuckling epic.

Even Sir Walter Raleigh, the eccentric potato-planting, tobacco-smoking, sea-faring hero of school textbooks, lived at Youghal, where he is said to have planted Europe's first potato. I could still picture a school illustration of Raleigh's Irish housemaid frantically dousing his smoking pipe with a pitcher of water, and it was easy to think of Raleigh as a cartoon cross between a pipe-smoking joker and a seaman's hero. But in reality Raleigh played a wholly unsavoury role in the history of Ireland, a history very rarely represented in British schoolbooks. Raleigh was granted forty-two thousand confiscated Irish acres during the plantation of Munster, as part of an Elizabethan policy of colonisation of the increasingly hostile native Irish. A bloody and ruthless military servant of the English crown, Raleigh was largely responsible for the treacherous cold-blooded massacre of six hundred surrendered Irish, French and Italian soldiers in Smerwick harbour in 1580, and prepared the ground for Youghal to become a bastion of the English colonial forces. Popular mythology, however, seems to have entirely ignored the mercenary, colonial side of the character, and Youghal itself prefers to cash in on the colourful aspects of the fictional hero. From the number of references, motifs and images of Raleigh on shopfronts, bars and nightclub signs, one could all but believe that Sir Walter is alive and well, dancing and drinking, in Youghal today.

~ ~ ~

Does a flower ever feel the residual creaking stiffness of the previous day's exertions as it unfurls its petals and turns towards the sun of a new morning? At the first shoulder-tapping warmth of the sun's early rays I moaned lethargically, cursed Mick O'Meara, and sat upright in the sleeping bag, stretching muscles sorely taxed by that thirty-six mile stretch. Like a distant whisper, low but clear, came the equally tired murmering of shallow, sticky waves. The tide at the edge of the Blackwater estuary had receded, leaving acres of shingle, mudflats and worm-cast littered ooze between *Sola* and the sea. Rolling the heavy kayak on an old half-inflated yacht fender, I trudged through the foul-soft, sucking muck, making painstaking progress seaward in stinky eighteen foot hops. Beyond the shingle, every step felt like treacle and smelt of rotten eggs, and a full half-hour passed before the soiled boat and its muddy occupant were reunited with the cleansing sea. In contrast to shifting a boat's dead weight on land, paddling it through water, even with aching limbs, seemed such a natural and relaxed activity. As if to reinforce the point, a light breeze caught my back and pushed me almost effortlessly south towards Capel Island, a brief punctuatory blip off Knockadoon Head.

My morning practice was to drink as little as possible at breakfast, because heading ashore at mid-morning, just for a pee stop, assuming I could even find a place to come ashore, always seemed such an awkward break in the paddling rhythm and a waste of time and energy. Sometimes, however, it seemed that fate tended to use just such gratuitous pitstops in order to season my journey with interesting and strangely relevant interludes or meetings.

On my one previous, landbound, trip to southern Ireland, I had become interested in the successful resistance of local people and environmental campaigners to the proposed building of a nuclear power station at Carnsore Point, and to the siting of a huge chemicals factory on the south coast. Hoping to make contact with some of the key campaign organisers, I had tried to phone various leads from Youghal the previous evening, but had so far drawn a complete blank. Now, at mid-morning, I found myself cursing that extra large mug of breakfast tea, and heading inshore at Glennawilling, where a mound of seawrack and an open channel revealed a shingle beach suitable for a quick toilet stop. Watching my approach from a small stone pier was a ragged, almost Christ-like figure, remarkable first of all for the clear intensity of his blue stare, and then for the speed with which he jumped up and dashed to haul me ashore.

Half-an-hour later, sitting with a ham and egg breakfast at his beachside cottage, it was difficult to decide whether I had blundered in there subconsciously seeking this character and his stories, or if he had been patiently waiting on the slipway for a listener to arrive, for he began – without prompting or preamble – to tell of his part in the campaign against the chemicals multinational Merrell Dow. Over coffee, Joe spoke of the driving power in his life, the discipline, teaching and saintly example of Padre Pio. But there seemed something about Joe that was also distinctly worldly. He had the gaunt messianic look of the archetypal martyr, the religious equivalent of a mercenary soldier. A veteran of countless crusades, he looked as though he had been starved, beaten, tortured, burned and just couldn't be kept down. He seemed frighteningly willing – and still ready – to fight to the end for a cause, perhaps any cause. One felt that here was a man who would be strong enough to tax the resources of the most brutal and persistent of torturers; perhaps even that he might relish interrogation and torture as a test of his own integrity. Beneath the Virgin portraits and Calgary statuettes, and among the Lourdes souvenirs and candlelit shrines in his cottage kitchen, Joe gave the uncomfortable impression of searching, still yearning, for a contemporary Grail to hunt, or a crucifix to fit to his own back.

According to Joe, despite the promises of a boost to the flagging local economy and a significant number of local jobs, the people of the south coast had fiercely resisted Merrell Dow's proposals to site a major chemical factory at Killeagh. Their concerns had been wide-ranging. Issues as diverse as the health of their children and livestock, the effects of chemical byproducts on sea-life and fishing and the general long-term quality of the environment were uppermost in their minds. They called on Merrell Dow to address their fears regarding the pumping of contaminated waste into the river and bay at Youghal, the transport of toxic waste on local roads, railways, by sea or by air, as well as their concerns about possible smoke pollution and fall-out over the surrounding land and sea.

Any successful community-based capmaign against a multinational company, or a major proposal like the construction of a chemicals factory, has to be a well-balanced hybrid between just enough carefully reasoned argument based on soundly researched facts, and as much gut-feeling and raw emotional appeal as possible. Without the latter there won't generally be enough crowd support or sufficient local feeling to push the rational argument through the various stages of consultation, objection and appeal which inevitably characterise a proposal of this magnitude. There was no doubt in my mind that Joe's talents lay firmly in the latter part of the equation. Objective fact and rationality were not the tools of his trade; when he believed strongly in a cause he shot straight from the heart and allowed others to worry about the facts.

Joe belonged to a generation whose consciousness of the chemicals industry was permanently tainted by disastrous episodes like the Thalidamide drug of the sixties and the barbaric military defoliant and irritant Agent Orange used so indiscriminately in chemical warfare in Vietnam.

As a protester and campaigner – what he termed a 'street fighter' – against the Merrell Dow planning application, Joe claimed to have been indispensible in mobilising local support. No doubt his tirades would have been highly subjective, and aimed at the chemicals industry in general rather than Merrell Dow's particular proposals, but morally indignant support tends to lend great impetus to an environmental cause which is simultaneously being well argued on a rational front. The mass protests, demonstrations and well-organised local opposition were certainly effective. Merrell Dow eventually pulled out before the case reached the High Court not, it claimed, because of the protests, but due to restructuring back at company headquarters. For the moment at least, the Youghal coast remained unspoilt, and Joe lives on to fight another leviathan.

Back down on the shingle-bank I slipped a lucky traveller's charm – a coin-sized, silver-haired angel which Joe had pressed me to accept – into my lifejacket pocket and paddled back into the sunny flow of my journey west. Then as I turned to wave back towards the shore, I caught an image which made the hair prickle on my neck, and which will stay with me longer than any lucky charm: Joe dropped to his knees among the seaweed, raised his arms high above his head then bought his hands together in prayer; just then the sun flashed an intense golden reflection from the glass window of his house, dazzling me with its glare, and apparently engulfing Joe in a blazing aura of sudden pious light.

~ ~ ~

By the time I reached the little fishing port of Ballycotton, fourteen miles in an intense morning sun had sapped rather than charged my energy cells. I was dazzled, light-headed and a little unsteady on my feet. I hauled the kayak up the beach, removed my outer gear and headed straight for the darkened sanctuary of the harbour-side pub. An angry exchange at the bar became quickly hushed as I entered the welcome gloom and ordered two pints of stout. The first one hardly wet the sides of my throat as I tipped it down. Then I settled to enjoy the second one, and perhaps pick up on a snippet or two of local gossip. The atmosphere was tense in the little pub. It seemed that local feeling was running high over the mysterious recent drowning of two government fisheries inspectors in the sea off Ballycotton. But no-one was very keen to talk about the accident, after I received a couple of hostile looks, I decided not to pursue that line of chat any further. Finishing my own glass, I sought out the shade beneath the pier for a cool snooze, but not without a brief thought for the safety of *Sola* in this suspicious town of edgy fishermen. My own suspicions were justified when I woke shortly after to overhear two or more voices discussing the kayak; but it seemed that, due to a rather bizarre optical illusion I'd managed to create in the pub, they'd decided they'd be better to leave the kayak alone.

'Ye should see the fella that's with thon yoke – a huge, wild-looking Scots fella he is – arms like fucking pistons.'

'Aye an' no wonder – they say he's going all the way to Cork in that thing!'

~ ~ ~

Indeed I was due to reach Cork harbour that very evening for an important rendezvous. Travelling by paddle power, subject to the fickle whim of sea and weather, made it difficult to agree to any meeting pre-arranged for a specific time and place. But with a ridge of high pressure remaining settled, and recent progress reasonably good, I'd made an exception several days previously, and committed myself to being at the Royal Cork Yacht Club at Crosshaven at seven that night. It was to be a final photo session with press, sponsors and charity fundraisers before heading west for the wilder, less accessible, less predictable Atlantic phase of the journey. Besides, it would mean the chance of a shower and a good meal, and I quietly hoped that my girlfriend Marie-Pierre – who was coming to Ireland on a week's holiday to try to follow part of my route by bike – might also make the rendezvous.

With the tide already on its second ebb of the day I left the procrastinating defenders of Ballycotton for a thirteen mile coastal haul to Cork. The coast was largely cliff-girt and serrated like the raw rim of a recent quarry. The low outcrop of Power Head looked like a giant sprocket-nosed chainsaw, frozen – in geological time – in the act of sending splinters of rock out to sea. Off Power Head, and in Power Head bay, the sea was churned rough by a stiff wind from the open southwest quarter, crosshatching the broad, eddying tides with a white-capped skin. This, with a slight cloud cover, was the first change from the pattern of blazing sun and sea fogs that had dominated Fastnet for over a week, and I couldn't help wondering if the Irish summer was already coming to a close. Shoals of mullet were riffling through the water of the bay, creating patches of exaggerated raggedness, difficult to distinguish amid the choppy surface patterns. At Gyleen, a cluster of cottages neatly thatched in rush and marram drew me inshore for a closer look. I heard a cormorant's throaty cackle, and watched as it spread its drying wings like a native American totem pole; and a small boy sat proudly guarding the carcass of a hammerhead shark which he told me had been beached, still alive, on the last tide. Making a mental note to check for hammerheads before my next swim, I continued to pass westward, letting the backing wind shush me eventually around the lighthouse at Roche's Point, and into the massive sea inlet known as Cork harbour.

Cork harbour is such a huge delta of sea routes that Cork itself could hardly be said to be on the coast at all. From the broad bay between Roche's Point and Weaver's Point – past Ringaskiddy, Spike Island, Cobh harbour and Passage West to the city itself – is a distance of almost fifty miles away from the open coast. With some relief I was heading, not for Cork city itself, but for the much more accessible port of Crosshaven. Riding the now flooding tide up the main channel, then branching left at Ram's Head, I coasted into the peaceful shelter of the Owenboy estuary. I was looking for the Royal Cork Yacht Club (RCYC). Established in 1720 it was probably the oldest and most prestigious boating association in the world, and the only one in Ireland to have a fully fledged Admiral.

At first I thought I must have taken a wrong turning; certainly I was among yachts – vast armadas of masts and hulls were moored, and others cruised back and forth in the estuary – but it wasn't quite what I'd imagined when I'd agreed to meet here. Somehow I'd pictured the RCYC as being a haven of mahogany and brass, sextant and lodestone, of clinker-built dinghies, and the gentle dunt-dunting of timber hulls. In their place stood ranks of smart racing and touring yachts, with lines beyond the wildest dreams of timber shipwrights, and sporting the glowing clownish colours of modern plastics, moored side by side along a maze of duckboard pontoons. In the immediate aftermath of the Cork Week major regatta series, there were catamarans straining at mooring shackles like full-blooded racing stallions, massive top-heavy powercruisers bristling with electronic gadgetry and crews with matching outfits; and hardly a boat among them that didn't look capable of housing a family of ten, or sailing non-stop around the world on a moment's notice. The predominant sounds were of steel rigging tapping on alloy masts, and deck shoes scuffing on slip-proof fibreglass, as I nosed *Sola* upriver in search of a mooring suitable for a humble kayak. Roping *Sola* to a pontoon cleat I clambered onto a floating walkway which led, through avenues of immaculate, towering bows, to the clubhouse. Later, showered and shaved, and in the cleanest of my grubby land clothes, I sat on the clubhouse verandah, sipping a beer and overlooking a dazzling display of waterborne wealth: the largest gathering I'd ever seen, of that most cliched symbol of western wealth, the private yacht.

It was only six o'clock, so with an hour in hand I left the yacht club for a walk into Crosshaven; and there, cycling down the main street, hair flying rough, on an overloaded hired bike, was Marie-Pierre. It was as if the whole operation had been stage-managed; an amazing coordination of time and place. Within minutes of meeting it was as if the last three weeks of living such vastly separate lives had hardly happened at all, and it was a wonderful feeling to know that we might now manage to overlap our routes for a few days along the coast of county Cork.

Half-an-hour later, back within the high security, ring-fenced perimeter of the RCYC, forces and figureheads were gathering for the reception. Dwarfing everyone, in stature and in rank, a unique figure in all Ireland, was Admiral Collins himself. At the waterfront bar waitresses served rounds of drinks on trays, while the progress of the Sola kayak and the fundraising targets of the Eyebank were reviewed and analysed like the tactics of a military campaign. Tannoy messages announced phonecalls for me, and meant regular disappearances to record phone-link interviews for various radio stations and newsdesks in the capital.

In a grand ceremonial gesture the Admiral shook my hand in his great meaty paw, declared how proud the RCYC was to be associated with the journey and fundraising efforts of the Sola kayak, wished me a safe passage along the Atlantic fringes, and presented me with the very exclusive RCYC yacht-mast pennant. The handshakes, photos, polite enquiries and restrained conversation that followed had just begun to drag on a little too long, when suddenly, above the modulated voices and the lapping of the sea, came the unmistakeable approaching grumble of large powerful motorcycles. Without the slightest hesitation, two sleek 1000cc machines with French number plates growled in through the yacht club gates and carved to a halt in a cloud of dust beneath the clubhouse bar. As four leatherclad figures dismounted, dusted themselves down and began to remove space-age helmets, the Admiral rose ominously to his feet. But Marie was even quicker. With a loud French squeal of delight she jumped from her seat and ran down the stairs towards the bikers, and I realised that we'd landed in the middle of a reunion between Marie and her family. Recently off the French ferry to Cork, Marie's parents and a couple of friends had detoured down to Crosshaven to find us, before setting off on an Irish tour of their own!

The formality of the little reception began to dissolve immediately as Marie and I began to hug and double-kiss our way through the road-stained new arrivals. And it was to the great credit of the various Irish dignatories and organisers that they were able to accept the unorthodox hijacking of the official reception in good humour, and to assimilate the whole unexpected episode into the evening. Within minutes the travel-weary French were sitting comfortably with drinks, while Deirdre (from Sola Lenses) made enquiries about local B&Bs for them. But the evening was drawing to an end. The official business was over; the photos had been taken, plans made and interviews recorded. For Marie and I it was time to catch up on news and stories, to share a meal with Deirdre, to book into a hotel for the night and to take stock of the journey so far. Reaching Cork, a quarter of the way round the Irish coast from Larne, was a minor milestone in itself; but in almost every respect the wildest, most challenging stretches of coast, and the strangest of adventures lay ahead.

CHAPTER 6

By Hook or by Crook

These pitiless caverns, too, were false and sly. Woe betide him who
would loiter there. The rising tide filled them to their roofs.

The Toilers of the Sea, Victor Hugo

At six o'clock I was woken by a string of long, low siren blasts from
Cork harbour, far below the window of the hotel room. It was a
strange awakening, without the dew, the thin sunlight and the
beachy sense of open space which had become so natural a habit
over recent weeks. But the dry warmth of clean sheets, and the
gentle cradling of a shared mattress were a welcome novelty. Marie
slept on soundly while I pulled aside the curtain to see what the
commotion on the water was about.

It was the sheer scale that was confusing. In the morning
half-light it seemed that a large, densely developed hillside town had
taken to the water and was sailing slowly up the estuary towards
Cork. The sirens sounded again, and I began to focus on tiny tug
boats, six fore and aft of the floating metropolis, working like
waterborne insects. Then I saw the hard, sweeping deckline which
cleanly split the upper half of the lighted citadel from its deep dark
hull, and I realised that I was watching the dawn approach of the
world's largest ship. The *QE2* was sailing into Cork harbour for the
first time to mark the opening of the newly completed twenty-five
million pound deepwater channel to the freight terminal at
Ringaskiddy. The freight container ships themselves were at their
moorings, but already a host of trawlers and tenders, yachts and
dories hovered and buzzed round the great Cunard liner as she
manoeuvred slowly up the channel. Each little boat's presence

further emphasised the incredible size of the liner. More than ten times larger than her nearest rival on the water that morning, it took an effort of imagination even to think of the *QE2* as a boat in the same sense of the word.

Within two hours I was paddling one of the world's smallest boats beneath the very bows of the world's largest. The immaculate black steel-plate walls seemed to throb with an almost deafening belly-rumble; her overhanging bow darkened the morning like a dangerous cliff-face; and even on an ebbing tide it took a full ten minutes to paddle the starboard length of the *QE2*. Of all places it seemed particularly fitting to meet such a historic ship in the Cork channel, for this was a channel that flowed thick with the history of ocean-going vessels and transatlantic liners. It is perhaps a cliched truth that Ireland's main export has always been her people; but the extent of that truth is sometimes forgotten. In 1847 alone over a hundred thousand people left Ireland, bound for North America. At times up to *four hundred* sailing ships could be seen there at Cobh, readying themselves for the long crossing to the New World. From the time of the famine until well into the twentieth century, the wharf at Cobh would have been, for thousands of emigrants, their first link with the wide Atlantic, and their last touch of Irish soil. For thousands more, sentenced to deportation to Botany Bay and other penal settlements in the nineteenth-century British colonies, their last experience of Ireland was of the prison fortress on Spike Island, opposite Cobh.

It was in Cork harbour that the British Atlantic convoys assembled during the French and American wars of the eighteenth century, and also here that the Americans made their principal Atlantic naval base in the Second World War. From here on the fourth of April 1838 sailed the *Sirius*, the first steamship to cross the Atlantic. At Cobh stands a memorial to the two thousand civilians who died on the *Lusitania*, sunk by a German submarine in the First World War. And even the *Titanic* – a name almost equally synonymous with ocean voyaging and disaster – recorded Cork as its last port of call. So strong in Cork's maritime history was the link with boats departing westward for the great Atlantic that the Cork 'Bosphorus' – the narrow sea passage between Loch Mahon and the Great Island – despite facing due south, is named Passage West.

By Hook or by Crook? That was the question asked of the old boats leaving Cork harbour. Were they sailing east for England, France or Holland by way of Hook Head, or west for the Atlantic by way of Crookhaven port? I wondered briefly, as I paddled towards the open sea, whether the *QE2* had come by Hook or by Crook, but was in no doubt that I was heading south and west by Crook, and ultimately bound for the Atlantic edge. Like a Chinese whisper, taking on independent life with each new telling, the Atlantic as a concept was steadily insinuating itself into my consciousness. Its history, its influence, its reputation were to become increasingly felt in meetings, places and events as I travelled west. It was no longer possible to ignore the proximity of the 'big water'; the thought that just around the corner began the largest ocean in the northern hemisphere. Part of me longed to meet the mighty pond as it washed, wave after wave onto Irish shores; but there was also an uncomfortable feeling of uncertainty as to what those waves would bring. How was I going to handle the great capes like Mizen Head? How exposed would the west coast be? And what did the Atlantic edge hold in terms of weather? Every mile westward, every new headland would bring those answers closer.

~ ~ ~

I was bound for an evening rendezvous with Marie at Dunworly Bay on the peninsula of Seven Heads, a full thirty miles to the west. Even the briefest glance at the map showed that the first obstacle in my westward passage would be the rather large and curiously named promontory known as the Old Head of Kinsale. Old it may indeed be, but surely no more so than the rest of the south coast sandstone. In fact, like so many place-names on the Irish coast, the name is a hybrid of Irish and old Norse, and is more of a warning to shipping than an acknowledgement of age. 'Old' comes from *Odde*, the Viking raiders' name for a long tongue of high cliffy land jutting into the sea. Kinsale, from the Irish *Ceann Saile* means 'the headland of the tide race'. The consensus of the lore of two ancient tongues, as well as the pendulous shape on the Ordnance Survey map, suggested that sea around Old Head would be something of a challenge; but it lay, as yet, seventeen miles distant.

I set off at a determined pace along a coastline of broken cliffs, gapped and cave-cracked through vertical fissures like the fixed grin of an elongated, toothy skull. Minor headlands loomed, then passed – Robert's Head, Flat Head and Barry's Head – increasing in interest westwards. But Old Head, with its tidal reputation, constantly dominated the western horizon and pressed heavily on my mind. After three hours paddling in a choppy sea, thoroughly whisked by a stiff breeze, I reached Frower Point. Rounding a fold of cliff and finding some brief shelter from the sea's restless energy in a tiny cove, I decided to land for a break and a pee-stop. There was no beach – no relief at all from the vertical cliffs that ran right around the point. So I left *Sola* floating, clipped a karabiner to her bowline and carefully scaled the rockface to a ledge suitable for an hour's rest. I tied *Sola*'s leash to my leg and lay back to snooze.

Within a half-hour the wind had risen to a force six southeasterly and *Sola*, bucking like a spooked horse as the larger waves swept round the cove, was tugging insistently on my leg. '*Come on! Come on! Wake up! No time to lose!*' The sea beyond the cove looked increasingly troubled. That wind was really stirring things up; but what worried me most was the prospect of meeting foul seas in strong wind-over-tide conditions off Old Head itself. The best option seemed to be to round Old Head *with* the tide race, rather than allow it time to turn against the southeasterly wind. Then there would be all hell to pay. There really was very little time to lose. Like a fireman answering an emergency call I pulled on my lifejacket, scrambled down the cliff, and set off immediately into a bouncing, boisterous sea. A further hour of hard paddling took me to Black Head, and beyond it to a curving, cliff-backed corral of water called Holeopen Bay, lying directly below the steep cliffs at the narrowest neck-joint of the Old Head. On the seaward edge of the bay the headland swelled again and where the present lighthouse stands, there was once a promontory fort, unapproachable by sea and defended easily by means of ditches and earthworks across the narrow isthmus.

The open holes of the bay are, of course, caves or, more correctly, sea-breached tunnels, which wind their tortuous, rotten-rocked routes through a half-mile of derelict geology to the west side of the headland. If only I could find a passage through one of these holes, large enough to paddle the kayak, I thought, I could cut several miles off the day's journey, and at the same time entirely avoid the wind-whipped tide race which would already be thrashing its way around the exposed buttress of Old Head. But there was now a boisterous swell even in the bay itself. The wind from the southeast forced large rolling waves into the rock-bound bay, to reflect on its cliffs and echo back on themselves in frustration. Conditions were far from ideal for the dodgy practice of entering an exposed cave mouth in a little kayak.

Probing along the rim of the bay, wobbling occasionally on reflected waves, I watched as successive wave-ranks glutted the mouths of the first two caves. Each wave broke upon the cave mouth debris, and exploded roofwards before being vomited out again with a canon-like *booommm!* by the air compressed inside. At the next pair of caves, what looked like recent rockfalls, part of Old Head's ongoing bid for island status, had left a shallow, uneven threshold at the cave mouths. As a result these entrance lobbies were wild cauldrons of clapotis, or wave reflection, whose interiors made an industrial carwash look tame. Visions of a kayak being cracked like an eggshell on a rogue rock, smashed upwards against the cave's roof, or jammed sideways inside the tunnel before being spat out in pieces on the first geyser-jet of high tide, filled my mind's eye. But gradually I began to notice vague patterns in the swell. About five large waves would come in causing great violence and mayhem. These would be followed by three, sometimes four, gentler, more manageable waves, some of which seemed to be disappearing into the fifth cave with much less reflection. A slight hope, I reasoned, might lie in being able to ride the reduced chaos of the smaller salvos, in the art of careful timing, and in the wave pattern remaining stable. Beyond the congested cave lobby, the rough area of break might itself form a natural buffer; and as the light receded with distance into the tunnel, so should the more serious wave conditions.

As the kayak bounced and bucked outside the next cave I timed the waves, grabbed the sixth crest and surfed into the entrance arena. With careful timing and rudder use I was able to avoid being smashed off the rocks, and, sure enough, soon reached a calmer area beyond. There was plenty of headroom at this state of the tide, and just enough sideroom to swing the paddles. But within forty-five yards I found my passage blocked by a massive mound of rock debris; there was no alternative but to reverse out through the churning break zone and think again. That particular 'hole open' had been closed! Eventually I found a small, narrow cave which, despite its reduced doorway, promised further reach than the others. A mysterious twinkle of light seemed to penetrate as if from a distant exit, and its echoing roar came from a deeper acoustic chamber. Could it be a 'hole open' at last? The problem, of course, was that the narrower entrance was even more prone to the wild sluicings of dangerous, angled swells, and timing on entry would have to be very precise.

Lunging forward, I crested the foaming front of an outcoming wave, slipped over into its wake and rode the following inrushing surge – careful to keep as straight as an arrow through the narrow entrance – then swept immediately left; one final critically timed stroke, and I was in! There was a sudden uproar of flapping wings as a volley of perhaps fifty startled rock doves shot from the cavern into the sunshine. The first bend took me out of direct line from the light source, and away from the cave mouth it grew rapidly dark. The beating of the sea made itself felt even inside the cavern, as the oscillating swells of the bay alternately raised and depressed the level of the waters with a respiratory regularity. The distant booming of large breakers continued to resonate through the muffling trumpet of the tunnel, and I paddled gingerly forward into the gloom. Gradually the air became stale and a feeling of slight panic settled in. It was the miner's sense of depth-under-land – the implied weight of being beneath thousands of tons of rock was immense. Somewhere high above me, gulls, rabbits, perhaps even people, went about their ordinary business, and a day in the life of an Irish peninsula continued unhindered. I had gone about halfway through the headland before I hit the rockfall debris, and as I could almost discern light from the exit I decided to try hauling the kayak over the blockage.

I cracked open a glow-stick to give five minutes illumination, and instantly the cavern took on an eerie green glow like the interior of a crypt. The vast ceiling was hung about with huge chunks of rotten rock which looked ready to fall at the first loud noise. Ahead of me lay a pile of these jagged rocks about six feet high, and extending for about fifteen feet. The water's lit surface reflected my light, hiding the depth below. It could be anything from six inches to six fathoms, I thought, as I slipped from the kayak into the water. Failing to find the bottom with my feet, I paddled astride the kayak until its bow touched rock. Then, in a combination of wading and pulling, swimming and towing, I progressed slowly over submerged shingle-banks to reach the main rock pile. Using leverage, see-saw motions and my lifejacket as a padded fulcrum, I was able to manhaul the kayak up and over the rock pile and, just as the glow-stick finally faded, found deeper water on the far side. And, round the next corner of the tunnel, natural light shone through the ragged portal which led to the west bay. *Yes!* I'd made it! This is what birth must be like from the baby's viewpoint, I thought, as I emerged into Holeopen Bay West, to the surprise of several grey seal midwives. 'It's a boy!' I shouted, ecstatic to reach the world of lightness, brightness and unrestricted space.

~   ~   ~

Beyond the sheltered water on the west side of Old Head itself, the bay of Courtmacsherry was whipped by southeasterly winds, force seven with a long fetch, shoving a wild tidal sea before them. Headland to headland across the bay was a distance of seven miles, but it took just over an hour to cross. It was virtually constant surfing, straining at rudder and paddle to keep the kayak perpendicular, and running fast in front of an awesome, tumbling swell.

'Never look back,' say the old sailors; certainly it was intimidating even to glance briefly sideways at the mountains of water piling up behind the kayak. You can't concentrate on what lies immediately ahead if you are always peering over your shoulder. Far better to focus on stability and direction; but even without looking, the sheer size of some of the waves could be gauged by the effortless way they tipped the kayak nose downward and almost sent me arse over elbow into a forward roll. The biggest waves came in runs of three. Desperately resisting the temptation to look back, I felt *Sola* being overtaken by yet another triplet. The first one welled up, tipping *Sola* forward as she rose, tail-high, steeper and steeper, in apparent slow motion as if she'd never clear the top. There was an agonising pause as she teetered on the brink, whole rear end in the air, rudder flailing helplessly, suspended as if she must surely snap along the backbone. But these were surging waves, rather than the plunging concave breakers of the beach surf zone. Rather than curl into a hollow tube, the wave's forward face simply heaved up gradually and reached a massive unsupportable peak before the terrifying collapse of the wave and the thunderous nerve-racking surf-ride which always followed. After what seemed an age, the main body of the wave swept on, and *Sola* dropped down into the following trough, only to begin the tailward sucking process all over again as the second and third waves passed through.

The Admiralty guide entry for Seven Heads warns of a 'bad sea close in during conditions of wind against tide', and by the time I reached Seven Heads the tide had certainly turned. There was frothing mayhem on the great white horseshoe of the tide race itself. But after a brief struggle in quickened eastbound water I was able to dodge even closer in than the bad sea itself, to find a narrow ribbon of manageable water on the eddy streams. Tentatively, I continued pressing west, keeping as close to the rocky, splintered headland as was possible without grounding. Occasional glances to my left revealed an awesome rumbling contraflow of white-capped tide, bound like a rattling freight-train for Old Head and all points east. Eventually I was able to tuck round between the Bird Island stacks, and at last gained the sheltered haven of Dunworly Bay, out of the reach of both tide and wind. The idea of being expected on arrival, of worry setting in if I changed plan or failed to turn up, had been a strange burden for me. But with the help of a rollercoaster sea crossing, and the Old Head tunnel I found I'd completed the trip two hours ahead of schedule. On the last of the day's ration of strength I sprinted across Dunworly Bay to an ancient, stone-hewn slipway, where Marie was waving a red jacket wildly in welcome.

~ ~ ~

Our clifftop camp had a panoramic and peaceful view west across Dunworly and Clonakilty bays to Galley Head, and at full evening tide a school of porpoises hunted and played directly below the tent. That little perch was, in itself, a celebration of open spaces and boundless seas; a place where, in the high-stake card-shark world of speculation and development, Nature still held a few trump cards. That evening, Old Ma Nature played one of her Jokers, a wild card by anyone's rules. He arrived on a rattling bicycle, climbed a mound behind our tent, and began an enthusiastic sermon on the inviolable purity of Dunworly Bay. Naked except for a brief loincloth, with jet-black hair tumbling in tight ringlets to his shoulders, a bushy matching beard, and skin tanned to mahogany brown by a life on the Dunworly clifftop, he had the appearance of an Old Testament prophet. He marched directly up to me and, apparently looking at an imaginary spot above my head, began his environmental tirade: 'Twelve years ago I was like all you others. I had lost the road. Wasn't I searching ... stumbling? Blind to the true way – the planet needs us all! *I am the guardian of this sacred bay.*'

From close up the combination of his dark weathered body, metallic, slightly crossed eyes, tangled-seaweed hair and beard, served to emphasise his evangelistic fervour; he was a cross between an intimidating merman and an aboriginal bushman. To hear him scream to the wind that he had been chosen by the planet to guard the nature spirits of Dunworly, was to appreciate the strength of whatever force had gripped him. He explained how the calling had been brought to him by a winged messenger. One day, while at prayer under the influence of a false religion, the bird had come through his open window and shat on the statue of the Virgin Mary. Since that moment, he claimed, he regularly received messages to be at the bay, where he sleeps, sits on guard, swims in the purifying sea, or balances on the cliff edge giving voluble sermons to anyone who might hear. It was *he* who had called the porpoises, *he* who had stilled the waves, and *he* who would later provide a sunset. I had the distinct impression that he would have rehearsed exactly the same *spiel* even if there had been nobody there, but by the time he had finished I was nervous even about dropping a used match, and pitied anyone misguided enough to desecrate the sacred bay of Dunworly.

~ ~ ~

Near the bay of Glandore, *Cuan Dor*, between Galley Head and Toe Head, was the location of *Tonn Clíodhna*, perhaps the best known of the 'Three Waves of Erin' of ancient lore. In its earliest incarnations this wave was known as the 'Wave of Dun Téite', named after a defensive fort on a seaward promontory of Galley Head. But in later folklore it was to become indelibly associated with the otherwordly stories and poems of Clíodhna.

The Wave of Dun Téite of the chiefs,
that was its name before in your land
till there was drowned in the wave in sooth
a woman whose name was Clíodhna.

Clíodhna, the *banshee* of south Munster, appears in various forms, and in many tales and poems of ancient Ireland. According to north Cork lore, she was sometimes seen leading fairies in a seductive nocturnal dance, occasionally in the form of a white rabbit, at the stone circle known as *Carraig Chlíodhna*. At other times she appears as one of the daughters of Mogh Roith, the powerful Druid of Valentia, growing up to inherit much of the secret occult knowledge and witchy-ways of her father. And in post-medieval tradition Clíodhna was seen as a dangerous seducer, luring men to their deaths with guile and trickery. In most versions of the lore, she is eventually – either as a result of magic music, a rival's curse, or simply as part of her own tragic destiny – drowned in a great tidal wave that swept over southwest Ireland.

In the best-known account Clíodhna Cenfind appears as one of the Tuatha de Danann, the beautiful daughter of Genainn, and elopes, or is carried off, from *Tír Tairngire*, 'the Land of Promise', by the young, curly-haired warrior Ciabhán. Perhaps the mystical Clíodhna had some prevision of her own watery fate, for she called to her father as she was being carried off in Ciabhán's bronze boat:

Keep watch for the day of my death!
I tell thee – this shall be my message:
there shall come a wave whose crest shall sparkle
and shall whelm thy home in thine island.

The great 'Wave of Clíodhna' is said to have risen up as an illimitable sea in the southwest, and forged landward towards Erin. Ciabhán had landed at Trá Théite, the Glandore strand, leaving Clíodhna asleep in the boat while he went to hunt deer in the woodland. It was then that the boat was swamped, and Clíodhna drowned in the mighty flood as it roared in, devastating and dividing the lands of the southwest, and taking many lives in its passage. From that day on, the great wave of Glandore was known as *Tonn Chlíodhna*, Clíodhna's wave.

> *Fifty ships went over sea*
> *the folk of the household of Manannan;*
> *that was no capture, in sooth:*
> *they were drowned in the Wave of Clíodhna*

The lore of the 'Wave of Clíodhna' is not only an expression of the ancient Irish idea that the deities resided in water, but a recognition of the seductive, often tragic lure of the treacherous sea. Even today, this area of the Fastnet coast, where the power of the Atlantic meets the currents of the Celtic Sea, and the great tides of the southwest divide to run eastward along the south coast of Ireland, the sea is seductively beautiful, but seldom tranquil, and always potentially dangerous. As a poetic reminder, the 'Wave of Clíodhna' still serves a useful role:

> *Not silent tonight is the strand,*
> *if the Wave of Clíodhna have arisen:*
> *it striketh a blow against resounding Banba*
> *after the woe of Genainn's daughter.*

Two hours of steady paddling from Dunworly slip, with a strong following wind, took me across Clonakilty Bay, past Dunowen Head and around Galley Head on a spring tide. The benign calm of recent days in east Fastnet seemed now a distant memory, and again a strong southeasterly wind shovelled the sea before it. For eighteen miles I surfed and rolled towards the twisted, tortured shapes of the Rabbit islands, where shingle storm-beaches and shattered rocks guarded the ruins of a solitary dwelling. The seaward sides of the islands were piled high with spume, ripped like eiderdown from the bodies of countless waves crashing their last upon ramparts of barbed skerries. Carefully I wove the kayak through the skerries, chest deep in spume, but largely protected from the sea's onslaught, snatching brief moments of precious rest before re-entering the fray beyond the Rabbits.

For three days the wind had blown from the southeast,

strengthening daily and stirring the Celtic Sea into a progressively more hostile mass. At least it was all going my way, I thought, but it was the style of its going that disturbed me. Paddling the kayak had become more akin to riding a wild animal than sitting in a boat. It was always frightening to sense the towering crests and tumbling wave-fronts piling up and driving rudely forward, and to feel the bucking responses of the boat. But the kayak itself was handling extremely well, continuing to prove herself truly seaworthy through a growing range of testing conditions. Occasionally, when the rudder was kicked out of the water by rogue waves, the kayak began to broach. But a swift and strenuous paddle-dig would usually compensate, and in general it was a rudder's sea. Paddling only to maintain critical surfing velocity (the speed of the passing waves), it was the rudder rather than the paddle which was used to hold the course, giving an exhilarating increase in speed in return for minimum effort.

In this way I flashed past Castle Haven, Horse Island and Scullane Point at around six knots. At Toe Head there was a tide race like a fairground carousel, a frenzied arena of popple and splat, hugging the fringe of the headland. Though not a particularly dangerous or technical area, it was one which gave me a thorough soaking, and threw up some fancy challenges to the normal balance regime. Just offshore lay a cluster of jagged rocks called The Stags, final resting place of many an unfortunate ship, the most recent of which was the *Kowloon Bridge* tanker which sank here in 1987 spewing almost two thousand tons of crude oil along the Fastnet coastline. Dodging between skerries, islets and channels, and narrowly avoiding explosive cauldrons of spray, I had an exhilarating romp in a wild, bright sea, until afternoon cloud fragments moved in to shield the sun, changing the entire mood of the seascape. From just around Toe Head I took a direct line for the Kedge islands, four miles off and shrouded in a mist of spray, assisted, but also slightly spooked by the unruly buffalo-lumps of sea which seemed to shove and jostle the kayak along. Happily the passage among the Kedge group turned out to be safer than it had looked from a distance; the islands' jagged forms tore spray and white foam from the body of the inrushing waves, tossing them aloft to hang in the wind, and spreading a mist of airborne spume about the islands. I landed briefly, in the islands' lee, because cloud and haze had now combined in a curtain of sunproof gloom, and the afternoon had turned chilly. Without the gloss of a brightening sun, a wind-thrown sea quickly assumes a much more menacing atmosphere and a kayak's cocky confidence begins to submerge.

A final two-mile sprint took me through the narrows between Sherkin Island and a rocky promontory marked by a white beacon, to Baltimore harbour. Beacon Point is a desolate headland, scattered with ruined cottages, traces of old worked fields, lazybeds and a lost way of life. The beacon itself, known locally as Lot's Wife, actually looks more like a chalky *dalek* straight out of 'Doctor Who' than a pillar of salt. Immediately beyond the narrow entrance, Baltimore harbour becomes a spacious, sheltered, natural haven formed by Sherkin Island, Ringarogy Island and the mainland promontory. Its separation from the open sea, and the conditions outside the narrows, give the harbour an atmosphere of timelessness. In the centre of the haven, bobbing slightly at anchor, was a classic image of nautical grace – the beautiful sharp-lined black and yellow schooner *Pride of Baltimore II*, newly arrived from Maryland, USA, and paying a courtesy visit to her namesake Irish port.

On the outskirts of Baltimore, I beached on a shingle rise, set up camp above it, swam away the aches of the day and settled down to wait for Marie to arrive.

CHAPTER 7

Brethren of the Coast

*... drink a health to the wonders of the Western World, the pirates,
preachers, poteen-makers ...*

Playboy of the Western World, JM Synge

Leaving Baltimore the next day, past the *Pride of Baltimore II*, by the
narrow neck of the natural harbour, I hugged the coast of Sherkin
Island, heading for the distant, mountainous mass of Clear, eight
miles southwest of Baltimore, and Ireland's southernmost
inhabited island. Twisted rock layers with colourful, inverted strata,
opening occasionally into fissures and small caves, formed the
beautiful east flank of Sherkin. Carrigclearmore islet seemed to
detach itself, then slide away behind me as I approached the shallow
Gascannane Sound, between Sherkin and Clear, on the strong pull
of an ebbing tide. I had been warned not to try crossing the Sound
on the flood tide, which reaches three knots and gives a nasty sea
especially during an opposing wind.

As I struck out across Gascannane Sound for Clear Island the
wind – a southwesterly today – was already approaching force four.
A headwind, it was hard graft in the kayak, but no real threat to tidal
conditions in the Sound. Wind-stirred, the sea began to dance and
sparkle; the kayak's bow threw off fireworks of brightling spray as it
dipped and thrust, and Fastnet reeled in a vivid sweep of colour.
Sherkin, now far behind, displayed its high and rugged south and
west coasts, with collars of white-laced sea off its salient points. A
glance eastward above the waves brought back images of recent
days – the profiles of Carrigatrough and the Kedge islands, now and
forever etched in paddling memory. Clear Island itself, from sea

level, was a high, mounded turtle-back, sloping slightly from a cliffy east to its lower, rockier west coast. And just four miles to the southwest, looking like a floating castle in a fairy tale, star of a thousand stormy forecasts, stood the Fastnet Rock itself. Its Irish name, *Carrig Aonar*, means 'lonely rock', and it is hard to imagine a lonelier posting than lighthouse-keeper on the Fastnet Rock. But long before it even had a lighthouse, it was known as the 'teardrop of Erin', being the last piece of Irish land seen by thousands of Irish emigrants to America, as they headed out to the open Atlantic and an unknown future.

Nowhere along Clear's east coast offered the chance to rest or land until, round a bluff promontory like a tenement street corner, opened the wide, sheltered inlet known as South Harbour. Its little bay had a fresco fringe decorated at low tide with arches and caves, and richer in bird life than anywhere I'd visited since the Saltee islands at the other end of Fastnet. Lazy grey seals humped reluctantly away from the landing slip as though I was the first boat to stop in a hundred years.

From a high bend on the steep winding road above South Harbour was a view perhaps little changed in centuries. A pastoral patchwork of pocket-sized fields clung to the island's slopes. Traditional stooks of hand-scythed hay, thatched and weighted against the wind, were neatly corralled in dykes of turf and stone. Rich purple fuchsia hung thickly from the turf walls like a crop in itself. Far below, beyond a golden hillside of gorse, a twin-masted wooden yacht lay peacefully at anchor in the bay, where *Sola* also waited. But Clear is neither heritage theme park, nor primitive backwater, as I was to learn when the owners of the little hostel, who also run the island cooperative and canoe club, invited me in for a chat. Over coffee and home-made scones Seamus O'Driscoll explained that the island still had a population of almost two hundred, fishing, fish farming and working the land on a scale which was appropriate to the island, its weather and its wildlife. As early as 1979 the Cape Clear Coop had been licensed by the ESB, the national electricity company, to produce and distribute its own electricity. Two generating windmills were sited on a hill in the centre of the island, and in 1984 the Cape Clear power supply system – a combination of wind, diesel and storage batteries – became the first of its type in the world. Electricity had made possible computer links, and there were already the beginnings of a scheme to link all the main islands round the entire Irish coast by computer modem and e-mail. It was a scheme which, in theory, should do much to overcome the barriers of weather, distance, costs and access to information which have made island life so difficult in past times.

Ireland was the first European country to carry out *aquaculture*, farming salmon in the sea as early as 1854. Over a century later, the industry's main problems lay in maximising the shelter from the open sea required by the fragile fish-cages, while minimising the pollution caused by various fish feed and treatment products in the sheltered sea inlets. Clear Island was now at the forefront of Irish fish-farming technology, demonstrating that sea-fish farming could be carried out in tanks *on land*, where there were no ocean waves, and where pollution levels could be more easily monitored and controlled. The sea water was even being raised into the tanks by wind-powered pumps: all the signs were that Clear was an island with a healthy future.

Replete with home baking and island hospitality, I left the South Harbour, bound for the famous Cape Clear itself, where I expected at the very least to meet a heavy and confused sea. Unlike the headlands of the south coast, notable mainly for their rugged edges and surrounding tide races, the southern tip of Clear Island is the first of the great Atlantic capes of the southwest seaboard. At Cape Clear one meets the dangerous combination of tidal conditions, and the full exposure to the Atlantic swell. And with a force six wind blowing it was bound to be rough. The Atlantic ocean is an awesome concept; an ocean of superlatives. Over thirteen thousand miles from north to south, and three thousand miles from Ireland to the opposite bank, it holds one-third of the planet's water. Receiving most of the world's big rivers, and about half the world's rainfall, it is at the same time both the wettest and the saltiest of all oceans.

The size and power of wind-generated waves is a function of three factors: the strength of the wind (force), the duration of its blowing, and the amount of open water over which it blows (its 'fetch'). The accepted oceanographic model is that a wind of velocity thirty knots, blowing over a fetch of 280 nautical miles for at least twenty-three hours, will produce a 'fully arisen' sea with average waves of thirteen feet, and largest waves of around thirty feet. But in the Atlantic ocean the wind, often hovering around gale force for days on end, regularly blows over a fetch of thousands of miles, raising enormous swells which dominate coastal conditions on both sides of the ocean, stirring the weather, scouring the shores and rattling boatmen. Some of nature's worst storms and biggest waves are spawned in the Atlantic, and many of the waves which break on the southwest coast of Ireland have come from Cape Horn, a full six thousand miles away.

Once a pattern of deep-ocean waves begins to radiate free from the wind-source that spawned it, the confused local chaos of apparently random sea-motion organises itself into fairly even lines of swell, consolidated wave ranks of greater length and increasing speed. As a rule, swell is less jagged than the waves of a sea pattern, and moves across the ocean's surface in great trains of waves, radiating downwind from their source in a pattern known as 'maturing'. Most ocean waves are deepwater waves, travelling unopposed for thousands of miles in water far deeper than their own wavelength. However, when they at last approach the coast, and enter a region of water shallower than half their wavelength their entire dynamic character changes. They begin to feel the bottom, to gather and steepen themselves in readiness to topple. Suddenly they are influenced by new factors such as tidal streams, inshore currents, reflection and interference; and in the general confusion they become possessed with a strong desire to break shorewards with great violence. A following current will increase the wavelength, decrease wave height and generally subdue an incoming swell pattern to some extent; but an opposing current or tide has the opposite effect, sharpening and steepening the face of the waves. A strong enough current, such as that found off some of the Irish Atlantic headlands, may well cause the waves to break like surf, even in deep water, and can be a considerable hazard to any small boat that insists on travelling round them without adequate preparation and research.

The first sign of the Atlantic edge was the steady pounding arrival of huge regular swell-waves from the southwest, already overtoppling their own crests in a welter of foam. Etched across their surface, for as far as the eye could see, were streaks of spume drawn out by the wind as it scoured the skin of the ocean. Here and there cross-waves, surging round the Cape itself, collided with the main swell-wave pattern. Where they met they exploded upwards like mortar shells in awesome luminous spray. The waters, crosshatched in complex patterns of ocean and inshore waves, tides and currents, mixed and merged, foamed and bubbled over with an amazing combination of living, coupling energies. All was starkly blue and white: sharp, angular and rapid. Sharpest of all were the waves themselves, swinging in every direction like Viking axeheads in mid-battle fervour. For me it was a wet assault, with several waves rising swiftly to smash me in the face or chest, with steep-mounded waves boosting the kayak high into the air, and the paddles struggling at times to reach the water below me.

The only witnesses to my struggle were the sea birds which seemed to swarm in great concentrations off the Cape. Storm petrels, skuas and at least two types of shearwater, all species of the open ocean, skimmed the waves here on the edge of the vast Atlantic. Their nonchalant presence among the crashing waves somehow made the rough water seem less threatening, as if a bright shining blue breaker, with a puffin bobbing on its forward edge, was any less of a hazard to life than a birdless black comber of the same magnitude. Indeed at times my concern was more for these frail-looking birds than for my own safety; I held my breath as, blithely, with an air of complete unconcern, tiny sparrow-like storm petrels bobbed on wave flanks within inches of massive breaking crests, just as a toddler might wander into the path of an articulated lorry.

Between the 'Bill of Cape Clear' and the Bream Point tide race, a particularly heavy and confused sea was running, such that I couldn't have ridden it for long. The kayak seemed to fly from wave crest to wave crest, and it was the wind itself which eventually pushed me around the great corner. Well-rested after my break at South Harbour, and with *Sola* bouncing superbly, I was soon nudged beyond the main area of fray, and free of Cape Clear's menace. Then the sea was behind me, bucking and pushing the kayak along the island's west coast with tremendous energy. The speed of some of the lifts and drops heaped the body with G-forces, and left portions of heart and stomach in mid-air. At times it seemed I was travelling as much up and down as forward, but within an hour from South Harbour I was cruising with the wind and tide at about seven knots back through Gascannane Sound. Relaxed in the knowledge that the worst of the day's waters were past, head filled with the images of a magical day, I surfed happily along the coast of Sherkin, re-entered Baltimore harbour, past Baltimore itself to Church Strand Bay having come full circle for the sake of a final evening with Marie-Pierre.

All too soon Marie's cycle tour had come to an end. For almost a full week we'd managed to meet and camp on the remote bays and headlands of west Cork, cooking on driftwood fires and watching the big, dark, southern skies of Fastnet. The little tent was going to seem very empty now as Marie turned her wheels back towards Scotland, and I continued to paddle west looking for Atlantic Ireland.

~ ~ ~

'Piracy on the High Seas' is among the oldest of recorded offences, having existed, like the related enterprises of smuggling and wrecking, at least as long as legitimate maritime trade. When Columbus discovered the West Indies he unwittingly inaugurated two centuries of Caribbean piracy. At first it was euphemistically known as 'privateering' and virtually endorsed by Queen Elizabeth I, who was torn between punishing and honouring renegade sea captains such as Sir Francis Drake and Sir John Hawkins, since their plundering of mainly Spanish ships brought gold and glory to England.

Those were times in which piracy was a glamorous way to be an outlaw; when a man could start his career as a pirate and end up as a Royal Admiral. Henry Morgan, the most famous of the English buccaneers, managed to tread a fine line between privateer and pirate for much of his life. In sixteen years of terror his boats sacked eighteen cities, four towns and thirty-five villages of the Spanish Main in the name of the English crown. Being particularly gruesome and bloodthirsty, his raids often far exceeded his Crown remit. The Dutch surgeon Exquemelin's records describe how Morgan delighted in barbecueing Spanish priests, hanging prisoners by their thumbs, and burning their faces with oil-soaked leaves until their eyes popped out of their skulls. His actions were nonetheless repeatedly sanctioned by King Charles II who knighted him in 1673. A brilliant seaman and tactician, Morgan remained a hero to both pirates and authorities alike, and eventually became Admiral Sir Henry Morgan JP, Governor General of Jamaica and uncrowned King of the Caribbean.

By the eighteenth century, however, England found herself largely a victim of the maritime monster she had helped to create: nowhere was safe from the 'Brethren of the Coast', and the Golden Age of Piracy had begun. Piracy was a glamorous and lucrative, if dangerous, trade for seamen disillusioned with the tyrannic discipline of naval life. Several European nations had established colonies in the New World, and soon the sea was awash with desperadoes from all of these. English buccaneers, Dutch *zeerovers*, French *flibustiers* and Spanish *piratas* dominated the Atlantic sea-routes, flaunting the unstable nature of international trade, fragile political alliances and colonial greed, and picking like hyenas on the casualties of sea-borne rivalries. Corsairs from the Algerian coast harried the ships of Spain as they neared their homeland, ambushed infidel vessels coasting along Africa, and even raided small ports along the south coasts of England and Ireland.

Many of these pirates were madmen and psychopaths; others found it useful to adopt eccentric and vivid character roles, often quickly acquiring reputations akin to a combination of pop star, lager lout and gangster in today's terms. The notorious Edward Teach, better known as Blackbeard, meticulously cultivated his fearsome image and brutal reputation as the devil incarnate. A giant of a man, he dressed always in black, and was permanently drunk on a mixture of rum and gunpowder which he also forced on his crews. His long beard covered most of his face, and reached to his chest in black pigtails braided with ribbons. In battle he wore an enormous sling filled with pistols and holsters, and a belt from which hung an assortment of daggers, cutlasses and yet more pistols. Tucked under his hat-brim were lighted, slow-burning fuses of hemp and saltpetre, ensuring he always had ready tinder, and adding to his smoky satanic appearance.

Blackbeard seems to have been almost indestructible. During a long and ruthless career he accrued a huge fleet and a vast fortune, and was bigamously married at least fourteen times. When he eventually met his end, at the battle of Okracoke Inlet off the Virginia coast, it took twenty stabwounds and five pistol shots to kill him; and legend has it that his decapitated body swam round the boat several times before finally sinking below the waves. Blackbeard was known to bury his treasure on land regularly. He would go ashore with one seaman, have the man dig the treasure pit, then kill him and bury him on top of the treasure. Along the Atlantic coastline of America lie many pirate skeletons, and large quantities of Blackbeard's treasure are still there for the finding.

The Golden Age of Piracy in the western oceans is long gone. Ordered, edited and sterilised by time, it has resulted in a collection of colourful adventure lore almost unrivalled in western literature and imagination. Pirates, from Long John Silver to Captain Hook, have become the stars of pantomime, light opera and swashbuckling movie epic; the archetypal sea adventurers of the age of sail. But on a global scale the criminal act of piracy has never really stopped. According to the International Maritime Bureau, whose Piracy Centre keeps a tally of every reported incident worldwide, there have in the past decade been more than a thousand convictions for piracy against merchant vessesls, not to mention the countless attacks on defenceless 'boat peoples' and refugees. The number of vessels seized annually by sea-going robbers doubled between 1994 and 1995 and continues to increase each year.

Piracy today, like the shipping trade on which it preys, has changed enormously and takes various forms. Often motivated by drugs cartels, political factions or terrorist groups with powerful automatic weapons, it can be big business. Fast boats, low in the water, can dodge radar detection, and have been able to seize vessels of a thousand tons or more while travelling at full speed. Most recorded attacks today occur in the Far East, in areas like the South China Sea where policing is weaker. Reports from the Sulu Sea off the Philippines, and from the Gulf of Siam tell of victims still being made to walk the plank into shark-rich waters, or having their throats cut to minimise noise or save on bullets. Yachtjacking is rife in the Caribbean; the coast of Florida is awash with wrecks deliberately sunk with cargo intact so that divers can recover the illicit goods at a later date; and Colombian pirates have tended to commandeer vessels for use as unmarked drug carriers. In 1995 a gang tried to capture a large passenger ferry in Denmark, and in the 1970s a plot to hijack a nuclear submarine was uncovered. Piracy has moved on to new targets and new arenas, and only rarely makes the news in the western world, but on a global scale piracy is every bit as real a problem in the twentieth century as it ever was in the eighteenth.

~ ~ ~

Baltimore, west Cork, is the home of the O'Driscoll clan. Even today O'Driscoll is the prevalent surname in the region; there are recurring facial features among people in the town; and each year in June there is a reunion of O'Driscolls from all over the world. Still visible too, are the ruins of the two great O'Driscoll fortified castles which protected the town during the turbulent raids and adventures of the fifteenth and sixteenth centuries – *Dun na Sead* ('fort of the jewels') beside the harbour, and *Dun na Long* ('fort of the boats') on the rocky shore of Sherkin Island opposite. There was a time, before the rise of powerful rival clans like the O'Sullivans and O'Mahoneys, when the O'Driscolls were a major dynasty, owning and controlling all the land and sea in west Cork, from Kinsale to the Kenmare River. Renowned pirates and sea-reivers, in the fifteenth century they made themselves both rich and unpopular by levying tolls and dues on ships travelling or fishing in the rich local waters.

> *Every ship that fisheth ... between the Fastnet Rock and The Stags [off Toe Head] is to pay ten shillings and two pence, a barrel of salt, a hogshead of wine and a dish of fish three times a day.*

Such extortion predictably led to ongoing, and often violent feuds with the men of neighbouring county Waterford who fished the area, but the last straw came in 1537 when the O'Driscolls seized a cargo of Spanish wine, bound for Waterford but driven into Baltimore harbour by a storm. The citizens of Waterford then dispatched a heavy revenge fleet to harry Baltimore town, and in the raid that followed both *Dun na Long* and *Dun na Sead* castles and the Franciscan friary on Sherkin were destroyed. Yet hostilities were not to end there. Almost a full century later a sea captain from Dungarvan, an old enemy of the O'Driscolls, led two Algerian pirate ships through the narrows and into Baltimore harbour. In what became known as the 'Sack of Baltimore', the Algerines screamed and pillaged through the town, looting, killing and burning, and carried away two hundred prisoners to sell as slaves along the Barbary Coast. As I packed the kayak, it occurred to me to wonder whether any deep-seated clan memories of vengeance, bloodfeuds and reigns of pirate terror, might have been stirred and revived among the O'Driscoll descendants by the elegant square-rigged *Pride of Baltimore II* as it sailed in through the Baltimore narrows the previous day, carrying over ten thousand square feet of sail. Baltimore clippers were originally built for speed and strength, they could evade stockades, out-sail enemies, and arrive in port with small but profitable cargoes, having 'clipped' hours if not days off the voyage time. *Pride of Baltimore II,* measuring over sixty feet in length was a superb replica of her eighteenth-century ancestor and, like the O'Driscolls themselves, the direct descendant of an age of cut-throat competition at sea.

~ ~ ~

That night I was invited to a beach barbecue on Sherkin Island. The Irish coastal equivalent of the bush telegraph had ensured that the people of Sherkin were expecting the *Sola* Round Ireland kayak long before I had even arrived in Baltimore, and Don and Anne Curtin had planned a little reception. Round the north end of Sherkin, I paddled between Spanish Island and the Catalogue islands in a sea freshly roughened by an embryonic gale, and the surf was breaking heavily as I reached Silver Strand Bay. From more than two hundred yards offshore I could smell the smoke of the beach fire and hear the shouting of the Curtin children, who had been posted on the rocks as look-outs. The surf broke on skerries in mid-bay, leaving a gentler passage ashore and a landing made even easier by being hauled in by several pairs of hands. On the beach Don Curtin was casually juggling fifty mackerel on an iron mesh, freshly caught and smelling delicious on the smoky breeze.

Curtin kids ran in and out of the Atlantic breakers like little Irish penguins. Steadily, groups of islanders arrived over the dunes, finding sheltered corners and coves near the fire, and occasionally stripping off for a dip in the sea. One tall quiet man stood apart in a pin-striped suit. Like a stooge from a silent movie, he stalked enigmatically to the edge of the sea, stripped off, pissed on the sand, and continued into the sea. When he reached chest depth, he simply turned round and reversed the process, replacing the suit without even drying himself, and wandered off to eat mackerel.

Around the fire, throwing occasional glances in my direction, were clusters of island men and exiles returned for the summer. Almost everyone I spoke to was called O'Driscoll. Perhaps it was a trick of the firelight, but the striped ganseys, high cheekbones and ruddy weatherbeaten faces of the islanders looked highly piratical to me, and the mysterious glances seemed to tell of some conspiracy afoot. Anyway, the chat was friendly enough, the beer refreshing, and the fish smoked to perfection. All the time the breakers thumped on the sand, wind wheezed overhead and people either huddled closer to the fire or disappeared back into the night.

Later still, in the first stirrings of a full gale, and at a time when most pubs would be closing their doors, the Curtins and I set off across the island to where the harbour nightlife lurks. The darkness was pure, untainted by street or houselights, but Don and Anne seemed to find their way instinctively along the narrow winding road. Don explained that historically the island houses have always been built in carefully chosen hollows and copses, so as to remain invisible from customs officers and sea-raiders. Sure enough, though I could smell the smoke of many peat fires, hardly a window-twinkle was visible from the road, and virtually nothing would have been seen from the sea below. Several houses have neither track nor driveway, their quick and dry access route being known only to the locals. This would delay the approach of unwanted visitors, and allow reluctant hosts time to disappear. It seemed unlikely, I thought, that TV licence dues would ever be collected on Sherkin Island.

Without an island policeman, there was a general sense of

acceptable anarchy, and, as far as the island's two pubs were concerned, the night was young. At the Garrison House a fire-haired girl with a voice like a wooden flute along sea cliffs sang 'Crazy Man Michael' and 'Annachie Gordon'. Then she broke the appreciative hush with a loud laugh, elbowed her neighbour and passed the guitar along like a peace pipe. The lights of Baltimore, glimmering across the bay, seemed to wink from another world. Above, through darkened lanes, we reached the island's oldest pub, the appropriately named Jolly Roger, a den of looters and rievers if ever there was one. A band by the name of Mór Porter held the floor, and could hardly have looked more piratical if they'd had hooks for hands. Sean Savage – in addition to having a fitting name – was the archetypal shaggy-haired, dark-bearded swarthy rogue; while Norman, with a bushy grey beard and three-cornered felt hat, looked as though he might have been blown in from Far Tortuga on the last Atlantic gale.

The crowd in the tavern were a colourful mixture of islanders, returned islanders, international travellers and even a few immortal hippies. And the music seemed to be nothing less than the vibrant soundtrack to Sherkin Island life itself. Through the smokey air, standing at the bar, and in every corner were O'Driscolls, the spitting images of those who'd been at the beach barbecue. When I caught their eyes, or blundered within hearing distance of a whispering group, they'd show a few teeth in a sneer or a smile, wink at me or just sidle off into the shadows. 'That's him,' they seemed to say. I was tempted to look below my beer mat for the 'Black Spot', but Don just shrugged it off as curiosity about a new face in the pub.

Night wore into morning. Occasionally I could hear rain and wind lashing at the windows, but inside the little tavern the milling horde of revellers were oblivious to the weather. The music and *craic* swirled and thickened, and seemed to hang in the air with the cigarette smoke. Murphy's Stout flowed like a thick dark tide; the tables were piled high with tall stacks of empty pint glasses, and full black ones. Toilet trips were taken quickly and efficiently on the front turf. Rain lashed and the gale howled on, but back inside the tavern they were soon forgotten. In the early hours of morning, when the atmosphere had mellowed a little, the doors of the tavern were firmly closed.

Choosing his moment, Don eventually announced that there was indeed a plot afoot: that several of the more piratical islanders had realised that the Round Ireland Kayak was due in O'Driscoll waters, and had decided, in honour of their forefathers to hijack it. Don stalled my disbelieving sneer with a raised finger: 'At least half the people in this bar are involved, including myself.'

With a broad, conspiratorial grin, Anne added, 'The fact is, you're *already* a prisoner. You have been since the barbecue! We wanted to help with the Eyebank fundraising, but, well, we have our own ways of doing things on Sherkin.' She explained that if I insisted on leaving in the morning, I would be immediately recaptured and brought back to Sherkin, and held under a ransom demand which would take effect from the morning. I was to be held on the island until a *thousand* pounds had been raised. There was a big cheer, and another round of drinks as they watched the message sink in, and I drank my first pint as a captive man. I smiled and thought to myself that there could certainly be worse places to be held hostage than Sherkin Island.

~ ~ ~

At about half-past four, with the music of the Jolly Roger growing gentler in the background and a morning light now defining the roadway, my captors and I made our way back across the island to sleep. Six hours later I woke feeling none the worse for a consumption of stout beyond normal prescribed limits, but with an uneasy memory of having forfeited my liberty. Pounding winds and horizontal rain persuaded the Curtin family that, preferable to Mass was a big communal breakfast fry-up, after which I decided it was time to slip quietly away.

It was a wild scene that met me on the hill above the harbour.

Waves were lapping over the harbour walls, boats tossed and strained at their moorings and gale winds herded the sea's most savage swells into the corral of Baltimore Bay. Not a soul stirred.

'Surely not kidnapping weather,' I chuckled to myself, and began to descend to the bay. Just then an incredibly decrepit car came raking along the track, heavily overloaded, reeking black smoke and trailing a loose exhaust pipe. It was the island taxi, filled to the gunwales with rowdy O'Driscolls, dressed in stripes, waistcoats, headbands and seaboots, complete with surgical eye-patches and painted scars which announced 'We Mean Business!'

They headed not for the harbour, but for the Jolly Roger, where they knocked back a few pints, waiting to see if I would actually attempt to escape. Still sceptical that they would launch a kidnap in that swell, I continued on down to the shore. Just as I pulled on my spray cover and prepared to launch the kayak from a slipway where the waves were rising and falling almost six feet, my heart missed a beat as I saw the Skull and Crossbones flag being hoisted on the foremast of the sturdiest trawler in the harbour, and a crowd of hardy onlookers began to gather at the pier.

Through bouncing waves and over ragged crests I headed into the centre of the bay, seeking a slight shelter in the area of sea immediately behind the *Pride of Baltimore II*, which was lying midway between Sherkin Island and the mainland. Any ideas of coming in too close were abandoned when I saw how the big square-rigger heaved and rolled in the gale-forced swell. Some poor oilskin-clad crewmen hung wretchedly over the gunwale near the bow where the ship rose and fell demonically. One moment the bowsprit was plunged underwater; the next it was shooting skyward with cascades of streaming water. I bobbed uncomfortably, but fairly safely on the chaotic surface, eyeing warily the *Pride*'s anchor cable – which was thrashing enough to slice me in two – and the breakers at the bay mouth which looked more than adequate to crush the life out of *Sola* and me. Altogether it was a pretty unfriendly scene.

With a start I heard the engine of a boat and whirled *Sola* round on a rising wave-crest. At first all I could see above the swell was the Jolly Roger flag, the traditional pirate signal to victims that their time was running out; the final warning to surrender your ship, or resist and be slaughtered. Then there was a foaming, plunging bow, punching towards me through the heavy waves, over the crest and deep into a trough. When it reappeared it was only minutes away. All around the bow, drenched in sea-spray but fired with Sherkin stout, was a motley band of rag-clad rogues, hanging overboard with boat hooks, rope-nooses and potato sacks, and hell-bent on hauling me in. Any vague idea I'd had about cooperating with the spirit of things soon disappeared when I realised that this screaming horde of stout-filled waterborne kidnappers was too deeply steeped in the ways of their ancestors to be entirely gentle with either me or the kayak. I cut through at a sprint from under the bows of the trawler, and the chase was on.

Being pursued by a powerful trawler manned by intoxicated pirates in a six foot swell is not my idea of fun, and it was towards the shore that I headed in case the whole caper went seriously wrong. They soon swooped down upon the kayak, almost swamping me with a bow wave. But it seemed that each pirate had a different idea of how I was to be captured, and clung to it singlemindedly. One swiped at me with a boat hook, which I parried with the paddle; another almost fell overboard trying to grab the tail of the kayak. I was half expecting the third to try boarding the kayak with a knife in his teeth, when suddenly I felt my paddle catch. It had been lassoed with a length of rope, the other end of which was secured to a deck cleat on the trawler. I had no choice then but to cling on hard as the trawler turned and spun back towards harbour. Roughly and at some speed I was hauled through walls of water, tumbling into troughs and exploding over crests until at last we reached the relative safety of the Sherkin shore.

It seemed an island memory had indeed been wakened on Sherkin, and complete pandemonium had broken out on the pier.

People with cameras or small children scrambled for safety as pirates, onlookers and anyone else within reach were being thrown unceremoniously into the sea. The mania spread and soon there were large numbers of drenched islanders bobbing in the harbour or drying in the sun. It took four sodden buccaneers just to lift the loaded kayak, but unconventional solutions to transport problems abound on Sherkin, and a tractor and trailer stood ready behind the pier. It had already been pressed into service for weddings, funerals, flittings and breakdowns, and despite a flat tyre and insufficient length of trailer, it wasn't going to back off at the prospect of shifting a kidnapped canoe. And so *Sola* was hauled off into captivity as I joined my own captors in the turquoise waters of Sherkin harbour.

Parrot burgers were on the menu up at the Jolly Roger. Dripping O'Driscoll pirates sat with pints of stout, occasionally lifting eyepatches to survey the bay, and generally looking as though great-grandfather would have been proud of them. The afternoon passed easily with music in the pub, a swim in the eight foot breakers of Silver Strand, and a visit to Matt Murphy's Marine Station. I began to think that perhaps captivity was the best thing that had happened to me yet. Captivity, after all, is a form of security, and I looked forward to a few restful days on Sherkin as the ransom was raised. Unfortunately that was not to be. A looting party was at that very moment causing mayhem in the mainland pubs, and half the ransom was collected even before the pirates had dripped dry. Half of the remaining pot was contributed in local donations and from the O'Driscoll pirates themselves. There was a great roar of laughter as I was encouraged at the end of a wooden cutlass to contribute a few 'Pieces of Eight' to my own ransom, and by late evening the full sum had been collected. In less than a day the crazy pirates of Sherkin Island had raised enough cash to fund four eye operations, and I, rather unexpectedly, was free to resume my journey in the morning.

CHAPTER 8

Atlantic Edge

And under the labour of their hands the ships went forward boldly on their journey, over the deep wet depths of the sea, and over the swaying ridges of the hilly ocean, and over the heavy sullen ramparts of the waves, and over the dark shower-dripping hollows of the shores, and over the haughty close-sided billows of the currents, and over the turbulent furious fierce horizons of the deep.

The Homeward Voyage, Anon, 13th-14th century

Between Cape Clear and the massive promontory of Mizen Head lies the great bight of Roaringwater Bay. Within it are some twenty islands, like jewels in a drawstring purse, with its neck open to the southwest and the Atlantic. *Roaringwater*: the name seemed increasingly appropriate as I left the shelter of Sherkin. The wind had not dropped below force six and, even among the islands, a huge swell remained from the previous day's gale. The constant roar of breaking water indeed filled the air as I wove between Inishodriscoll, Skeam East and Skeam West, like a little needle stubbornly towing a yarn of furrowed sea. Little houses with slipways, gorgeous hidden gems of beaches, and a few small boats working shellfish creels gave a small inkling of what the bay must have been like in more prosperous times; but since the decline of the pilchard fishing and processing industries, and the mackerel and herring fisheries which followed, the population of the islands in Roaringwater Bay has declined steadily, and now only a few of the larger islands like Sherkin and Clear are inhabited at all.

Beyond the Skeams, heading for the broken, skerried forms of the McCarthy islands, the sea was more potent and hungry than I'd seen it along all the south coast. The McCarthys lay due west, along the line of wind and swell, and although I could see the sea smashing right over their backs, I headed directly into the group, hoping for a tiny eye of shelter within their horseshoe grouping. Sure enough, just as someone right next to a bomb blast may occasionally escape the worst damage, there was just shelter enough inshore to make a brief landing on the largest of the McCarthy islands.

The swell exploding on the western edge of the island was sending curtains of spindrift – myriads of bright, sea-spawned, wind-borne micro-particles – over the land to the sheltered bay on the other side. Flecks of foam swirled above the island like wayward gulls, telltale rags of the sea's wild power. I walked ashore on deep soft mats of sea shrubs, between sharp serrated rocks, caught unawares several times by virile blowholes gushing spouts of pressurised water from crevasses among the campion. I tried to picture what I could of the bay and the route ahead, but saw and heard only its endlessly roaring water. The noise of breaking waves, one of the great elemental sounds of nature, was so loud, so pervasive, that it seemed to fill the mind entirely. I cast around for a suitable metaphor and found none. The ocean can sound at times like anything from a sleeping child to a six-lane motorway; but on days like this it was beyond comparison; it was uniquely and overwhelmingly just the pure noise of roaring water.

Leaving the McCarthys safely was a matter of gauging where the swell mounted, tumbled and broke, and where it merely rose up unbroken; a single mistake of timing could easily lead to more than just waves being broken on the seaward ramparts of Roaringwater Bay. Bobbing nervously in the safety zone behind a sharp-crested rock in the bay, I studied the incoming swell with all the concentration of a matador. Groups of swell are called 'sets'; long intervals between sets are known as 'lulls'; and the pattern of sets and lulls – the surf-beat – is nothing more or less than the language of the ocean itself. A recreational surfer will learn useful phrases of the language as a matter of sport, while an inshore fisherman of the

Atlantic edge becomes fluent as a matter of survival. I was still far from fluent, but had become, as a matter of necessity and constant practice, reasonably competent in the art of quick, practical translation and soon began to decipher portions of the roaring semantics of the bay.

The swell was coming through in ranked sets of six waves, with a period of about ten seconds between each, and a lull of about eighty seconds between sets. Within each set the middle wave was usually the largest, exposing all the shallowest reefs of rock in its passage and breaking, with a daunting volume of both noise and water, on the inshore skerries. It was with a mental imprint of this pattern that I began to skirt the white foam that marked the outer edges of some of the danger zones, weaving the kayak as close as I dared to the areas where the largest swell waves would begin their breaks, rising and falling on the waves as the sets tumbled through. I angled my bows across the foam-cordoned no-go areas only during the brief ceasefires between sets, careful to count the seconds and to keep a wary eye on the western horizon as I powered the kayak into the bay. Within minutes I had cleared the broken water of the McCarthy islands and was heading west towards Long Island.

The island was bleak and unremarkable, like the rising back of a dull-coloured fish. But the crossing itself was impressive for the sheer unmistakable power of the rollers that were now coming up the bay. Coming in a-beam were veritable hillsides; slow slopes climbing to perhaps thirty feet. From the summit of each was a daunting view of an endless procession of others. Those waves which found their progress obstructed by island edge or rock skerry, blasted against them in extravagant outrage; but otherwise, in mid-channel, they simply bulldozed determinedly onward. Wave after wave, I was constantly amazed that the kayak – dwarfed by these chunks of unbroken ocean – was not simply swept, like a piece of dust, back into the bay; instead she crept repeatedly up the long smooth flanks of these great beasts, until gradually I gained the outstretched form of Long Island.

The final passage of a day brim-full of bright images of Atlantic power, took me past the wild, magical shapes of Goat Island and the Illaunricmonia group, and round Castle Point in search of an evening camp. The mountainous land of the southwest begins at the biblical-sounding Mount Gabriel, providing shelter from the wind and western swell. On a shingle bay at Gabriel's foot I set up camp, hung clothes to dry in the last hour of the evening sun, and rustled up a driftwood fire to cook on. At ten o'clock the coastguard forecast '... from Carnsore Point to Dursey Head ...' came over on the VHF in a broad Cork accent. The reader cleared his throat, apologised, cleared his throat again, then said 'Oh damn it all! I've taken up the wrong papers. Excuse me one moment if you please.' He was several minutes away looking for them, during which time the radio was completely silent, and when he eventually re-started I was in such a fit of giggles that I missed most of it anyway. At high water I checked the kayak was safe from a grabbing swell, then relaxed into a deep and long-overdue sleep, the sleep of an escaped prisoner with a delayed hangover.

~ ~ ~

What do butterflies get in their stomachs when they are nervous, I wondered as I left the haven of Galley Cove, bound for an encounter with the Goliath of southwest Ireland, Mizen Head, which one Irish writer has described as 'a giant spoke of a headland that sticks up like a boar's tusk above the rugged lip of the Irish coast'. Galley Cove had been peaceful, sheltered and sunny; a place to read, snack and collect my thoughts before 'the Mizen'. But a week of westerlies, seldom dropping below force five, had induced an unusually large Atlantic swell off this exposed corner of the country, making progress along the broken coast tortuous and terrifying. Brow Head frowned down on me as the sun dipped behind a cloud, and I blundered past on a large patternless reflecting swell. Already I could feel the pull of a four knot tide towards the great cape, but it was the swell that concerned me more. Reports warned of almost unnaturally large accumulations of sea and a fierce tide race off Mizen Head, and I began to brace myself for an epic paddle.

The sun was bright and low as I approached the Mizen, and although a massive sea was now heaving round the cliff, its surface had a warm, reassuring glow. For over two hours, paddling forward meant alternately climbing skywards at an uncanny angle, feet towards the sun, struggling to gain the wave crests, then tipping into a dive and skimming down the westward slopes of successive swell mounds. In sections where the swell reflected directly from the cliff-walls, there were explosions of multiple crests and deep pits of compounded troughs, slowing my progress with the desperate need to pull every support stroke in the book. The main race poured westwards with a thundering urgency. The sea dictated the pace, while I merely clung to it and battled to stay upright like a drunk on an escalator. Meanwhile, the Mizen steadily unfolded its pattern of twisted, banded sandstone cliffs, glinting pink and white, and tilting towards the sun.

From a low angle, ahead and to my right, the sun shone fiercely, taking the edge of terror from the sea, and relaxing my face with its warmth. The whole surface seemed to have taken on a dazzling golden shine like burnished brass, and my eyes were half-lidded in the glare. Then, just as I was beginning to enjoy the massive rollercoaster motion, the whole scene darkened, and out of the sun came a huge sailing ship. I can only describe her as a three-masted galleon under full sail. Her vast curving wooden bow was heeled over to port, parting waves of white water as she ploughed forward, directly towards me. I remember briefly being stunned by what a superb replica she was; how solid she looked; impressed by her speed under sail; and more than a little worried by her apparent collision course with the Mizen Head cliffs; but my immediate reaction was to kick the rudder, dig the paddle and get the hell out from her path. For several minutes I sprinted hard towards the cliffs. When I looked back there was only the sun and the swell and the kayak.

Strange tales of events at sea, often based on the testimony of sailors returning from long voyages on distant oceans, form a major part of the literature of the western world, from Homer to Hemingway, Coleridge to Conrad. Coleridge's *Rime of the Ancient Mariner* is a classic example of the combination of the poet's genius with the sailor's imagination. It is characteristic not only that the old sailor in the narrative was the sole survivor of his strange odyssey, and therefore had no-one to contradict his version of events, but that he went on recounting his tale despite the listener's obvious desire to get away. Ever since men first ventured over the sea, sailors have been returning with colourful tales of lands, peoples, creatures and phenomena outside the scope of normal experience. Some of these sailors – often subject to extremes of weather, fear, loneliness or malnutrition – inevitably misunderstood their own experiences, or so enhanced them with onshore eloquence and drink, that their stories have to be taken either with the proverbial pinch of salt, or re-interpreted in the light of modern knowledge. Yet many of the old sailors' most unlikely-sounding tales, stranger than many of their fictions or superstitions, were directly based on accurate accounts of true experiences. How many sixteenth-century landlubbers, for instance, would have believed tales of fire-belching mountains, floating castles of ice, flightless birds or flying fish?

Throughout the history of sea-tales many stories have been told of ghosts seen from ships, or even of ghosts on board ships. Joshua Slocum claimed to have met the ghost of the pilot of Columbus's *Pinta* on board his yacht. But perhaps even more famous are the tales of ghost-ships such as the *Marie Celeste*, cursed forever to sail the seven seas; or the *Flying Dutchman* with her satanically posessed Captain Vanderdecken. For over three hundred years there have been accounts from all over the world of sightings of the *Flying Dutchman* scudding before the gale. Old sailors believed that just to see her meant bad luck, and that the first man to spot her would soon die. In some accounts sailors have been close enough to see the tortured white-bearded forms of her cursed crew hauling frantically at the sheets and calling out for help; but, in almost every instance, before anyone can get within range the ghost ship disappears into the storm.

Had my *galleon* been a ghost-ship; a brief and spectacular glimpse through an Atlantic time-warp; a spectre from the lost days of sail? Or was it just the illusory product of my sun-soaked imagination? The sheer vividness of the vision; the detail of the ship and its movement; the suddenness of its appearance; and the fact that my mind was fairly alert at the time, all suggested to me that the plunging galleon, sailing full tilt on a fatal course towards the Mizen cliffs, was indeed a blast from the distant past. But I'll never know for sure. Fortunately perhaps, I had no time to go ghost-busting just then; no alternative, saving a few bewildered backward glances, but to shake the image from my mind, concentrate on the fairly crucial task in hand, and to paddle on round Mizen Head.

The Mizen lighthouse came into view, perched high on a precipice like a fortress, linked to the main headland by a bridge across a treacherous geo. A lighthouse on a headland, like a policeman suddenly appearing at the door, never fails to stir the adrenalin in me. Both are indelibly associated with serious events and potential trouble; they concentrate the mind on what you might have been doing wrong; and I began to focus anew on Mizen Head with the respect it demanded. I was riding the biggest swell of my life, off the notorious Mizen, on the edge of forty thousand square miles of ocean, with nowhere to land within sight in any direction. With intense concentration I stayed within the main tide race, which curved northwest and crossed Dunlough Bay with no perceptible loss of power; and off distant Three Castle Head it showed again as a mosaic pattern of shadows, foam and white-capped water mounds. Edging carefully into Dunlough Bay, I found a more rounded swell and was able to relax a little. But the bay was entirely cliff-fringed. Even through binoculars I couldn't see one cove, beach or slipway at which the kayak could be landed even in an emergency.

I was already tired and weakening, but the only option remaining was to re-enter the tide race and struggle round the next headland, hoping to find a sheltered haul-out in Dunmanus Bay. So there followed another headland, another battle in clapotis waves, and a tide race of even fiercer proportions. Arrogant wave masses forced their way around the headland, creaming over the skerries at the mouth of Dunmanus Bay, and knocking the kayak around like a piece of driftwood. Even Dunmanus Bay offered no immediate prospect of a camp. Its southern shore was a wilderness of cliff and rock, where high mountains tumble down to sea level, culminating in cliffs, arches and geos. The smallest shore boulders were the size of family cars, and looked impossible to land on in the big dumping swell. It was a further hour, limping along with leaden arms and aching back muscles, before I found a little slipway – incredibly steep, but at last sheltered from the swell – at a cove named Doonen Coos.

Above the slipway the hillside was ablaze with fuchsia. There was fuchsia woven among the hedgerows, individual fuchsia shrubs growing from the old turf-dykes, and tough little wind-pruned fuchsia bushes overhanging the gullies along the clifftop. Everywhere I looked the deep red of thousands of little dew-bulb flowers seemed to glow against the greenery of southwest Ireland. It was hard to imagine the landscapes of the southwest without the ubiquitous fuchsia, weeping its dark red tears, like an emblem for a sad Irish socialist. And yet, paradoxically, the fuchsia is about as Irish as a banana palm; *Fuchsia magellania* originated in South America, where it was first recorded by a sixteenth-century botanist called Fuchs. It was brought to Europe in the eighteenth century; and tradition has it that it was Cornish copper miners, working in areas like the mineral-rich Beara peninsula, who first brought the fuchsia to Ireland. The soils, and the mild, damp, oceanic climate of the southwest suited the little shrub, almost as well as its home slopes on the foothills of the Andes, and it has grown profusely throughout the southwest corner ever since.

Among the riot of fuchsia, there was a square of grass to camp on, fresh water to rinse my salty clothes, and plenty of blackthorn bushes to dry them on. A rich smell of peatsmoke and *muirburn* hung on the air, and the patterns of red and black fruit on the coastal brambles hinted strongly that autumn had reached Atlantic Ireland just before me. One perfect little fuchsia hung demurely over a steep burn by my tent, sobbing deep-red flowers and saying 'Don't go any further; stay here with me.'

~ ~ ~

After Mizen Head the eroded coastline of south Cork gives way to a series of long mountainous peninsulas, roughly chipped at their seaward ends to form rugged islands such as Dursey, the Skelligs and the Blaskets. *Rias*, deep fjord-like sea inlets, the drowned valleys of an even more ancient mountain range, separate these peninsulas, forming the great bays of Bantry, Kenmare and Dingle. Southwest Ireland then, is like a 'handclasp' of rias and great rocky headlands. Five bony fingers of land reach desperately out to sea; and equally long sea digits interlock with them in a firm and intimate grip. Along this coast the highest summits of Ireland sweep down to challenge the restless Atlantic along a coastline of stunning beauty and tremendous, often dangerous, energy. To travel around the extremities of this coast, even in gentle weather, is to measure your luck and judgement against the very edge of the Atlantic itself; on the other hand, to follow the convoluted coastline into the great rias would have meant a threefold multiplication of the paddling distance. I opted to stick to the Atlantic edge.

Thrusting boldly, thirty-five miles out into the Atlantic between Bantry Bay and the Kenmare 'River', the mountainous watershed of the Beara peninsula not only separates the Corkmen from the Kerrymen, but divides the sea areas of Fastnet and Shannon. Even the sea itself cleaves here almost as cleanly as a river separates round the parapet of a bridge. The main Atlantic tidal surge reaches the southwest of Ireland and splits in two off the Bull Rock, west of Dursey Island. One branch, which I already knew well, runs southeast to the Fastnet Rock, and onwards along the south coast to Carnsore Point and the Irish Sea; the other runs north to the Blasket islands and on up the western Atlantic coast.

Dursey Island is a high rocky lump separated from Beara by a channel barely two hundred yards wide. It is connected to the peninsula, from which it looks as though it has simply broken off, by Ireland's only cable-car link. Swinging like a dew-drop on a fragile thread, a hundred feet above the sea, the little aluminium cabin hauls its way precariously through space with a maximum load of 'Six passengers, or one man and a cow', maintaining an umbilical viability for the island. Many of the Dursey islanders are fishermen with their own boats; but the tidal channel known as Dursey Sound is treacherous, often churning with white foam like a river rapid when opposed by a strong wind, and can isolate the community for weeks at a time. From kayak level the cable-link looked like some kind of crazy mooring, designed to stop the island drifting away on the tide; and although I could already feel the steady quickening of the waters beneath me as I closed in on Dursey Sound, I infinitely preferred the security of the kayak to the thought of a ride in a swinging tin box!

After rounding Crow Head at the tip of Beara I'd found myself heading quickly towards Dursey Sound on a fast-moving belt of foam-streaked sea. The Atlantic had grown dark and gloomy, bringing a treacly stiffness to the water, but its momentum, pushing northwards, made it easier just to continue rather than attempt to scrabble ashore. In fifteen minutes I'd covered two miles, while the Sound narrowed quickly from a mile to two hundred yards, sucking all the tideway through its pinched funnel. Dark Dursey Sound began to flush like a river, its edges speeding by more like banks than shores; and the kayak became a galloping pony as I passed beneath the cableway. And yet, just a few strokes later the ride was over. On a widening, weakening flow the kayak and I emerged from Dursey Sound unscathed.

As I paddled north I could see three strange rocky islets back to the southwest of Dursey with arched caverns through them. According to local legend there was a family on Dursey many, many years ago who had a beautiful, coal-black bull and cow. The cow gave more than sufficient butter and milk for the family, and in time they were blessed with a little black calf. However, an impatient servant girl, while milking one day, struck the cow with a stick, whereupon it mooed sadly to the bull and calf, and all three plunged into the sea. To this day the three islets off Dursey are known as the Cow, the Bull and the Calf; and it is off that same Bull Rock that the tide splits to run north. It was upon that very tide that I was soon heading away from Beara, bound for the Skellig rocks, and Ireland's Atlantic edge.

SHANNON

Dursey Island to Slyne Head

260 miles

SHANNON

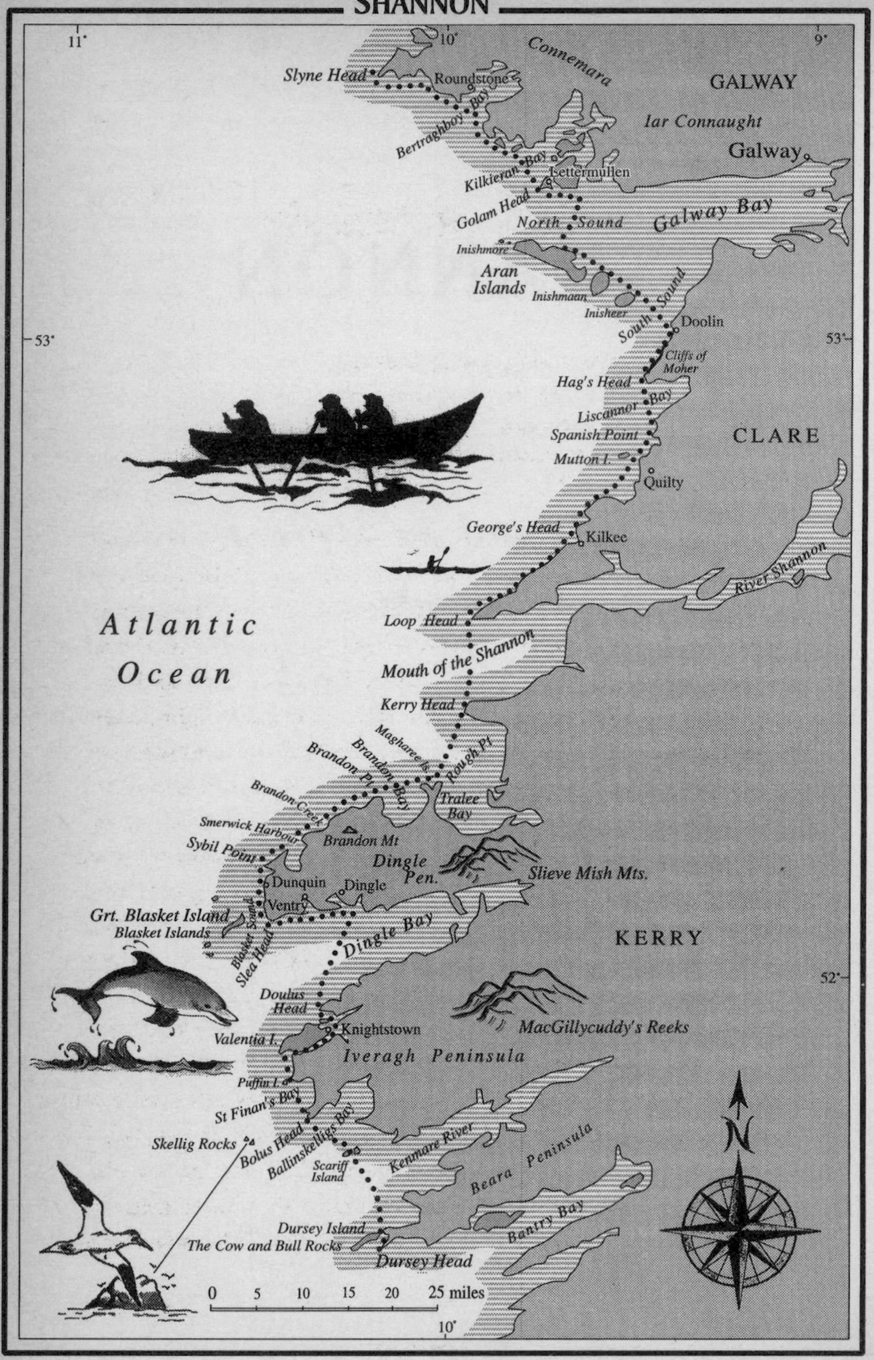

11°
10°
9°
53°
52°
Slyne Head
Roundstone
Connemara
GALWAY
Bertraghboy Bay
Iar Connaught
Galway
Kilkieran Bay
Lettermullen
Golam Head
North Sound
Galway Bay
Inishmore
Aran Islands
Inishmaan
Inisheer
South Sound
Doolin
Cliffs of Moher
Hag's Head
Liscannor Bay
Spanish Point
Mutton I.
CLARE
Quilty
George's Head
Kilkee
River Shannon
Atlantic Ocean
Loop Head
Mouth of the Shannon
Kerry Head
Magharee Is
Brandon Pt
Brandon Bay
Rough Pt
Brandon Creek
Tralee Bay
Smerwick Harbour
Brandon Mt
Sybil Point
Dingle Pen.
Slieve Mish Mts.
Dunquin
Dingle
Ventry
Grt. Blasket Island
Blasket Islands
Blasket Sound
Slea Head
Dingle Bay
KERRY
Doulus Head
Knightstown
MacGillycuddy's Reeks
Valentia I.
Iveragh Peninsula
Puffin I.
St Finan's Bay
Skellig Rocks
Bolus Head
Ballinskelligs Bay
Kenmare River
Beara Peninsula
Scariff Island
Dursey Island
The Cow and Bull Rocks
Bantry Bay
Dursey Head
N
0 5 10 15 20 25 miles

CHAPTER 9

A Sea of Monks

Tell her to find me an acre of land,
Parsley, sage, rosemary and thyme,
Between the salt water and the sea strand,
Then she'll be a true love of mine.

'Scarborough Fair', traditional

In the iconography of the Atlantic edge the Skellig rocks rank supreme; ten miles offshore, rising sheer from the sea like petrified icebergs, they are the dominant and distinctive totem of the western seaboard. It has been said that this is where Europe ends. But in many ways this is also where much of Europe began, and was sustained, though at times only as a lonely glimmer of light on the western fringe of a long dark age. Storm-lashed, steep and soil-less, the Skelligs would seem to defy the very thought of habitation; and yet some of the main cultural threads of Irish, and wider European, civilisation can be traced back to this most unlikely outpost. From the sixth century, for at least a further six hundred years, Christian monks lived and prayed in the tiny beehive-shaped stone cells that cling to the upper reaches of Skellig Michael, six hundred feet above the sea. During the flowering of Christian culture in Ireland, scholarly monks on the Skelligs and other outposts were acknowledged to be among the most educated men in all Europe, collectors and guardians of vast archives of scholarship and literature. At the end of the Dark Ages they set out to travel and disseminate that learning throughout Europe. So not only were the Skelligs once inhabited, they were also one of the first centres of academic excellence, the Dark Age equivalent of a University of the

Atlantic; and south Shannon in the sixth century was a shimmering sea of Celtic monks.

A line traced over the twin peaks of Skellig Michael, across the sea to Little Skellig and on through the Lemon Rock, like a quizzical blip on the ECG of a nervous canoeist, would extend along one straight sea-path to meet the Irish coast at St Finan's Bay, county Kerry. From my camp on the hem of a sheltered patchwork of small, steep fields above the tide-scoured bay, the Skelligs – in single file – appeared as a composite feature on the western horizon, pulling, teasing at the kayak like a magnet. I knew that a journey to the Skelligs, ten miles into the Atlantic's own realm, would be no mean feat in a kayak. Atlantic weather can change within hours, and yet it would take two to three hours just to reach the Skelligs. Would the weather hold? Would the swell of recent days have dropped enough to allow me to land on the rock? Would I then be able to return, or might I become trapped for days on the rock? All these questions rumbled through my mind as I anxiously tuned in to the coastguard's evening VHF bulletin and BBC weather reports. Local conditions contrasted strongly with those in England, where temperatures of thirty degrees were melting road tarmac and causing water shortages, but nevertheless seemed reasonably hopeful for the morrow. As the waves lapped at St Finan's Bay I lay down to sleep under a soft, seeping Irish sky, with a breeze ruffling the tent flaps, and a patter of gentle raindrops falling on the flysheet.

~ ~ ~

St Finan's Bay is a bight formed by Bolus Head to the south, and Puffin Island to the northwest. Its sweeping embrace translates the power of the Atlantic swell into a series of determined curved waves which often break with erosive force on the little beach. Once famous for its sandy bathing beach, cross tides and a severe undertow have now removed the last of the sand, and warnings to swimmers are posted on the landward access routes to St Finan's Bay.

Sunday morning dawned on low tide at St Finan's Bay.

Waiting for the tide to rise, I wandered inland hoping to find a shop and telephone. At the Keel crossroads a little blue *Telefon* kiosk stood between a tiny tin-shack grocery shop and a large solid chapel. The latter, swelled for morning Mass, accounted for the closed door of the former, and for the deserted atmosphere that hung over the crossroads. Neither person nor vehicle stirred.

Trrrünnng! Just as I touched the phonebox door-handle, the phone began to ring. And no sooner had I answered the call then the church began to disgorge its bustling crowd of Mass-goers; immediately the door of the little shop swung open to catch the overflow, and with the brisk suddenness of clockwork, Keel crossroads sprang into life.

'Is Cath O'Sullivan there?' repeated the thick Kerry brogue on the phone. Slightly bewildered, I shouted across to the church throng, now jamming themselves tightly into the bulging shop. The message was relayed several times through the crowd, and sure enough one Cath O'Sullivan was produced. She squeezed by me in the kiosk doorway with a quick giggle at my pink trousers, and a curious smile which seemed simply to say 'Well, why did you answer it, if it wasn't for you?'

A visit to the shop after Mass was clearly a high-spirited social event which seemed to have more to do with cramming a record number of people into a tiny space, than with exchanging money or goods across the counter. It was therefore to be expected that some geezer elbowing through the crowd in a pink nylon suit, answering other people's phonecalls and asking to buy bread and chocolate, would cause a few raised eyebrows, and become the subject of a certain amount of lively debate.

'He's tryin to see can't he get all round the country in a little canoe – by sea!' explained one man, triumphant at having grasped the elusive concept.

'What would he want to be doin that for?' piped up another sage. 'Sure, doesn't everybody *know* that the sea goes all round Ireland?'

A wave of a laugh filled the little tin shop.

'It's a circo–circle–*circum*-navigation, so!' decided another.

'No, isn't that what the Jewish sailorboys have at birth!' came the reply from Cath O'Sullivan, to yet more laughter.

It was with a large entourage still locked in academic debate over the finer points of oceanography and comparative religion, and with a loaf of hard-won bread under my arm, that I returned to St Finan's Bay. There, the kayak itself silenced all further discussion, and the look on every face was even more eloquent – 'No, surely that can't get all the way round Ireland.' To the further bafflement of onlookers, I proceeded to unpack all but the kayak's essential safety gear – hauling long-lost items from her deepest recesses and storing them in the tent – for only with the boat as light as possible could I possibly hope to haul her ashore on the Skelligs.

'How long will it take you to reach the Skelligs?' asked a serious old man.

'About three hours, with any luck,' I replied.

'Oh, your poor mother!' piped up Cath O'Sullivan. 'Or are you married even? Oh, but who in their right mind would marry the likes of you going into the sea like that!'

I tried to assure her that I was neither married, nor had any intention of 'going into the sea'; but my defence fell on sceptical ears, and Cath shook my hand in a very final-sounding goodbye.

~ ~ ~

The wind was in the northwest, where it had lurked for several days, so that within an hour beyond the sheltering breakwater of Puffin Island I began to feel the increasing influence of an accumulated swell. The kayak began to bob and dip on the lumpy Atlantic, like a cork in a bathtub; and I knew there'd be no respite for the next seven miles.

Lemon Rock, the small, protruding tip of a treacherous skerry lying midway to the Skelligs, was visible from a long way off because of the shrapnel of shattered waves which it threw upward in arcs of white. Somehow passing the halfway mark is always significant on a difficult journey; it gives the chance to check time and progress, and it means that the route to your destination is now at least shorter than the route back to start point. However, on a there and back journey, every step past the halfway there mark means a further two steps to come back! By the time I reached halfway I was already several hundred yards adrift of Lemon Rock, and among a boisterous bright sea on a generous scale. A living landscape of vivid water bounced and surged, breaking occasionally over the kayak with drenching effect. Each large breaker meant a sudden sideways shunt of the kayak, a brief wobble or support stroke, and a cold heavy flush of seawater. The unnerving booming of the swell breaking on Lemon Rock slowly faded into a more general roar as it fell away behind me. Two miles further on, the sea was big enough to mean frequent waves breaking aboard, and white-caps as far as the eye could see – requiring both concentration and much physical effort – though not yet big enough to make it necessary to turn back.

It was not until I was within a mile of its cliffs that Little Skellig at last stood out as a distinct mass from Skellig Michael. Towering above the white-capped waves, a bright guano-limewash highlighted the saw-ridged form of the high-rise sea bird colony. At first sight what looked like a plume of volcanic smoke hung over the island's four hundred foot peak; but greater proximity brought better definition: thousands of gannets were swarming in a flight-cloud so dense as to reduce the daylight. The sky was filled to saturation with white, whirring adult birds. The whole island too was alive with creamy-headed gannets; every available ledge on the serrated cliffs and pinnacles had been claimed.

Gannets, sometimes called solan geese, are large birds by any standard – the size of flying tom-cats, with five-foot wingspans – consuming considerable quantities of fish, and producing proportionately copious amounts of excrement. And Little Skellig, one of the largest gannetries in the world, is home to no fewer than twenty-three thousand pairs! As I paddled directly below the wheeling, thickening gannet cloud a simple biological equation became clear: most of what goes in must come out; and all of what comes out must come down. All around me guano-bombs began to splatter the sea's surface. Several near misses were followed by a large green *Splat!* which covered thirty square miles of Kerry on my deck map. Then, time and time again, in rapid succession, I was being hit: on the kayak, on my jacket, my hands and – most disconcertingly – right on the head! It was like being the unarmed quarry in a paintball wargame as I battled onward, unable to retaliate, running a gauntlet of guano. The foul-smelling liquid skittered over my forehead, ears, neck, and soon spread in fishy runnels to the few places which hadn't already been directly hit. Fearful of the potentially disastrous effect of a direct hit in the face, I was keeping my eyes shielded and low and thanking Mother Nature that noses are designed with the nostrils facing downward, but my hair and head received a thorough covering. When a warm green gob dropped down my neck, I shivered in disgust, and finally abandoned the detached ornithological term 'guano'. Under full siege the only appropriate term is *shit! shit! SHIT!* and my paddle strokes increased to full panic level to escape from the lee of Little Skellig as soon as possible.

I emerged from the gannet cloud thoroughly caked in a rapidly hardening whitewash, looking, I supposed, like a scale replica of the island itself, and unable, for the moment to do anything about it. Beyond the slight shelter of Little Skellig, the sea took on an extra dimension. A large swell had built up and was breaking heavily in places, sometimes from a height of five feet – well above eye level when you're sitting in a kayak, and quite daunting when eight miles from land. The sudden need to perform decisive bracing strokes – sweeping the padde across the water's surface to gain the extra support necessary to right the kayak using a hip movement – gave the situation an extra edge of tension. Skellig Michael now lay across a final mile of heavy water, its dramatic shape and massive berg-like presence tempting me ever onward.

But the bright, bouncy morning was gone; cloud had closed in and the wind had increased to force five, and I began to doubt whether it would be possible to land on the rock.

Beneath the towering rocks of Skellig Michael I surged and stalled, rising and falling on reflected waves. A twelve foot swell was pounding against the landing platform, fully exposed to the sea's assault. One moment I was level with the waves worrying the concrete step; the next I would be plunging downward until the platform was several yards above my head. To have tried to land there would have risked serious damage to the boat – and probably also to me. Skirting the rock gingerly, I found a second landing site, away from the sea's main force, at a place named Blind Man's Cove, where a flight of steps from the lighthouse ended in a submerged concrete block. But even here the swell was flushing in with great force, before sucking suddenly back to reveal a great void above the ubiquitous tearing rock. Alone there was no way to land without damage to the kayak; and as the kayak was my only ticket back to St Finan's Bay, I couldn't take that risk. With a sinking heart I began to realise not only that I'd be unable to explore the Skellig, but that, after almost three hours in the kayak, I wouldn't even be able to stretch my legs and have a pee. The long low line of the mainland, from Dursey Head to the Blasket islands, was just a distant smudge on the eastern horizon.

Well, the wind strengthened and the sea grew yet bolder, and the long journey landward became one of my roughest and most protracted ever. Fighting a severe drift to the southeast; cowering before occasional bullying squalls of force seven which whipped at the paddles and terrorised my balance; braving again the dreaded gannet cloud, it was a further three and a half hours before I regained the sheltered water of St Finan's Bay: a total of seven hours constant hard paddling. Seawater and sweat added a vicious sting to the already aching pressure-sores on my bum, and several people watching with binoculars from shore will have seen the grimaces on my face as I groaned closer with every last stroke. At last I felt my bows touch land. I slumped forward in the seat and laid my weary guanoed head and arms on deck, a sodden, hungry, frustrated, shit-caked, gannet-smelling wreck.

'You've been to the islands?' guessed a curious child on the beach. 'Did you see any gannets there?'

Luckily I hadn't the strength left to catch and throttle her.

~ ~ ~

It was a short, strikingly beautiful Shannon day's hop from St Finan's Bay to Valentia. With morale boosted by a fine send-off, and Cath's gift of a home-made cake, I pushed strongly to stem the three knot tide through the narrow channel inside the Puffin Island bird sanctuary. Clownish puffins and tiny, hardy storm petrels rafted and skimmed past me on the tide, while I struggled perversely to gain ground in the opposite direction. But beyond the Puffin tide-pull, I warmed to the paddling rhythm, and began to move like a rocket boat; the Skellig rocks to the southeast drew steadily apart, and Valentia Island came into view.

Valentia has no known Iberian or Mediterranean connections; the label is simply an anglicised corruption of *Beall Innse*, the name of the long narrow sea channel that separates the island from the Kerry coast. Indeed Valentia Island has an Atlantic pedigree almost as impressive as the Skelligs. It was the European terminus of the first transatlantic telegraph cable in 1855, and remained a vital link in world communications for over a century. The pioneering Valentia Radio service is well-known to Atlantic sea-farers. And of course the Valentia Weather Observatory, familiar to devotees of the BBC Shipping Forecasts, is the major monitoring point for Atlantic weather systems. Be it good news or bad, Kerry, the most westerly land of Europe, is always the first to get the Atlantic weather.

I passed into Beall Innse, and beneath the Valentia bridge at Portmagee, along a sheltered backwater like a large oxbow lake. Fringed and protected by high mountains, the land here was lush and green, with little fields hedged and dyked right down to sea level. Banking round Reenard Point and into Valentia harbour, I suddenly heard the roaring of a large crowd, and blundered in on the tail end of a seine-boat race. Traditional wooden boats, long and slender, each rowed by a team of thirteen men, the seine-boats soon pulled quickly away from my sluggish company. The Valentia Regatta commentator briefly interrupted his tannoy flow to announce: 'The Round Ireland Kayak ... attempting to row twelve thousand miles round the coast of Ireland ... a big hand please for this grand effort.' *Twelve thousand miles!* That was at least ten times the figure I'd estimated, and the thought of a further nine trips through Shannon helped me decide that it was time to pull into Valentia for a pint and a recount. At the quiet side of the harbour a lobster fisherman gave me two huge steaks cut from a conger eel which had wedged itself into one of his creels.

'They're bad bastards, the congers,' he said. 'They'd take your hand off soon as look at you. Bite always goes septic too. Dorty teeth, ye know. They caught the biggest one ever, just out there by Beginnish. In 1914, I think ... Seventy-two pounds it was. Nearly bit the boat in half, so they say.'

After some quiet reading, and a meal of Beginnish conger, which tasted like juicy cod, I walked into Knightstown, capital of Valentia, where the pubs were throbbing with life in the aftermath of the regatta. Teams of salty oarsmen lined the bars, and one pub was running a continuous video loop of the day's races. Eventually the seine-boats appeared on the screen with, sure enough, the colourful kayak tagging along behind like a donkey at the Grand National. It was, if nothing else, a good ice-breaker, and soon several jars of Valentia stout were washing down the lingering aftertaste of conger.

At Valentia, as in many areas of Ireland, history seems to blend with superstition to produce a rich sauce of stories – not blandly factual, but vividly real, and strongly connected to the land and sea they describe. In the hands of the best storytellers the ancient tales hybridise with current affairs to produce delightfully ambiguous mongrel images: mischievous fairies tempting people to their deaths by leaving lottery tickets on exposed clifftops; leprechauns in balaclavas, sipping poteen and brandishing kalashnikovs; and mermaids, or *moruach*, with domestic violence problems, constantly swigging brandy salvaged from shipwrecks, and seeking out coastal farmers as husbands rather than returning to their even harder-drinking mermen partners.

The early Christians lived on Church Island, and the Vikings settled on Beginnish, I was told, as if they had been contemporary neighbours sharing gossip and waving to each other across a narrow channel. Oliver Cromwell, I gathered, built two forts here to guard the deep water shelter of Valentia's natural harbour in the 1600s; oh, and John Paul Jones, eighteenth-century Scots-born pirate, and founder of the American navy, often visited. Almost in the same breath there were claims that Mogh Roith, the one-eyed druid magician who beheaded John the Baptist, once lived on Valentia; there were stories that Beginnish Island is haunted by the ghost of a drowned pirate whose grave is in the Valentia woods; and tales of a local woman who had a one night stand with a man from the sea, and gave birth to a son who could never sleep except between tides.

~ ~ ~

Doulus Head, the seaward rampart of Kilellan mountain on the south side of Dingle Bay, is an impressive piece of geo-architecture by any standards, but especially so when viewed from a bobbing kayak on the metallic blue waves of Doulus Bay. Wild goats cling to its rocky ledges; colonies of guillemots, razorbills and kittiwakes give it a businesslike atmosphere, and the waves of Shannon whittle incessantly at its foot. But even Doulus pales a little when set against the backdrop of mighty Slea Head, the Blasket islands and the mountains of the Dingle peninsula. At first sight, across a stretch of blue water, Brandon Peak, Beenoskee, Stradbally and Slievanea looked ancient and venerable, almost mythological, marching forty miles out into the Atlantic. At the very end of the peninsula stand Mount Eagle and Slea Head, where Mor, daughter of the sun, is said to have married Lír, god of the sea, in a ceremony of magical sunset colours. Here, on the western edge of county Kerry, two hundred miles closer to the sunset than mainland Britain, is Europe's most westerly point; and the Blasket islands, ranging westward yet like stepping stones into the Atlantic itself, have often been called 'the next Parish to America'. As I rounded Doulus Head, it was tempting to strike out for the Blaskets directly, but first I wanted to head for Dingle harbour, where I hoped to catch a sighting of the famous wild dolphin who had been frequenting Dingle Bay.

It was overcast, but fairly calm as I began the twelve mile crossing of Dingle Bay, singing deck-songs and constantly keeping an eye on the sea's surface, hoping in vain for a glimpse of flipper or fin. Three hours later, it was a strange sight that confronted me as I passed between the two towers that mark the entrance to Dingle harbour. A ragged assortment of boats, yachts, dinghies and even a sailboard seemed to be dashing from corner to corner around the bay, like rugby players chasing a stray ball. Another regatta? I wondered, but no; they were all frantically searching for the Dingle dolphin, launching off *en masse* whenever the slightest fluke or fin was sighted.

Suddenly there was a great cheer, and the whole motley throng was heading towards me like a pack of foxhounds, pointing fingers and wielding cameras. Turning quickly round I saw the massive silver head of an adult bottle-nosed dolphin rise at the tail of the kayak with a 'Fooled you!' grin. After examining the rudder, he rolled on his side and slowly inspected the kayak, which was several feet shorter than himself. He seemed to enjoy the bright-coloured boat and its dipping paddles. By this time I was surrounded by tour boats, literally draped with people and cameras, all of which were trained on me, waiting for the dolphin to show. Feeling claustrophobic, I sprinted for an open sea-space, and noticed that just below the surface the dolphin raced along with me, occasionally arching his back to breathe, and effortlessly matching my speed. For ten minutes he shadowed the kayak, regularly popping his head above water to give quizzical glances, apparently studying both myself and the kayak; then just as I reached the shallow edge of the bay he was gone.

I camped on the outskirts of Dingle town, with a view over Dingle Bay to the Kerry mountains, and watched the sun slowly setting over the natural harbour which Fungie the dolphin had made his home in recent years. I felt supremely content and at peace with the world. Dingle, a lively, colourful fishing town, made famous in 1970 by the glorious scenery of the film *Ryan's Daughter*, and bustling with international tourists, offered the prospect of a pint and some good music. But there was more to my warm feeling than that; I seemed to have lost all sense of the heaviness and fatigue which had dogged me since failing to land on the Skelligs, and I was certain it had something to do with meeting the dolphin.

The strange, almost mystical, links between dolphins and man are hard to explain away. There have been several recorded cases of people with psychological problems experiencing almost miraculous improvements after close personal contact with dolphins. Sufferers from anxiety, severe depression, under-confidence and even anorexia, have compared meeting a dolphin to a religious or renaissance experience with apparent healing power. Almost all such reports mention two factors: first, that the dolphin seemed to relate directly to the person trapped inside the human body; and second, that when the dolphin spent time with someone, they felt, in a special sense, chosen. Surveys of ambitions have shown that more people dream of being able to touch a wild dolphin in the open sea, than meet a pop idol or jump from a plane. It seems to be a sort of unformulated ideal of freedom, a metaphorical reaching for the wild; perhaps even a genuine *need*. Irishman Brian Keenan, held hostage by Muslim fundamentalists for four years in a tiny concrete cell in Beirut, dreamt that his mattress was a raft on a vast sea surrounded by dolphins. 'They would roll out of the water and look at me with their mystic eye,' he wrote, 'and I wanted to reach out and touch them and know their comfort.'

It is not a new phenomenon. Encounters with friendly dolphins feature in many of the world's mythologies. Fifteen hundred years before Christ, the Minoans believed that dolphins bestowed spiritual blessings on human beings; they became symbols of joy and music in Minoan art; they were deified also in ancient Greece, where to kill a dolphin was punishable by death; and, according to Haida Indian legend, man was born from the belly of a dolphin. Pelorus Jack, a remarkably friendly piebald dolphin, well-known to sea-farers in New Zealand's Cook Strait in the nineteenth century, received special protection by an Act of Parliament. Such occasions were once rare, but in recent decades there seems to have been a great increase in the phenomenon of friendly dolphins; of solitary dolphins choosing to attach themselves to certain locations, and inviting and enjoying human company in the sea. There was Donald, who frequented the Isle of Man in the 1970s; and Simo, whom the harbourmaster at Solva, Wales, thought was the reincarnation of a fisherman friend whose ashes had been scattered at the exact location where he first saw the dolphin. There was Jean Louis of Brittany, Percy of Cornwall, Turke of Yugoslavia and Freddy off the Northumberland coast.

In the early 1980s Dingle fishermen began to notice a dolphin occasionally escorting boats and ships passing through the bay. Assuming he was attracted by free fish, they would fling him oddments from the catch, until one evening – as if to prove he had no need of their hand-outs – the dolphin tossed twenty-two pollack back into one of the boats. They called him *dorád*, Irish for 'dolphin', and later Fungie, and became used to him greeting the boats with a fish in his mouth or cavorting alone in the bay. Word spread locally of the dolphin of Dingle Bay; soon divers arrived to swim with him, and fishing boats began to moonlight as Jacques Cousteau-style dolphin-watch vessels. Fungie came to wider public notice in the mid-1980s with Heathcote Williams's book and Edinburgh Festival performance of *Falling for a Dolphin*, and has been attracting visitors to Dingle ever since. There are cetacean cafés, porpoise parlours, and dolphin stalls throughout the little town, and several trawlers have traded in the fishing to become full-time fin-spotting tour boats. The remarkable thing about Fungie is that, no matter how much of a star he becomes, he is still a wild dolphin, a true creature of the ocean and coast, neither trapped by nor dependent on man. He can be as elusive as any other wild creature, disappearing for days on end, and will one day disappear forever. But when he appears or performs in Dingle harbour it is because he chooses to do so; when he surfaces amongst a gaggle of tour boats, it is because he chooses not to skulk on the sea floor or hunt pollack among the rocks. And, for whatever reason, he has chosen to stay in Dingle harbour.

~ ~ ~

A gorgeous blossoming sunrise began to reflect in the lightly rippled, gently steaming waters of the bay's high tide as I paddled out from shore. Every paddle stroke seemed to echo out across the water in the dawn stillness. I reckoned that the best time to be alone with the dolphin would be early morning, before the first tour boats. I had wolfed down a few chocolate biscuits, loaded my waterproof camera, and by six was approaching Fungie's puffing spouts, easy to see and hear across the sleepy water. He came to investigate immediately, but was less overt than the previous day. He approached from the front, then disappeared. Then he was behind me ... moving closer ... a glimpse of fin, then gone. I saw him surface by some rocks, perhaps twenty yards away, then dive again. Suddenly he was right below me; then – *Wow!* he seemed to explode from the water, to pour skyward, *up – UP – and over* the kayak in a looping curve like a watermill wheel. 'Good morning to you too!' I shouted.

Instantly my heart was thumping, blood coursing, senses alive; but there was a strong sense of missing out on the real world of the dolphin, of seeing only half the picture from above the water's reflecting surface. Tying the paddle to a cord, I grabbed a huge breath of air and tipped the kayak over, upside down. As the

The avenue of palm trees adds to the Treasure Island atmosphere of the Saltee Islands, county Wexford.

Being towed by a lobster boat near the Saltee Islands, county Wexford.

The kayak passes carefully through a sea-breached tunnel beneath the Old Head of Kinsale, county Cork.

Final preparations before the day's launch from Seven Heads Bay, county Cork.

Piratical duo, Mór Porter, brighten the hours of captivity on Sherkin Island, county Cork.

Atlantic swell and strong local tides combine in Dunmanus Bay, Mizen Head, county Cork.

Icons of the Atlantic edge, the Skellig rocks appear on the western horizon in county Kerry.

Fungie the dolphin surfaces at the rear of the kayak, Dingle Bay, county Kerry.

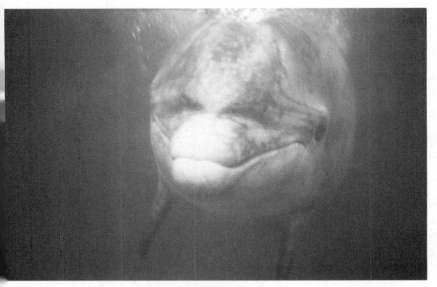

Fungie re-appears 'smiling' beneath the sea's surface in
Dingle Bay, county Kerry.

The Blasket Islands
from Dunquin,
county Kerry.

Sunset on the ripples of low tide, Connemara.

County Mayo seascape near Portacloy.

Zap! An unusual shaft of light recalls the legend of St Patrick at Doonbriste, Downpatrick Head, county Mayo.

Rainbow over coastal campsite on a pocket of turf in Port Bay, county Donegal.

Kayak and makeshift camp on the holiday seafront of Portrush, county Antrim.

Journey's end.

initial cold shock eased, and the bubbles cleared, there he was, hanging vertically in the milky morning water, tail downward, with his head cocked slightly in a crooked smile. He seemed much bigger than before, perhaps twenty-two feet long, and sturdily built. The skin, which I'd imagined as being smooth and perfect, was in fact criss-crossed with scars, especially on his forehead and back, where he had apparently come too close to boat propellers. With a slight tail movement he circled round behind me, then reappeared face to face, still grinning, but now upside-down as I was. Choking on a stifled laugh, I grabbed for my paddle and rolled the kayak upright, spluttering for a new breath, and chuckling aloud in the morning air: *what a joker!*

Just as I was preparing to capsize a second time, Fungie surfaced at the rear of the kayak, nibbled the rudder then raised his whole head, nodding open-mouthed in a toothy clownish smile. He rubbed his flank along the side of the kayak, then with a quick sprint and stop managed to suggest that, when I was quite ready, we ought to move along. Soon we were tanking through the bay together. My paddle was pushing seawater on one side, and gripping dolphin on the other, scraping a zigzag line down his itchy flank which he rolled and lifted for attention. He seemed to be very itchy indeed, and while being scratched by the paddle would have his eyes half-closed in apparent contentment as he cruised along on his side. Occasionally I hooked the paddle in front of his dorsal fin and surfed along, using the rudder to steer as he picked up speed. Round the bay in wide arcs, we cavorted, entirely oblivious of time or place, until I became aware of the first of the day's visitors. With several cameras and camcorders trained our way, we pulled another couple of circuits and had a final itching session. But eventually I had to turn for shore and breakfast, and Fungie's working day had begun.

All through breakfast my mind was full of dolphin questions, and wild dolphin energy. It was like suddenly discovering you're awake, when everyone else is still sleeping; as if so much had passed in such a short time that it would take perhaps years to make sense of it all. What, I wondered, was the source of the dolphin's joyful spirit, its apparent ability to dissolve time and care with something pure? And what was that 'something': was it pure joy, or pure love, or something else completely? Why does it seem so obvious that a dolphin smiles? A scientist once wrote that 'If zoology were a religion, then anthropomorphism would be its cardinal sin,' – meaning, among other things, that dogs and dolphins do not smile. But I already had grave doubts about the extent to which we ought to license scientists exclusively to define Nature for the rest of us. Now I knew for certain that not only could a dolphin smile, but that its smile is highly contagious. Leaving aside the possibility that the solitary dolphins are actually nautical engineers, sent to spy on human boat designs at close quarters, or cetacean anthropologists collecting data on human beings themselves, couldn't they possibly be a sort of inter-species missionary, sent to put mankind back in touch with certain basic values? Jovial playmate or Atlantic evangelist, Fungie seemed to have infused my whole awareness with a spirit of pure *fun*. From the little it takes to satisfy the human spirit at such times, perhaps we can fathom the depths of our loss, and how much we have yet to regain.

After a business day in Dingle, catching up on mail, messages, telephone calls and local media interviews, I was glad to be back on the bay by late afternoon. Leaving Dingle meant saying goodbye to Fungie, but from the wayward, unfocused sailings of the bay boats and tourist launches it seemed that the dolphin was attending to business of his own elsewhere. As I passed the two towers he was still nowhere to be seen. I was just thinking that a few punters would be looking for refunds when I glanced over my shoulder and saw him. He was about a foot below the surface, following my rudder but surfacing only to breathe; and then he seemed to disappear. Making a rough attempt at a telepathic farewell, I did a final wide circle on full rudder, then reluctantly, with a feeling of leaving something unfinished, headed west for the Blasket islands. I had left the bay boats far behind, and had almost reached the Crow

Rock, when suddenly there was a loud *psshhhh* of expired air and the dolphin launched himself like a torpedo from the grey deep. There was a broad back and a graceful tail flick, then just a hole in the water which healed like mercury. It was the last I saw of him; a final goodbye; and as he vanished, so did any negative feelings I had.

'Goodbye, Fungie!' I yelled, and put new strength into the journey west.

CHAPTER 10

Island Fever

Sometimes the sky looks sickly. Its face is wan. A thick dark veil obscures it. The mariners observe with uneasiness the angry aspect of the clouds.

The Toilers of the Sea, Victor Hugo

The best of the day's weather had already passed over as I left Dingle, drawing behind it a rapidly thickening cloud base and a sudden drop in temperature. A stiff breeze from the southwest had whipped up a sizeable clapotis, the restless waves reflecting against the rugged shoreline, and made for slow wet progress in the kayak. Leaning and adjusting the bow and the kayak's speed I tried to alter the motion to avoid taking onboard too many splashes, but as the clapotis grew this became a lost cause. Every few minutes a full wave would hit the bow at just the wrong angle, setting up a flying sheet of brine that would lash across my face, stinging my eyes with salt and dripping icily down my neck. Within a short time I was soaked and shivering.

Twenty miles away, on the south side of Dingle Bay, the coast was disappearing fast; even before I reached Ventry Bay, a deep Atlantic front was advancing from the west, swallowing up all in its path. It gulped the Skelligs, followed by Doulus Head and the Iveragh mountains. To the west it had already taken the Blaskets and Mount Eagle. And soon the grey squall had enveloped me, its swirling hag-breath whipping the sea into a frenzy and driving rain horizontally into my face. I struggled to pull on my hood, but there was little point in continuing. I was making no forward progress at all. Altering course inshore, I decided to weather the squall from within the haven of Ventry harbour. As the front gathered and advanced towards the Kerry mountains, Ventry darkened quickly and dramatically. The landscape suddenly seemed to have shrugged off all the evidence of past millennia, and looked as if the great legendary Fenian battle might have had taken place only yesterday.

It was in the third century that Fionn MacCumhaill eloped to Ireland with both the wife and the daughter of the King of France. Seeking revenge, the kings of France and Spain, and the King of the World pursued him to Ventry harbour, filling this very bay with their massed fleets. For a year and a day the Fianna kept them at bay, during which time the King of Spain was killed in battle, and the King of France went insane. But the invaders had a giant with them, who had killed too many Fianna, and had to be stopped. A group of Ulster warriors challenged him, and in the fray that followed all were killed except the King of Ulster's son, who clung to the giant until they were both drowned in the incoming tide.

Crede, a beautiful woman from the east of the country, had fallen in love with Cael, one of Fionn's poet-warriors, who had written a verse about her homeland. Following him to Ventry, she worked as a nurse to the wounded in the battle. Then, after the last great skirmish, when Fionn had killed the King of the World, Crede walked among the dead and found the body of Cael washed up on the strand. She lay down with him then, and she too died in the Ventry tide.

In an hour the squall front had passed, leaving me shivering and damp, and the sea bright, restless and otherworldly. Thinking to myself that, in the stories of the Fianna, sea-strand and shore, and even the cries of the gulls, were as significant as the heroes and the adventures themselves, I paddled once more towards the west, half-expecting the bodies of the dead Fenian warriors to float past on the tide. At Slea Head, just around the great shoulder of Mount Eagle was a magnificent sight. A final scattering of islands on the outermost edge of Europe, the humpbacked forms of the Blaskets were lined up like Fenian galleys sailing eternally west.

Testing the sea, in the aftermath of the squall, I coaxed the kayak over the lumpy water that surrounded the steep bluff of Slea Head, across the cameo beach of Coomeenoole, and tucked in for shelter beneath Dunmore Head. The sea was stirred, and the tides of the Blasket Sound ran strongly, but the weather looked settled for the evening, and somehow I seemed to have the energy and the will left to attempt the crossing. From the little island off Dunmore Head to the village strand of Great Blasket is a distance of only two miles across the notorious Blasket Sound. Known as the 'dirty sound' to the old islanders, its treacherous shallow tidal waters claimed at least two ships of the Spanish Armada in 1588, and more boats over the centuries than perhaps any similar passage in all Europe.

Even from kayak level I could see the tide race that extended out from Garron Point on Great Blasket like a scythe blade, and hear the intimidating roar of its broken water as it rushed and chicaned southward. On a counter current I surfed round Dunmore Head, then changed course radically for Beginnish Island, keeping Blasket and its race, for the moment, well to my left. To be caught up in the race would mean a bumpy one-way passage in a stream of breaking water down the east coast of Great Blasket, past the ominously named Fatal Cliff, with little chance of making landfall. Now heading for Beginnish, with Inishtooskert in the background, I was checking my transits avidly for any signs of drift, and only when I was sure I could make headway against the spring tide bound for the Gorram race, did I finally turn and head directly for the Great Blasket strand.

~ ~ ~

The Blasket islands are fantastically atmospheric, hauntingly beautiful, and yet seem, at first sight from the sea, to forbid the very idea of human habitation except on the most temporary basis. Great Blasket itself is a huge mountainous ridge of rock and peat, whose eastern side ends in the thousand foot Fatal Cliff, and whose whole coast offers no more than a couple of exposed coves where a boat might land in fair weather. There are no streams, no trees, no soil; and the whole island lies scoured in a restless tide, and buffeted by the Atlantic swell. It is no coincidence then, that the entire population of Great Blasket concentrated itself into one small steep village on the island's northeast corner; it is the only habitable patch on the whole island. In addition to being within sight and boat access of the mainland, the village site is sheltered from the prevailing winds. Here alone there are freshwater springs, small patches of arable land and a beach for launching currachs, collecting seaweed and driftwood, and landing animals. The people, placenames and much of the way of life of the Great Blasket Island have become familiar to many people who have read the remarkable books written by Blasket islanders in the first half of this century: *The Islandman* by Tomás O'Crohan, *Twenty Years a-Growing* by Maurice O'Sullivan, and Peig Sayers' *Peig*. Classics in the Irish language, these books represent the culmination of the islanders' art of storytelling, while also preserving for posterity a record of the Blasket way of life. There is, however, in all of the island books, a sadness, blended with philosophical acceptance, that the days of the Blasket Island population were numbered.

'People will yet walk above our heads,' wrote Peig Sayers, 'it could even happen that they'd walk into the graveyard where I'll be lying, but people like us will never again be there.' In a remarkably similar phrase, much parodied in Flann O'Brien's *Poor Mouth*, Tomás O'Crohan's *Islandman* says, 'The likes of us will not be seen again.'

At their peak, the Blasket islands supported a population of almost two hundred people, who tilled land, raised cattle, sheep, donkeys, scoured the island cliffs for birds' eggs, and its shore for shellfish, and traded produce at occasional markets on the mainland. They were the most westerly people in all Europe. In skin currachs, locally called *naomhógs*, and later in open wooden boats, they fished the notorious Blasket waters for anything from basking sharks to lobsters. Shipwrecks in the Sound brought occasional bounty to the island, from timber for building to bales of cloth and boxes of fruit. All three of the Blasket books tell of the great boost to island living standards during the First World War, when the sea brought a regular harvest of goodies from merchant ships torpedoed in the Atlantic. During the famine years of the mid-nineteenth century, the Blaskets and other Irish islands, having access to a wide range of food resources (sea birds, eggs, rabbits, seaweed, shellfish, fish) suffered slightly less than their mainland counterparts. But the conditions that made island life viable were to decline steadily during the following century. Young people left to find work on the mainland or abroad; the population aged and dwindled, and the little island boats could not compete with the arrival of the big trawlers. In *Island Home – The Blasket Heritage* George Thomson writes:

> *... fleets of steam trawlers appeared in Blasket waters, scouring the sea bed and ranging ever further afield as stocks were depleted. The inshore fisherman, with only a canoe, was no match for the big companies now fiercely competing amongst themselves in the uncontrolled expansion of deep sea fishing. In 1921 there were 400 canoes in the district west of Dingle; in 1934 there were only 80.*

By 1960 the island was empty, the islanders settled in Dunquin or Dingle. Several of them maintained huts as occasional shelters to be used while fishing the surrounding waters, and continued to put sheep on the islands in summer, but the village had died. It wasn't the weather, but the slow draining wounds of emigration and economic disadvantage that finally forced the islanders onto the mainland in 1953. It was ghosts and emptiness I expected that evening as I ran the kayak's bows up amid dumping surf-waves on the sweeping sandy beach of Great Blasket. But immediately there was a smell of peat smoke, and on climbing the dune I could see people moving among the ruins of the village; there was even a boat in the little harbour. A new generation of fair-weather islanders had appeared. Lobster fishermen and shepherds had made the island their summer base, camping in some of the better maintained of the original houses. One house at the north end of the village had been restored and was serving as a café and hostel to which visitors come from all over the world. Many of the visitors are descendants of the original islanders; yet others have perhaps read one or more of the books which made Great Blasket famous.

As night fell on Great Blasket, I made camp on the grassy cliffs above the strand, with views out across the Sound to Clogher Head, Sybil Point and the rocky spurs of Kerry. The aroma of peatsmoke drifted across on the breeze. My plan for the morning was to explore Inishvickillaune and the rest of the Blasket group, but already I felt the tell-tale throat-ache and early stiffness of an imminent cold. I woke late the following morning, soaked in sweat and aching all over, in the grip of one of the worst bouts of flu I've ever suffered. I summoned the strength to make a mug of tea, but without even getting out of the sleeping bag, soon had to rest my head again. All day long I drifted in and out of a fevered consciousness; aware one moment of the tide being high and waves crashing on the strand below, and then later of the tide being out. At early evening I woke with a start, completely delirious, disorientated and unable for several minutes to work out where on earth I was. Wads of toilet roll, used to stem the flow from my nose, lay strewn around the tent and the sleeping bag was clammy with sweat. The struggle to rise, change into dry clothes and step out for a pee, made me feel like I'd paddled fifty miles, and no sooner had I got back into the tent than I fell back into a troubled shivery sleep.

Twelve hours later I woke again with a terrible thirst, but the fever had gone. The limitations of a tent as a sick-bed were immediately obvious. Sleeping bag, mat and groundsheet were all damp and clammy; every lump of ground seemed to press into my aching bones; I had no medication for flu symptoms, and I had run out of water. Wearing every scrap of warm clothing I walked along the island's stone-pitched, overgrown track to the village in search of water.

The older houses of the village were arranged in rows, north to south, with their gable ends towards the sea. Set into the steep hillside, the doorstep of one was level with the chimney of the house below. And several of the houses beneath the road had their roofs at road level. Old stories tell of hens roosting in the thatch, or of children scouring the roofs in search of eggs. One man found a fledgling in his breakfast, and another islander fell through his roof while chasing his mother's cow. At the top of the village, overlooking the terraced house roofs and the Blasket Sound beyond, is *Tobar na Croise*, a well supplied by a natural spring, and never known to have run dry. It gives only a slow trickle of water, and so was always known as the place for lingering and gossiping with neighbours as the buckets filled at a leisurely pace. It was here that I met Micheál, a lecturer. With a trunk full of Irish books, a case of whiskey and a primus stove, he had installed himself for the summer in one of the felt-roofed ruins below. He collected shellfish, bought lobsters from the fishermen and had cigarettes sent over weekly from the mainland. Unwashed, unshaven, and wearing what looked like a sackcloth cassock, he seemed to have settled completely into his summer-retreat mode.

''Tis the finest water in the village, surely,' he said. 'But it won't cure what you've got, not in a month of Sundays. Come on down below, now, and I'll fix you a drop of something better.'

In the unlit hovel Micheál warmed a glass of water on the primus, added some cloves and molasses, then tipped the whole cloudy mixture into a half-full bottle of Irish whiskey. He swirled it around, held it up to the light of the window like a medieval alchemist, warmed it again over the flame, then poured out a tin mug full for each of us.

'That's about the right dose for the flu,' he said clinically. 'I've been taking this three months now for my cold; and praise be to God it hasn't done the least bit of good. *Sláinte!*'

Ouf! It was pungent powerful stuff, and went straight to the head.

'Will you take another?' said Micheál, laughing at the expression on my face.

'Well, I don't know if–'

'Sure, there's no harm in the second dose; it's the first drop that destroys you!' he chuckled, already calmly preparing an even stronger brew.

After the second dose, I returned to the tent with my senses reeling; if not quite cured, then at least slightly numbed to the deep aches and shivers of the previous night. Micheál's cloves had cleared my nose; the miserable shivers had given way to an inner warmth and a smiling contentment, and the convalescent view from the tent was still unrivalled. At the edge of the white beach, a gentle surf stroked the sand. The sea in the Sound was constantly changing colour from turquoise, through royal blue to black according to depth gradients and the shadows of roving clouds. Little rocks and offshore skerries wore smart surf-collars in the inky sea, and the Atlantic light gave fickle moods of olive freshness to Beginnish and its sparkling shingle beaches. Even the clouds were attractive, weaving and playing over Brandon mountain, Mount Eagle and the MacGillycuddy Reeks; and it suddenly seemed that Kerry, with its mountains, islands and wild beaches was bound to be the most dramatically beautiful of all Ireland's coastal counties.

On my third day on the Great Blasket the forecast was for force six southwesterly winds. The sea was high, tide races roared dramatically, and the skerries were ring-fenced by explosions of spray which hung for long moments in the air. The small visitor ferry was cancelled, and twice the lobster boats made tentative forays to the island's northwestern edge, assessed the power of the swell on the skerries, and retreated to the Blasket slipway again. On the headland a gentle troupe of donkeys, abandoned and redundant as on many Irish islands today, huddled and sheltered among the rough grasses.

All morning I lay on an elbow in the tent watching the sea; coughing, nose-blowing, and still watching the sea. All in all, I thought – absentmindedly eating all the perishable food, popping camera and radio into waterproof bags, and packaging the loose items around the tent-mouth – neither the sea-conditions nor the wind looked likely to deteriorate; and my flu would probably feel a bit better when I was on the move again. I knew that the ferry cancellation probably had more to do with the fact that the ferryman had a new German girlfriend at Dunquin, than with the sea conditions, and felt that I could at least get across to the mainland. By mid-afternoon, with a lot of careful consideration – though not entirely wisely – I had decided to break the stagnation of my Blasket flu; to pack the kayak and escape from the island. The plan was to aim for Clogher Head, four miles away on the Dingle peninsula, and to re-assess the size of the sea from there. Beyond Clogher there would be a couple of options for shelter if needed, but perhaps I could tackle Sybil Point and reach a less exposed section of coast beyond. It was a plan which was set to undergo pretty drastic reduction by the day's end.

~ ~ ~

I was hesitantly launched through a snatching surf on the Blasket strand, by Micheál and some of the islanders. For their benefit I'd acted confident, committed and healthy, persuasively outlining my plan and route. But by the time I'd cleared the surf, waved a couple of times and reached Beginnish Island I had begun to absorb something of the leaden greyness of the sea, and feel the real power of the swell. Already my mind had closed to Sybil Point and Clogher Head as destinations, and switched to Dunquin – a mere three miles across the sound – as the only sensible target. Beyond the slight shelter of Beginnish was a large and steep-sided sea with an atmosphere of real savagery in its blackness. The tide race at the edge of the deeper channel was running at full strength, with an opposing wind, and a current set up by three days of southwesterlies flushing through the Sound. On top of that, wave reflection from the hostile cliffs of Dunquin made for an almost unnaturally savage and confused area of water.

My stomach felt like it was being tossed about loosely, and my head was thick with flu. Days off the water had eroded my confidence in the kayak, and even the paddle felt heavy and unfamiliar. Flu-like symptoms seemed to have infected everything around me. The sea itself looked sick; and the eeriest symptom of all was that it seemed to have become mute. Despite the breaking waves, the rocky shore and the exploding clapotis – all of which would normally have been quite oppressively loud – the sea had lost all sound. Even the colours were all wrong; the sky was green, the cliffs mauve and the sea a deep sickly purple. Every feature of the seascape was reminiscent of a poor-quality silent movie, or a feverish nightmare, and I resolved to get out of it as soon as possible.

And yet how could I get ashore? Wherever I looked the sickness I felt in the sea became real as it met toothed skerries and black towering cliffs. I veered round carefully, paddling parallel to the cliffs until clear of some dangerous skerries, then broke out of the tide race and desperately propelled the bouncing kayak towards my only hope for a landing, the *naomhóg* creek at Dunquin. Here, at the foot of an incredibly steep, winding concrete path, was a little slipway. The angle of the slip itself made landing impossible in those conditions; but glad at least to be out of the fray, I pushed on through elbow-deep mounds of sea foam and forced a slightly indelicate, uncontrolled landing on a nearby 'beach' of slimy, sheep-sized boulders. So relieved was I to reach shore – any shore – that I stumbled out of the kayak, caring little if I cracked a shin or bruised an ankle.

So the intrepid canoeist, risking life and limb in the Blasket Sound gun-run, had achieved a full *three* miles in order to shiver among the rotting, low-tide, lobster bait of Dunquin. Weak as a kitten, I sat on the kayak deck, hunched and despondent, staring out to sea and wondering where I'd ever find the strength to haul *Sola* above high water mark. A couple who had been watching the waves from above Dunquin slipway, began to descend the steps towards where I sat on the kayak. *Oh no!* I thought: my head ached, my nose dripped on my map of the Blaskets, and I dreaded the standard polite enquiries about how far I could paddle in a day, whether I got lonely, or how healthy I must be. I feared my present comments on all those counts would prove unconvincing.

But I was to be pleasantly wrong. Not only was Brian Fryer-Kelsey a giant of a man, with an enthusiasm to match his bulk, but he was a canoeist too. The founding member of the Donegal Ducksqueezers kayak club, his imagination was immediately fired by *Sola*, my Irish journey and the very idea that someone could get all the way round Ireland in a kayak. If he and his wife Maureen could possibly be of any help, he assured me, I had only to ask. Striding over the boulder beach like a JCB, Brian carried *Sola* virtually single-handedly above the tideline, dragging me along behind, and arranged her safely for the night. The walk up the steep winding track from the slipway almost finished me off, but up at their car Maureen had prepared large paper cups of rum, warmed with water from a thermos flask, and very soon I felt the damp dregs of fluey gloom begin to leave my body. Once under the wing of the Fryer-Kelseys I became quickly aware of the subtle but irresistible whirlwind of hospitable support that is their style. They gave me a towel to dry my hair with, gathered up used maps and books, promising to dry them out and send them home for me, then whisked me off on a car tour of the peninsula. A fierce surf hammered on the Kerry beaches, and Clogher Head and the Ballyferriter bays, where I'd hoped to find shelter, were full of hostile churning waves. We visited the amazing drystone-built Oratory at Gallarus, and found the ruined *Ryan's Daughter* schoolhouse; we had a drink at Kruger's Inn and a steak meal in Ballyferriter. By ten o'clock the whirlwind had blown full circle and, having arranged to look up Brian and Maureen when I reached the north, I was back once more at Dunquin harbour, camping, alone again, but fired-up with an infectious human enthusiasm and warmth.

CHAPTER 11

Naomhóg

Is it right or left for Gibraltar,
What tack do I take for Mizen Head?
I'd like to settle down near Ventry harbour,
St Brendan to his albatross he said.

'St Brendan's Voyage', Christy Moore

Along the coastal counties of the Atlantic seaboard, from Kerry's Kenmare to Sheep Haven in Donegal, traditional boats of a design virtually unchanged since the retreat of the last Ice Age are still in practical daily use. These are the Irish currachs, among the last surviving descendants of the oldest type of watercraft in the world, the skin boat. The original currachs, made from animal skins stretched on a hazel-rod framework, like the hide on a dolphin's ribcage, have been replaced by tar-painted canvas or calico over wooden laths. The exact pattern and shape changes slightly from county to county, and according to their use and purpose, but, in general, Irish currachs have a strong family resemblance, and share many of the same time-honoured features. They are long and narrow, round-bottomed and keel-less, with pointed bows. Propelled with long oars, they glide over, rather than cut through the water. Being supple, they give easily in breaking water, and with skilled handling can survive in some surprisingly violent seas. For general seaworthiness, efficiency of propulsion, and ingenious use of minimal materials, the Irish currachs, like the eskimo kayaks or the native American skin canoes, are exquisitely distilled products of the boat-builder's art, requiring a minimum of tools for construction and maintenance. Currachs are perhaps closer in design to canoes than any other craft, and indeed the word is translated as 'canoe' in the English versions of the Blasket Island literature. In common with canoes and kayaks they are only millimetres thick, light enough to be carried to and from the sea on the heads of their crews, and therefore need neither winch, pier nor harbour – landing and launching from places heavier boats would simply be unable to use.

Possibly the finest of all the currach species – the queen of the skin-covered boats – is the Kerry *naomhóg*, whose true home is the precipitous harbour of Dunquin. Just over twenty-six feet long, and only five feet wide at the middle, the *naomhóg* has seats for four oarsmen, each pulling a pair of oars which pivot on gunwale pins, and has room for a mast and sail for use in a favourable wind. For generations *naomhógs* were the main form of transport for the Blasket islanders. Launched from the beach, or the tiny Blasket slipway, they ferried people, livestock and goods to and from Dunquin in all but the worst of weathers. Livestock were either towed, swimming behind the currach, or laid in the boat with their hooves bound and tied. Every Sunday, whenever weather permitted, the islanders rowed *naomhógs* to Mass at Dunquin's chapel. Maurice O'Sullivan, in *Twenty Years a-Growing* vividly describes how, as a small child, he was terrified to see a huge black beetle marching towards him on the slip. 'Have no fear,' said his aunt, 'that is a currach they are carrying down on their backs.'

I saw six black shiny *naomhógs*, side by side above the harbour at Dunquin. Stored on stools, upside down to prevent them filling and bulging with rainwater, they looked, at rest, more like a huddle of black slugs after a downpour than O'Sullivan's beetle.

~ ~ ~

Neither *naomhóg*, lobsterboat nor ferry were on the water that day as I set off from Dunquin, sliding out from the boulder beach on a strong undertow and meeting my first wave of the day square on the chest. Sea conditions at Dunquin, and in the Blasket Sound beyond, had changed little since the previous day, but I was facing them in better health and spirits, and was ready for a long day's sport. Off Clogher Head the sea was rough, oversized and determined. For a considerable distance around all of the rock outcrops there were deep accumulations of foam, herded into mounds by incessant clapotis of a frightening scale. Feeling very small and underpowered compared to all that was in process inshore, I kept well out to sea, giving Clogher as wide a berth as I dared. When I rose on the swell I could see ahead the sandstone mass of Sybil Point, named after Sybil Lynch, who eloped with an Englishman and was drowned by the rising tide in a sea cave while hiding from her angry father. At Sybil I came closer inshore, but again had to fight through a massive area of wave reflection around the exposed point. The kayak seemed to be semi-submerged for most of the time, and the spray cover began to leak badly, meaning I had to stamp my foot constantly on the bilge-pump just to stay afloat.

From Sybil Head, where I'd hoped to find some shelter, the whole coast ahead looked inhospitable and impossible to land on, fringed with deep foam and clapotis as far as the eye could see. Progress through severe clapotis, with every second stroke used as a support measure, or an outrigger on which to lean the kayak's shifting centre of balance, is as slow as battling against a tide; so that clearing that stretch of foul cliff, headland after headland, became a prolonged agony of concentration and technique. The Three Sisters, conical hills sliced in half by the sea to leave a trio of curiously matching gable-ended cliffs, seemed to take ages to draw level, then sneered derisively down at my efforts until eventually I cleared their reef-fringed corner and the clapotis eased as I entered Smerwick Bay.

Near Dunacapple Island, on the far side of Smerwick Bay, I picked up the rough water once more, and the exposed coast for four miles around Ballydavid Head became another battle; not a desperate struggle, or an emergency dash, but a tedious wet slog along a rough and difficult coast whose obvious beauty was being stifled by the persistent leaden greyness of cloud and sea. The one thing which spurred me forward was the certainty that somewhere beneath the great mass of Brandon mountain, nestled Brandon Creek, a tiny inlet which would give a safe landing and shelter for the night. As I paddled on I found my mind filling with thoughts of Brandon himself, holy voyager of the Atlantic.

~ ~ ~

There is a Kerry story about a nineteenth-century sailing ship on passage to America which dropped anchor one night about two hundred miles west of the Shannon. In the morning it weighed anchor again, only to find the wheel of a horse-cart caught onto its hook. This is proof, the story claims, that Irish people were travelling to the New World many centuries before Columbus; for they were going to America – *by road* – before the Great Flood!

'The telling of outrageous lies is still a Kerryman's prerogative and duty,' says Kerry writer Des Lavelle, and though there may be more than a little poetic licence in the story of the wheel it is now at least generally accepted that Columbus was far from being the first European to cross the Atlantic Ocean. Early Celtic tales are littered with references to *Iarghal*, 'the land beyond the sunset', and it is almost certain that Norse voyager Leif Erikson had reached America several centuries before Columbus. Even Columbus himself sought out an Irish sailor, living in Galway, who had seen the 'red land'. This man sailed west again with Columbus in the *Santa Maria* in 1492, and his stone memorial slab is in the church of St Nicholas in Galway town. It is likely that many of the earliest transatlantic voyagers made a one-way trip, being either disinclined, or unable to return to Ireland to tell the tale. The first plausible account of a return voyage to America is that of St Brendan the Navigator in the year 501, almost a millennium before Columbus.

Brendan (Brandon) was one of Ireland's most important saints, classed as a saint of the second order, and one of the most inspiring characters of Irish history. He seems to have combined a life of fascinating adventures with a successful career in a way that very few people even today manage to do. In addition to becoming an abbot, and having a profound influence on the Celtic church in Ireland, and in wider Europe, he gained a great reputation as a traveller, and more specifically as an ocean voyager. All round the northern and western coasts of Europe, and even Africa, references to Brendan survive in the names of places which he visited in small, handmade, skin-covered boats.

Several Latin texts dating back to AD800 make references to his voyage across the Atlantic ocean. The most important of these, known as the *Navigatio Sancti Brendani Abbatis*, described how St Brendan and a party of seventeen monks sailed to the Promised Land far across the ocean in a boat made of ox-hide leather. The long, hard journey recounted in the *Navigatio* took seven years and involved many strange adventures; but the monks were able to reach their destination, and to re-provision their boat before setting sail again for Ireland. At first reading, the adventures described seem as bizarre and unlikely a collection of sea-faring yarns as one could ever hope to find. The monks come across an island paradise completely filled with birds singing in harmonies; they are chased by a sea monster breathing fire, before being rescued by yet another monster; then they reach an island like a blacksmith's forge, where they are pelted with fire and rocks; encounter a huge pillar of crystal floating in the sea; and they become lost in a great cloud before reaching the Promised Land.

But those involved in a great adventure inevitably describe their fears, joys and discoveries in the language of their own culture and personal and religious background. Legends and tall stories therefore often disguise important elements of experience and fact. Academic authorities have pointed out that the practical detail contained in the *Navigatio* make it seem far more like a first-hand account of an actual voyage (or series of voyages) than a mere fanciful tale. Seen in another light the most colourful episodes in Brendan's voyage bear a remarkable resemblance to geographical facts. If the monks had taken what is today known as the 'stepping stone' northern route to America, then the Paradise of Birds could conceivably have been the Faroe islands, an ornithological treasure even today. The sea monsters could have been whales or walrus, or other large sea mammals at that time unfamiliar to the monks. The burning rocks were perhaps molten slag from a volcanic eruption on the coast of Iceland; the crystal pillar could have been an iceberg; and the cloud coincides with the notorious fog banks which fishermen and sailors still encounter today off the coast of Newfoundland.

The practical objection, that materials and equipment capable of transporting a group of monks across the Atlantic and back, simply did not exist in the sixth century, was convincingly dealt with by Tim Severin in 1977. By journeying to America in a boat constructed entirely with materials, tools and techniques known to have been available to Brendan, Severin and his crew proved at least that such voyages would have been physically *possible*; that Irish monks might quite conceivably have crossed the Atlantic a thousand years before Columbus.

The Dingle peninsula of county Kerry, between Smerwick Bay and the mouth of the Shannon, is often referred to as Brandon Country. It was here that Brendan was born, and here that he launched and completed many a sea voyage. Along this coast St Brendan is commemorated in the names of almost every significant natural feature: Brandon mountain, Brandon Head, Brandon Bay, Brandon Point and Brandon village. Brandon Creek is a tiny cleft in the line of massive cliffs that guards this whole coast. The Atlantic heaves and swirls within its constricted space, booming out from the sea caves and fissures at the mouth of the creek; but here at least a boat can find shelter, a haul-out from the open Atlantic beyond, and a road that winds down to sea level. I was safe here for the night.

~ ~ ~

After a short chat with the crews of two currachs fishing at the mouth of Brandon Creek, I steered the kayak to head northeast up the Brandon coast, past the massif of Brandon Head itself. It was a grey, and still darkening, morning, with cloud building on the western horizon, and a wind gradually rising. The currach teams had warned of a 'big sea' on its way, and I wanted to push as far north as possible before it hit. The first eight miles along the rough Brandon coast repeated the conditions of recent days; hard work and slow progress in a badly reflecting swell with nowhere to haul ashore. Mighty Brandon mountain veiled its venerable peak under a hood of pious cloud, looking for all the world like an effigy of the saint himself.

A brief rest and snack in the lee of the mountain, then I set out six miles across Brandon Bay to the Magharee islands, the Seven Hogs, scattered carelessly in my path, among the foul tides and swirling shoal waters of Rough Point. Only a week previously a currach fisherman had drowned at the Magharees, and I wove among them with extra caution. Finding a bank of shingle, I landed the kayak to stretch my legs, gulp some chocolate and bale out some water; but the tide was rising quickly, in strange surges which seemed to lick hungrily at the kayak, and I soon set off again.

Two hours, and a further eight miles of hard paddling, brought me around the exposed, crumbling sandstone cliffs of Kerry Head, the southern jawbone of the mouth of the Shannon. Another headland, with its attendant ring of heavy clapotis – the pattern had become almost routine – but a glance behind me revealed that this time I was truly running before the storm. The first foot-soldiers of a rapidly darkening rank of congested cloud and wind-pushed sea had reached Kerry Head from the west. The sea was going my way, which meant that it was possible for me to continue for the moment; but it was unsettling to glance behind at the dark grey backcloth of looming clouds and towering waves which seemed to draw ever closer, and now occasionally passed me. Sometimes a wave would lift the kayak and surf her forward in a helter-skelter of foam as it overtook. But more often they broke across my shoulders, swamping the rear end of the kayak and flooding in through the spraydeck. In the bouts of frantic foot-pumping which followed, the rudder would be momentarily neglected, and the kayak would begin to broach in the path of the following wave.

The Loop peninsula, seventeen miles across the mouth of the Shannon, was almost obscured in the dark gloom which was steadily enveloping the coast. And, in any case, a crossing in such deteriorating conditions was out of the question. It was time to throw in the towel; to get off the water before the big sea, forecast by the currachmen of Brandon Creek, arrived in earnest. At first glance the entire coast was an endless line of skerry and reef, low-lying, swell-washed and rocky, with no apparent hope of a haul-out. Then, rising momentarily on the shoulder of a passing wave, I caught a brief glimpse of two currachs and a pile of lobster creels on a patch of shingle, perhaps fifty yards inshore, and I knew there must be a safe, hidden passage to them through the skerries. So I doubled back, scoured the rocky fringe and, tucked in between two particularly savage-looking reefs, I found a sheltered channel, perhaps only three or four yards wide. If the currachs can land here, so can I, I reasoned, following the channel through a dog-leg to a tiny cove where the tide lapped gently, unruffled, up a shingle beach.

Two currachs, shiny black as the devil's hearthstone, lay upturned across trestles above the tide line. Beside one of them were two tar-melting pots, some ruined sticky tarbrushes, and a set of yellow oilskins and seaboots from which someone had simply stepped out, and walked away. Beneath the other boat a second set of oilskins, neatly folded, hung from the inverted seat to air and dry in the breeze. There was one pyramid of carefully stacked lobster creels, and a second load simply thrown in a pile. Smiling, I pictured a slow, meticulous older fisherman, and an impetuous younger lad, keen to meet his mates in the pub at Ballyheige; the absent owners of the beached currachs. Discarded bait and fragments of broken shellfish littered the shingle, stinking

strongly and providing a free buffet meal for the rats of the
foreshore. The currachs on their wooden stands are safe from the
teeth of the rats, in the same way that the Greenland eskimo kayaks
are placed on stone-built plinths out of the reach of the dogs who
would happily gnaw the dried skins.

With evening falling quickly, I wasted no time in setting up
camp. Within minutes of my rigging up a clothes-line the rain had
started, but at least it would rinse the stale salt from my togs.
Jogging naked across the shingle beach, I moved the apprentice's
boots and oilskins to beneath his currach, then slid for a wash into
a stream tumbling onto the beach. Though it had sounded
deliciously fresh, the stream proved to be rancid, a mixture of
pig-slurry and silage probably running straight from a nearby
farm. In seconds I was immersed in it head to foot, and it was too
late and cold to go in search of somewhere else to rinse. I had to
dry myself, rub my hair, and put on my clothes, reeking like an
angry skunk

At the end of a thirty mile day, when every mile has been
gained in spite of the weather conditions, and the kayak rests on a
new beach, on the coast of a different county, there is some small
pleasure in marking the little line of progress on the large-scale
map of Ireland. It may well be the first pleasure of the day, for the
colder, damper aspects of Atlantic voyaging are low on the
hedonist's pop-chart. Those philosophers of human wanderings,
who claim that happiness lies essentially in the pursuit, rather than
the attainment, of a goal – that it is better to travel than to arrive –
have never forged through a wind-lashed sea for eight hours,
soaked to the skin in chilly brine, dreaming of nothing more than a
sheltered bay and a dry sleeping bag.

It was dark as I pulled the tent around me and attempted to
resuscitate a dehydrated meal of chicken curry. Lighthouses at
Loop Head, and Carrigaholt on the Shannon, flashed undaunted
as yet another bank of cloud and rain scudded in from the black
Atlantic, noisily slapping at the wet walls of the tent. Once in the

warm familiar cocoon of the sleeping bag, I began to slip gently into oblivion. Paddling along the exposed coast of north Kerry, especially in the aftermath of recent illness, had been more of a strain than I'd expected, and my body felt as though it had been through a mangle. Without time to plan the day ahead; without hearing a weather forecast; without even finishing my meal, I was borne away on a current of sleep which made the great Shannon itself seem like a sluggish backwater.

CHAPTER 12

Before the Storm

Every storm is preceded by a murmur. Behind the horizon line there is a premonitory whispering among the hurricanes.

The Toilers of the Sea, Victor Hugo

The two currachmen were early at the shingle harbour. Hardly a word passed between them as they strode to the trestles, ducked beneath an upturned currach and stood up with it on their heads. It is a sight that has been called 'a short procession wearing a huge communal hat'; but on that grey morning the measured, determined solemnity of the two pairs of black-clad legs, mutely synchronised beneath the black boat, gave the event the air of a bizarre pall-bearing funeral march. One glance at the sea beyond explained the lack of spring in their collective steps. Like me, the currachmen were in for a day of *dreich*, cold sea-work, with little joy in it. On such days Ireland is a bitter wind-lashed place.

Perhaps because of the relative frailty of the craft, a currachman's awareness of the weather is second to none. To see lobster currachs frantically pulling in their pots and heading for shore, is a surer gale-warning than any falling barometer. At that very moment, a deep Atlantic low was winging its way across the weather charts towards Shannon, forecast to hit the coast of Clare later that day. A gale warning was in force, and it looked as though this one might settle in for several days. The currachmen would be hoping to haul and salvage their lobsterpots; and I wanted to get to county Clare, across the gaping mouth of the Shannon, before the gale struck.

The currach was flipped from their shoulders into the

shallows. Without pause the front, older, man stepped neatly into the little cockleshell, fitted narrow wooden oars onto metal gunwale pins and sculled while the younger man loaded ballast stones, smooth enough not to damage the skin, but oval enough to lie at rest, into the bottom of the boat. Then, with an almighty shove he too stepped into the currach and fitted his oars. Backs towards the open sea, the two men leaned into their first stroke, and the little currach shot over the water faster than any rowed boat I've ever seen. During the whole launch, the pair had exchanged neither a word nor a glance. I got the distinct impression they could have done it in their sleep. Round the dog-leg channel they rowed in perfect harmony. The long oars were slender to avoid wind resistance, the blades hardly wider than the handles. These men were experts, each pulled a pair of oars, handles overlapping in an exaggerated crosshanded style, sending the currach easily around sharp rocks with minute adjustments of stroke length or angle; and I noticed that as they reached the open coast both simultaneously raised the oar handle on the windward side higher than the other, so that the different angle would compensate for the tilt of the light boat away from the wind. It was an absolute joy to watch.

~ ~ ~

Crossing the mouth of the Shannon, at the widest point of the longest river in the British Isles, seemed a long and painful process. Loop Head, on the far shore, drew a modest bathrobe of cloud around itself, and flashed at me only occasionally. Having forgotten that the Shannon is also a major shipping lane, I was bounding along on the physical equivalent of autopilot when I first heard the rumble of a tanker bearing towards me, completely oblivious to my presence. I changed course towards her stern and let her rumble on past, and paddled on a little more wakefully for the next hour and a half. Loop Head, when it arrived, rehearsed the full Atlantic-headland-in-a-clattering-swell routine, noise and all. Its high cliffy profile was widely ringed with broken lumps of ocean, rebounding on the hard southern edge of county Clare, before rejoining their ever-incoming Atlantic cousins. So I'd crossed the Shannon, but if I didn't get round Loop Head now I could be gale bound on its southern edge for days. The head itself was a dark mass of split and broken rock, surrounded inshore by a band of diabolically disorganised waves. The kayak rolled and climbed through dips and rises of black water and, but for one short anarchic passage between two great towers known as Dermot and Grainne's rocks, seemed to be tossed like a pancake from crest to crest. Then Loop Head began to sheer away astern, and the swell regrouped and swept in a more orderly fashion up the coast of Clare.

The west coast of Clare, from Loop Head to Galway Bay, is one of the most forbidding in all Ireland. It is largely cliff-girt, very exposed in westerly winds and has no significant natural havens other than the slight bight of Liscannor Bay to the south of the uncompromising Cliffs of Moher. Both on the map and in the flesh, Clare seemed all cliffs, all headlands, dark and heavy beneath well-laden clouds. In the course of ages the waves of the Atlantic have washed away all the softer material, leaving huge pillars of hard rock standing stubbornly all along this shore; but they too will fall in time. Between the cliffs were lower stretches of formidable surf-fringed reefs, and it began to look as though, in those conditions, there would be no possibility of landing a kayak before Kilkee, a further twelve miles or three hours distant. *Could I outpace the gale?*

What might otherwise have been a rich display of rock stacks, arches and caves, fell flat in the monochrome cloud light. The only features of any colour or movement to distract the mind, were little fishing boats slinging their last nets, or winching in lines of crab and lobster pots before the storm. Each of them in turn altered course towards me to shout across a gale warning, often with genuine concern, rather than matey banter, in their voices, and I noticed that the fast, clipped accent of Kerry had given way to a softer Clare brogue. Eventually the unfolding coast threw out Castle Point, and released Bishop's Isle, and I knew then for certain that I could reach Kilkee before the full storm. But already the forerunners of that storm had reached the coast, and even as Kilkee Bay opened before me I could see little except the great reef of surf-battered rock which forms the bay's natural breakwater: '... as ugly a ledge of rock as the most fastidious taste in that class of scenery could desire,' said Richard Lovett, writing of Kilkee in 1880. What he described as '... the most fashionable watering place of the district ... a pretty semi-circular beach formed of good sands, and protected from the inrush of the Atlantic ...' was, of course, now hidden in rain cloud.

The surf smashed manically on Lovett's ugly ledge, and I had to weave a carefully precise route to avoid being picked up and hurled onto its ramparts. But once I'd lined the kayak correctly, and let the swell sweep her through a gap in the reef, I found the bay behind it relatively sheltered. The rain clouds, fresh in from the Atlantic, looked as sodden and tired as I did, hanging so low and heavy that it seemed as if they must surely be slowing me down. And perhaps I burst one with the tip of the paddle, for at that moment, only yards from the Kilkee shore, the rain began to fall in sheets. Groaning with each of the last few paddle strokes, I closed my eyes as the rain drummed on the decks of the kayak; then with my head filling with wicked, lustful hallucinations of hot tea, real food and a dry seat, I ran the bows up on Kilkee's north slipway.

~ ~ ~

Quite by chance, I had made one of the most homely and hospitable landfalls in the whole of county Clare, directly beneath Maura and Ronan Grady's guesthouse – a cross between a daytime nursery-playgroup, an extended happy family and a B&B. It was never exactly clear which category was meant to apply to me, but I was quickly rescued from the relentless rain by the gently insistent, fatherly figure of Ronan Grady. We sat in the warm kitchen drinking cups of scalding coffee, while I dripped inoffensively onto a big soft towel laid on the chair for that very purpose, and Ronan periodically disappeared to check the water level in his hot tank.

'There'll be plenty now, I'd say, for your bath,' he announced, as though thawing out wandering storm-bound canoeists was a routine occurence in the Grady household.

As soon as I sank up to my neck in the steaming bath, I knew it was exactly what I had needed. The rheumatic aches and muscle strains that had been with me since the Blaskets soaked away along with the salt and grime and pig slurry. One thing worried me though. With all the exercise of recent weeks, any spare padding I'd had on my rear end had now virtually disappeared. While this was okay in itself, it meant that the sores which had formed between my bum bones and the kayak seat had been under increasing pressure, and had now become huge, angry craters of pus. My lazy tendency to leave problems alone in the hope that they'd eventually conform to nature's plan and heal themselves, was not working. Seawater, far from being the universal panacea that old sailors claim it to be, is actually acerbic, corrosive and rot-inducing; constant immersion in it was certainly doing no good for the seeping red sores under each of my buttocks.

There was, however, a general feeling of something akin to a cease-fire: an understanding that the damage had at least temporarily stopped, and that everything could now begin to mend. Around me in the bath floated my dirty washing, and upstairs my VHF radio battery was re-charging. On hearing the tea-time shipping forecast, Maura had prepared a bedroom for me, and set an extra place at the table. 'You'll not be going out to sea in that!' she decided; and I slept well that night, between clean sheets, while a full gale raged over the little town of Kilkee.

Next morning was a business day, spent on the backlog of land-bound commitments associated with running a sponsored kayak journey. It started at breakfast, when Clare FM radio and the *Clare Champion* newspaper tracked me down at the Grady's. Later there was a chance to make all the phonecalls I had been neglecting. All day long the storm swept over Kilkee. Huge Atlantic billows rolled swiftly above the rooftops like rain-bearing Zeppelins;

sudden grey squalls alternated with dazzling spells of bright sunshine in typical Atlantic chequerboard pattern. The wind was a constant force seven, occasionally gusting higher. It harrowed the bay, tearing up the sea and causing massive explosions of white swell on the Kilkee barrier reef, and on George's Head. Even Moore Bay, the sheltered crescent beach that had made Kilkee a famous resort since Victorian times, was fringed in a hacking surf. It was not a matter for debate; Maura was right, I wouldn't be going to sea in that.

I must have seemed a strange figure among the holidaymakers of Kilkee, wandering around town clutching a VHF radio for forecast updates, and casting furtive, regular glances around street corners towards the sea like a nautical Peeping Tom. I could still tell you which shopfronts get the best VHF reception, and which cafés have the best view of George's Head. The Gradys continued to make me feel very much at home, constantly drying my wet clothes, providing home-made soup and a bed on a drop-in basis, but when the forecasts began to concur in predicting a slight and brief drop in wind for the following morning, I knew it was time to repack *Sola*. There was indeed a drop in wind, and it was indeed very slight. It slowed perhaps to force six, and compensated by bringing in grey walls of slashing rain and veils of wet mist. I delayed until late morning over a good breakfast of soda bread and marmalade, and over saying goodbye to the Grady kids. Little Cormac asked if there would be caves on the way, and made me promise to name the first one after him.

~ ~ ~

Cormac's Cave, then, is the first sea cavern around George's Head, reached in a heavy sea by some delicate negotiation of breaking swells between the Kilkee reef and the headland itself. It is hardly likely to become a major visitor attraction, nor even warrant a name in the next edition of the Ordnance Survey. And as I passed its mouth a big comber rolled out of the southwest and, tripping neither on reef nor skerry, filled half the cave mouth with its surge.

There was a great deep *booomm!* of compressed air, and the whole wave mass was spewed out of the orifice in a halo of spray and vapour. I made a mental note never to stop for a snooze in Cormac's Cave, and paddled on.

Even after only a day's absence it felt good to be back in the kayak; she was warm, comfortable and, with the addition of a second spraydeck, for the moment remained dry inside. But, for all that, she was a small cork bobbing along a shadowy line of towering broken cliffs in a vast grey sea. It was not at all a good sea to be out in. The swell retained much of the wind-generated power of the storm, only today it was harder to see. In such poor visibility it was difficult to decide even which direction it was surging from until it broke, with deceptive violence, upon hidden reefs. And, as in recent days along this exposed coast, there seemed nowhere one could risk a landing, for fear of broken bones and shattered fibreglass. The crashing of waves from deep within the cloud betrayed the presence, just out of harm's way, of several small islets along the route; the surf outlined them audibly with a muffled thunder. Eventually, after four hours on the water, I could hear surf on *both* sides of the kayak, and knew without seeing, that I was passing close inside of Mutton Island, about eleven miles north of Kilkee. Carving hard right, into a bight sheltered from the southwesterly swell, I was happily surprised to find a haven called Seapoint, near the hamlet of Quilty, where I could land undamaged. It was four o'clock, high tide, and I simply stepped out of *Sola* and pulled her easily onto a patch of grass where a small brass plaque gloomily recorded that two ships of the Spanish Armada were wrecked in this bay in 1588.

In what had become a neat, polished routine, I hurriedly pitched camp, changed clothes and brewed a drink; and was huddled behind the quay, drinking hot chocolate as the rain swept over when a pair of fishermen walked past.

'By Jesus there's still a few of them on the loose, Pats!' said one, waving a big gloved hand in my direction.

'Round ... Ireland ... Solo,' said Patsy, reading from the kayak's stickers. 'How many of ye are there in that then?'

'Just the two of us; myself and the boat.' I tried to sound cheery and confident.

'Well, I wouldn't give much for *your* chances. But I'd say the *boat* might make it!'

When they returned from checking their mooring, Patsy and Dan told me of an infamous pair who'd stopped at Quilty some years before whilst rowing round Ireland in a traditional currach. They were shown regularly on TV, sculling powerfully out of various west coast bays, or pulling in at island harbours, and giving interviews from their currach. But what everyone assumed to be a pile of safety gear covered with sackcloth near the stern of the boat, was in fact a well-disguised outboard motor. Patsy was doubled over with approving laughter as he described how the pair would row out to the first headland, whip off the sackcloth, fire the motor into life, and head for the next pub along the coast. 'And do ye know this,' said Dan, 'I think they are probably going at it to this day!'

'Have you something to put with a mackerel?' said Patsy, handing me three small ones before I could make sense of his phrase. 'Good wind for the morning,' he said.

'That's just perfect,' I said laughing, 'a meal and a forecast combined; thanks a lot!'

'Eat well, so,' said Dan. 'Welcome to Quilty.'

I lost no time in beheading, betailing and begutting the little mackerel, and fried them up with beans and Kilkee potatoes, wondering if any of the poor survivors of the sixteenth-century Spanish galleons had been so well received. Despite the prominence given in school history texts to Sir Francis Drake's famous scuttling of the Spanish Armada, only two ships were actually sunk, and two captured, by the English navy. A further fifty-four ships were destroyed, and the thousands of men on them perished during the months that followed on their miserable escape attempt north and west around Scotland and Ireland.

It is little wonder that so many ships of the Armada were wrecked that year on the west coast of Ireland. For on the sea charts of the day the entire west coast was shown as a straight line, north to south, with just one small inlet at Galway Bay; whereas in reality the Atlantic seaboard is as convoluted a maze of headlands, islands and dead-end bays as could be found in the whole of Europe. If the Spanish fleet sighted Ireland, and from the first northwestern headland sailed due south, it's a wonder that they didn't all end up directly on the cliffs of county Mayo. In fact they became embayed, or ran aground, at several locations down the west coast, and there met a fate every bit as terrible as the sea itself. By all accounts there were few survivors. Of those Spaniards who had not already died of disease, starvation or wounds on board ship, some were drowned or battered to death on the rocks as the ships ran aground; but far more were murdered as they came ashore. Word had gone out that they must be slaughtered, and so they were. Many who escaped the British army parties scouring the shores were beaten to death by the Irish peasantry for their clothes, their valuables or simply through misunderstanding, fear and superstition. Tradition has it that a few survivors, wrecked perhaps near some of the less savage of the coastal communities, met with a kinder fate, eventually mixing in marriage with local girls and introducing the particular dark Iberian colouring that still surfaces occasionally in the western Irish gene-pool. But on the whole, the episode was not one of which Bord Fáilte, the tourist board, would have been particularly proud.

~   ~   ~

Next morning Patsy had been out early, fishing the mackerel shoals at dawn to provide bait for his lobsterpots, and was on his way in for breakfast as our boats grazed gunwales at Quilty quay. His deck was a mass of blue-silvered bodies, the metallic sheen of life only just leaving their scales.

'Enough is as good as plenty!' he said. 'Ye know, they're a strange one, the mackerel; always swim towards the wind – some years they'd go so far offshore that we don't see them at all. And you know the daftest thing of all?' He glanced at me over a box of mackerel. 'They can't float like a normal fish can. No float bladder you see, got to keep moving fast all the time or they sink. 'Times you'll see the whole surface boiling with shoals of 'em. You'd have seen that yourself now?' I nodded, not wanting to interrupt his flow. 'In spring I'd be setting the nets for them. They have the scales on their eyes – blind you know – can't see a hook. But now the scales are off, they're like piranhas! – take a bite at anything that moves – even bits of other mackerel.'

'That must make the work easier,' I suggested.

'Not at all! Not at all!' said Patsy, stuffing the three last big ones down the back of my lifejacket. 'Sure, don't I have to work like a Kerryman just to keep them off the hooks, for fear the boat will go down under the weight!'

Still chuckling, and with mackerel tails brushing the backs of my ears, I set off into a gentle, rounded swell. 'Bad wind tomorrow!' shouted Patsy, as I waved and headed north for Hag's Head and the infamous Cliffs of Moher. The wind was down around force four and, except where it met shallow reefs or cliffs, the sea had become a gentle procession of high-domed southwesterly swells. As I rounded Spanish Point, the first buttresses of the Cliffs of Moher were already beginning to rise from the grey sea across Liscannor Bay, as were the long western ramparts of the Aran islands. But soon they were all gone, receding into a deep bank of cloud which infected the day from the west. Swollen rain clouds, like embayed Atlantic galleons driven onto a lee shore, spilled their cargoes over the coast of Clare.

It took almost three hours to cross Liscannor Bay, by which time some pretty savage rearing and breaking was going on for some distance out to sea beneath Hag's Head. A change of heart and a wide detour took me almost a mile out to the west, first on a course for the Arans – Inishmaan, then Inisheer – then bows pointing once more towards the cliffs of the mainland. My sweeping curve took me out to where two little trawlers were fishing the shoal water on the edge of the turbulence, dipping and rolling in the restless swell as they tried to haul a net.

'Hey! Are you that Round Ireland canoe yoke?' They shouted across a garbled, disjointed message: 'There was a piece in the paper about you ... There's a bit of a forecast on the way ... Here's a crab for your tea ... and if you see a fishing boat dawdling about out there, tell him not to bother coming home – his wife's divorced him.'

~ ~ ~

My first view of the Cliffs of Moher, then, was from well out to sea; and as I approached the cloud lifted clear of their tops to reveal a quite magnificent rock face, stretching away in both directions. For five miles here Ireland is without a coast, and county Clare pours cleanly, vertically over a seven hundred foot precipice to the Atlantic breakers below. Cheated of a more gently shelving landfall, the ranks of swell shouldered roughly against the cliff buttresses before turning and taking their unspent energy back seaward; and as I eased inshore and began to paddle north, their frustrated, reflecting motions made the kayak rise and fall like a fairground carousel horse.

The great undulating rock wall stretched on and on like a vast pennant trailing in a breeze; and occasionally along the clifftop – like frantic ants on a slab of cake – I could see the dwarfed forms of people. Ireland's answer to Dover's White Cliffs, and just a short trip from Galway town, the Cliffs of Moher have long been an imperative stop for round-Ireland tourists. Above me, I imagined, would be a large car park, burger vans, donkey carts and vendor stalls: fast snacks for now, souvenirs for later, and postcards to prove you were there. A coach disgorges its cargo of camera-laden holidaymakers for a short stop on a busy schedule. Photos are taken of the dizzying drop, of the untamed Atlantic below; and the tiny, coloured speck which would eventually show up like a blemish on the developed prints would be me: green if I remained upright, and yellow if I happened to capsize. It ocurred to me that I ran a significant risk of being hit by any wish-laden lucky coins cast from the clifftops. According to my quick 'O' Grade physics calculation, a fifty pence coin dropped from the clifftop would take about six seconds before it cannoned right through the fibreglass hull at a speed of forty miles an hour.

Close inshore beneath the cliffs, six-hundred-and-fifty feet beneath O'Brien's Tower, was a zone of shallower water where the swell concentrated itself into deep corrugations before dumping savagely at the cliff-foot and receding with a vicious undertow. After a brief look I decided against trying to land here, on a pocket-handkerchief spit of shingle, and turned to head back into rounder unbroken water. Suddenly I saw a currach with two oarsmen, heading straight towards me with great urgency, the bow rising and falling in the swell like a pit-head pump-iron. At times they were out of sight in the deeper troughs, but I turned and paddled towards them, meeting them out where the sea rose and fell with a little less exuberance.

'Thanks be to God you're all right!' said the older man, bent heaving and puffing over his oars.

'We thought you'd be needing some help there,' added his son, with just the slightest note of disappointment in his voice. It turned out that they'd seen only my head bobbing in the swell, and thought that a tourist had fallen from the cliff. I thanked them for taking the trouble to check, and the father handed round cigarettes as I leaned unsteadily on their low gunwale. Their currach was of the Aran style, with its stern cut off square, and its bow – which they called the 'bird' – raked up in a high angle, like an Indian canoe. It was strongly built, though not as neatly finished as the *naomhógs* I'd seen in Kerry. I had watched them handle the boat with an enviable skill, and an obvious mastery of the conditions, but I wondered nonetheless whether it might not be *them* one day who would need rescue. Although both were light, keel-less, seaworthy craft, propelled by manpower alone, the kayak and currach had many important differences. The kayak was completely sealed. Small amounts of water in the cockpit could be evacuated using the foot-pump, and if capsized by a breaking wave it could be flicked back upright using an eskimo-roll technique without me even leaving my seat. In addition it contained a certain amount of buoyancy fore and aft beyond sealed bulkheads. The currach, on the other hand, had no integral buoyancy, and was potentially vulnerable to capsize, puncture on a sharp rock, or swamping in a large wave. Its crew were self-confessed non-swimmers, wearing heavy tweed clothes and boots, and had no lifejackets; it seemed their only concessions to safety, apart from their own skills and intricate local knowledge, were a St Christopher medallion, and a tiny phial of holy water carried beneath the currach's prow.

'It's better to be lucky than to be wise,' said the father, quoting an old Irish proverb.

'But don't you worry about a strong offshore wind driving you out to sea?' I asked.

'Oh, you need never have any fear of going as far west as the wind will take you,' answered the father, baiting me, 'because sooner or later surely a westerly will spring up and take you back home again!'

'Very good,' I laughed, 'but what happens in a capsize?'

'Well, you would likely drown,' came the matter-of-fact reply. 'This is a bad stretch just here for the boats swamping, now.'

'Are currachmen drowned here often then?'

'Just the once – each!' he finished with a smile. (In fact no fewer than three men were to drown in separate currach accidents during the three months that I was in Ireland.)

'It strikes me that those big boots and jerseys would sink you straight to the bottom,' I teased.

'Aye, maybe so,' he returned, 'but only for a few days. After a week or so, you see, the body bloats full with gases and floats back to the surface again. Not a pretty sight.'

He told me the story of an old currachman of his village who had been fishing alone one still evening in a bay where, only a week before, the crews of three currachs had been drowned in a freak storm. All was quiet. The wind was dead and the thick evening sky pressed heavily on the sea. Suddenly *whoosh!* a man's body, swollen with the gases of death, bobbed to the surface right in front of his currach. Although shaken, he quickly crossed himself, and reached for a boat hook and rope with which to secure the body. Then *whoosh! ... whoosh!* In a rush of bubbling water two more corpses surfaced on one side of his currach, one vertically with the flesh hanging rotten from its face, and its gloved hands reaching out as though towards the boatman. In all, eight sea-bloated bodies surfaced in the small bay around his currach within the space of an hour. Without either stopping or looking back, he rowed as hard as he could all the way to his home beach, put a sharp rock through his currach and never went to sea again.

I quoted from Synge's *Riders to the Sea* where the islander says: 'A man who is not afraid of the sea will soon be drownded ... for he will be going out on a day he shouldn't; but we do be afraid of the sea, and we do only be drownded now and again.'

'Yes,' said the currachman. 'I've heard that; that's the true wisdom for you. By God, but you're some man for the stories! If you've finished the interrogation you'd better be making for Doolin. I'm beginning to wish we'd never rescued you!'

'I was thinking of making for Inisheer,' I said,

'By God, boy, there's a gale on the way; all the fancy lifejackets, pump-feet and eskimo-sausage-rolls in the world won't get you there tonight! Do you like a bit of music? Well, Doolin's the place, so. Good luck to ye now!'

~ ~ ~

Doolin harbour lies in a tiny coastal indentation, protected slightly from the Atlantic swell by a lump of rock known as Crab Island. Riddled limestone terraces tilt gradually towards the sea, decorated in occasional bays by little sand beaches, seductive but treacherous. The sea-waves sluice in round Crab Island, then exit again beneath their successors, causing a deceptively strong undertow. The tragic drowning of eight young people here, after a music festival in 1983, was still prominent in local memories and conversations about the sea.

At the stone pier a colourful, disorganised collection of travellers lay, sat and strolled around, waiting for the little *Happy Hooker* ferry to the Aran islands. Rucksacks, tents and coloured mats had been piled in a mound, and on top sat a young Spaniard dressed in a raincoat and shorts, plucking chords on a mandolin. They were like the first daubs of primary colour on the grey canvas of sea and stone that had been the day. But the ferry didn't come. Gale-bound on Inishmore, it wouldn't sail now until the morning. The little multicoloured whirlwind eventually picked itself up and, undaunted, bimbled back to the Doolin pubs, looking almost like a carnival procession, as they straggled along the narrow road.

Twenty years ago, during the early years of the folk music revival, the village of Doolin had been the traditional musicians' mecca. Many of today's big names, like Sean Cannon, Christy Moore and Matt Molloy were young unknowns who used to come to the quiet fishing village, just down the road from Lisdoonvarna, to meet and play, perfecting their art and honing their skills. But the secret leaked out that 'genuine' Irish music was to be heard at the little fishing hamlet at the foot of the glen, and the tourist trade got into gear. Tourists began to arrive by the coachload, and the smell of big money was on the sea-breeze. Hostels, B&Bs, cafés, restaurants and craft shops sprang up everywhere; and within ten years the village had changed entirely. It was full of accents and languages, and busy with people more interested in holiday snaps, ice-creams and souvenirs than in fishing or real live music; so the 'real live musicians' upped and left. Doolin settled into its new role as a tourist village, and ferry port for the Aran islands.

It's a pleasant enough place, Doolin, and still has a reputation, of sorts, for good music. Two pubs and a café all advertised *Live Music Nightly* on colourfully painted wall signs; but now the show is directed by the pub landlords and the business community. They know that the music brings in the tourists; the tourists bring in the money; and the season is short. They are 'making hay while the sun shines' and, well, who can blame them.

In O'Connor's Bar, once the turf-reek had cleared a little, there was a great mixture of nationalities and faces, ranging in colour from peat to petal, were stacked around the walls and tables. They were listening intently to an accomplished duo on accordion and guitar, singing songs of famine, emigration and heroes of the turbulent troubles. There was no need to understand either the language or the history of the Gaels in order to sense the emotions which the music tapped into; and there was no doubt about it: these players were good. But the very special atmosphere of a good Irish music pub – when the *craic* and tunes are spontaneous, unpaid, unpredictable and wild – was missing. O'Connors was packed to the eaves, but not with a pub crowd: they were an audience. And this was much less a 'session' than a performance or concert. While I knew that everyone there – from the smiling dark Spaniards crouching on the floor, and the giant blond Vikings at the back, to salty, cynical Brian from the tent at the beach – would go home with fine memories of a good night, I could not quite shrug off a slight disappointment.

But then, perhaps it was just me. Doolin was rapidly becoming yet another dustbin for my hopes of progress. The day before had been a complete blow out, with gales whipping up the sea in Galway Bay. Twice I had walked through the rain into the village, made some phonecalls, had a pint, and walked back again to the tent; but my heart was set on getting moving again. So many times I walked out across the limestone plateau, clint-cracked and grike-fretted by erosion, gazing out across a dark and furrowed sea to Aran. Each time I returned desolate and frustrated, knowing the battle it would have been to survive in that sea, and shelved my hopes at least until the next forecast.

'All ships, all ships, all ships. This is Valentia Control.' After blowing the dust noisily from the microphone, the coastguard proceeded to cancel the scheduled morning forecast at seven due to a distress call on air. Somewhere out in that gloom a ship was in trouble. I heard the Valentia forecasts at ten o'clock, one o'clock, four o'clock and finally seven o'clock in the evening, then gave up on the damp stuffy tent. Up at the Doolin pub I drank and sang with a group of pale Glaswegian lads and dark Iberian senoritas, clearing the air and chasing off some clouds with a raucous crazy version of 'Dirty Old Town'.

CHAPTER 13

The Happy Hooker

I am alone, and I want to be alone, with the clear sky and the sea.

Nietzsche

There are very few things more exhausting than paddling against a strong headwind; few conditions less motivating than black cloud and grey rain; and perhaps nothing less conducive to small boat travel than a complete soaking. And yet, with an early start, frequent short breaks, and the frustration which comes of having been tent-bound for days, it is still possible to notch up an impressive mileage. On a day when the wind blew at force six, and the sky could only be distinguished from the sea by the black hollows and white wave-caps of the latter, I was to clock up thirty miles with the manic energy of a coiled spring unwinding, to end the day on the coast of county Galway.

The wind had dropped a notch on the previous day's gales, and moved back into the southwest, slightly reducing the swell piling into Doolin harbour. But the light of day hardly seemed to penetrate the cloud, and the wind-driven rain curtains remained tightly drawn. It was anything but pleasant canoeing weather, however I hoped at least to reach Inisheer, the smallest and closest of the Aran islands. At eight o'clock my would-be saviour from the currach was down on the Doolin pier. Sniffing the wind, he decided to forego trap-hauling beneath the Cliffs of Moher, in favour of scouring the shore for flotsam and wreck in the aftermath of the big westerlies. Cautiously he agreed that I should be able to make the Aran islands, as long as I could find them in the murk, and wished me luck.

I set off into the deep grey wash of the South Sound of Galway Bay, heading for the position where Inisheer had last been seen. The cloud continued to regroup and thicken, and rain came over in sweeping bands, but it was a fine feeling to be pushing energy through the paddle again, firing the kayak and the whole journey forward rather than stagnating slowly on the edge of the international vortex of Doolin. Instead of gradually accumulating a tent-bound dampness, I was soon unambiguously drenched. Waves forced up the sleeves and down the neck of my jacket until my woollen jersey beneath was saturated; but for the moment it was enough just to be mobile. I must have been roughly in mid-Sound when the *Happy Hooker* emerged from the cloud, riding raggedly on the shifting swell, and gave me a cheery 'Thomas the Tank Engine' toot as she powered towards Doolin. The tide in the Sound should now have been against me, and I was forcing the kayak into a strong headwind, so it was with some surprise that within a further half-hour land emerged from the mist.

One danger of landing on a strange island in poor visibility, as St Brendan himself discovered, is that it might actually be a large whale. The presence of rocks, beaches, soil, even trees, might mean nothing other than that the whale had not dived for some time. If a boat were to land all of its crew, and tie a mooring to the whale, and the whale later plunge down into the sea, the boat would be lost with all hands, as was nearly the case in Brendan's *Navigatio*. The wise and cautious seaman then, since the time of Brendan, always sends a man ashore in advance, to test the 'island' by emptying out his pipe embers, or starting a small fire on the shore. If it is a whale, it will feel the heat, submerge, and a lot of trouble will have been saved.

I landed on a sheltered sandy beach, in the lee of the wind and swell, and – using a little petrol from the stove – started a small driftwood fire to brew some hot chocolate. The island didn't move; I wasn't yet sure that it was Inisheer but at least it wasn't a whale. It seemed likely that it was indeed Inisheer when a tiny aeroplane buzzed in from the cloud and came to a stop somewhere on the landmass behind me. Ten minutes later it took off again, presumably on a hop to the next island of the group, Inishmaan. And I followed shortly after.

As I passed the northern tip of Inisheer and stepped off into the isolation of mist and cloud once more, I knew from the map that I was crossing the two mile sea-gap known as Foul Sound. At first the sea was pushing boldly through the Sound, and I paddled a careful route broadsides to the southwesterly advances of the wavefronts. But I was putting full strength into each stroke, and soon reached the more sheltered shore of Inishmaan, the second, in both size and position, of Aran's three islands. In the centre of a recessed bay, a chapel and pier materialised slowly from the gloom. A large ferry from Galway was disgorging a cargo of daytrippers onto the island, so I opted to continue around the sheltered northeast quarter of the island and perhaps make a crossing to Inishmore.

The third Sound, *Sunda Ghriora*, Gregory's Sound, is named after St Gregory of the Golden Mouth, a humble, unhappy saint, who measured his own worth against Aran's great holy man St Enda, and found himself inadequate. Legend has it that Gregory became a holy recluse, confining himself to a cave beneath a pile of huge boulders on the shore of Inishmaan, directly opposite Inishmore. There he anguished and agonised over his sinful past, and in a fit of grief bit off his lower lip – and a golden one grew in its place. At the time of his death, still deeming himself unworthy of burial on St Enda's sacred Inishmore, he asked to be abandoned at sea in a barrel. But the barrel then washed up on the shore of Inishmore, so that the lonely Gregory was indeed finally buried on Inishmore, high on a headland overlooking the sight of his self-imposed exile and the Sound that now bears his name.

After pulling on my hood, I squeezed the kayak out from the rocks and began to head for Kilronan on Inishmore, four miles from the tip of Inishmaan. The wind had increased, and was blowing contrary to the ebb tide now draining out of Galway Bay between the islands. The rain, now heavier and more constant, had flattened the swell a little but the entire Sound was a seething mass of white horses. Nineteenth-century emigrant ships, leaving Galway for America, used to pass through *Sunda Ghriora*, sometimes having to wait for days in the shelter of the island for a favourable wind on which to begin their Atlantic crossing. Often there would be Aran people on board. They would already have said a very final farewell to their relatives on the islands, who they would almost certainly never see again. It must have been a cruel and heart-rending experience to lie at anchor so long within sight of grieving relatives on the shore and the island, which had, until then, cradled their whole world.

One fast wet hour later I surged round the big breakwater of Kilronan pier and beached, on a rapidly falling tide, beneath the village capital of the Aran islands. Shedding my outer layer of clothes, I removed my woollen jumper and longjohns, wrung pints of water from them and put them back on again before going in search of a snack and a beer. Kilronan is a quaintly authentic island village, built heavily in stone, securely set into a sheltering hill above a superb natural harbour. Mile upon mile of drystone walls surround hundreds of tiny pastures, each field created from bare rock, and enriched yearly with a man-made soil of seaweed, dung and lime-sand. Steep, winding, cobbled tracks lead through Kilronan itself, and out of the village in both directions. Running tourists through the village, and out to the cliffs and fortress of Dun Aengus, is a lucrative trade for a man with a donkey and cart. Car drivers complain that these rough surfaced roads ruin their tyres, but the owners of the island's donkey fleet counter that the hooves of the donkeys wouldn't get enough purchase on a steep, tarred surface; and so the debate goes on, and it seems that neither the cobbled lanes nor the donkeys are likely to disappear just yet.

Over a pint of stout and a large plate of sandwiches, I sat in a pub overlooking the harbour, my damp shirt steaming as though it were about to explode. It was mid-afternoon, and I'd covered about thirteen miles from Doolin. Beyond the harbour wall the sea looked – well, no worse than before. If anything the swell had calmed a little, although the visibility was down to about a mile. The little pub was filled with an interesting mix of fishermen hiding from the sea and weather, islanders sheltering from the rain, students improving their Irish and tourists waiting for a ferry. Many of the tourists, having been caught in a downpour while out at Dun Aengus, were as wet as I was. Everyone seemed relieved to be out of the weather, and the cheery international atmosphere was a welcome break from the lonely grey sea. But when yet another of the big Galway ferries docked at the pier and began to pour out another wave of visitors, I decided that I'd make one final crossing before the day's end.

~ ~ ~

It was under the bemused gaze of tourists, ferrymen and fishermen alike that I donned my kayak gear in the Kilronan rain, hauled the kayak down to the tide, and paddled out of the harbour, once more into the wind and rain of Galway Bay. Eight miles across the North Sound, the long, low fragmented coast of Iar Connaught, county Galway, lay hidden from view. I headed on a rough northerly bearing and, even allowing for the effects of the wind, and the ebb tide setting westwards, calculated I should hit the Connaught coast somewhere on or near Gorumna Island. It never feels entirely comfortable to head away from a safe shore, into a mysterious oblivion, when all you can see are restless white-crested waves in every direction; and no matter how carefully you have worked out a course with map and compass, a shred of existential scepticism always remains. Is there really a coast out there? Could the compass be wrong? If the world really was flat after all, where would the edge be?

The wind was persistent and furious, but at least it was no longer a headwind; it bundled the kayak forward usefully, if a little roughly, from the rear left quarter. Visibility dropped to about half a mile and, after only an hour of paddling, I felt completely disorientated. Putting all faith in the magnetic bearing, and in the confidence that I could keep paddling for as long as needed, I bent my head into the rain and forged on.

There was no way to measure progress, but I gained ground slowly wetly northward. The wind, as its fetch from Inishmore increased, whipped up a larger sea, and all around me white crests curled and toppled. Matthew Arnold came to mind:

> *Now the wild white horses play,*
> *Champ and chafe and toss in the spray.*

In many ways these were the archetypal 'white horses', rearing up with manes flying in the wind. Tradition has it that a fleet of Spanish ships, becalmed for many weeks on an ocean voyage to the New World, had to throw their magnificent horses overboard for lack of drinking water. The Spanish *caballeros* thought so highly of their horses that they even believed horses had souls, and were horrified at the tragic loss of the white beauties. In the rough weather that inevitably followed the calm, the *caballeros* dreamed that the horses came back to haunt the ship in revenge. They told these dreams to sailors, who later often imagined that they saw the demented white horses, the *caballos blancos*, bearing down on them in wild storms.

All around me was nothing but a waste of sea, a livid grey whipped up here and there to white foam; and then beyond it, like a theatrical curtain, the surrounding cloud banks, the chaos and the flurry of wide Galway Bay. Although I was tiring quickly after twenty-five cold rough miles, the balance of effort on the whole was mental rather than physical. Constantly I was fending off thoughts born of cold, fatigue and insecurity. What if I capsized and got separated from the boat? One thing was certain: a flare fired in emergency would be lost in deep cloud within seconds. How long would I last? What were my chances of being found? Where would I wash up? I knew that in past times men drowned off the Aran islands were often carried by tides, and washed ashore as far away as Donegal, one-hundred-and-sixty miles north. Word would be sent down the coastal grapevine, but often it was only from the clothes –

the intricate patterns of the Aran fishermen's jerseys were unique to each family – that the corpse was identifiable. Many fishermen's bodies, of course, were simply never found; and there were families in these western islands where generations went by with hardly a male member dying a natural death on land, or needing a burial in earth.

Surprisingly, I think, since it was such a fact of sea-faring life, families from these islands had a remarkably superstitious attitude towards drownings. One prevalent belief was that the sea always claimed its due, and could not be robbed. A drowned corpse would not be allowed into a house; nor could timber from a boat wrecked with loss of life be re-used. And many a drowning man was left to his fate, for to rescue him would have been to deny the sea its quota, and sooner or later someone else would be taken in his place. I wondered if anyone descended from the old islanders still held to these spooky philosophies of surrogate drowneeship. If so, I hoped at least that they were not employed by the lifeboat or the coastguard!

~ ~ ~

I could hardly have picked a more torn or fragmented section of the entire Irish coast on which to make a lucky-dip landfall. As it runs westward, the coast of Iar Connaught disintegrates, almost dissolves, into a tangle of bulbous peninsulas, convoluted bays, islands, causeways and, finally, hundreds of tiny islets. There are neither roads, railways, harbours nor even a lighthouse to provide a coastal waymarker. Apart from a handful of dwellings, and long rough tracks snaking down from the nearest road, Iar Connaught meets the sea in a smudge of anonymous fragmented rock and turf. From the point where a leaden sea could just be distinguished from the slate-grey sky, a band of bile-coloured no man's land appeared and very slowly expanded to become a stretch of featureless coast. It looked more imaginary than real. And yet, if I had imagined it I would surely have endowed it with at least some features or shapes. The coast looked like a grubby smear at the back of a shirt collar, and was just about as inviting. I landed, close to low tide, on a shingle beach within a semi-circular bay, fringed by rocky islets which almost entirely absorbed the swell from the sea. The fingers of the sea, seeking, searching among the pebbles and shingles of the beach and rock pools, managed, within a few yards, to pilfer away the vast energy of the open ocean.

I thought it likely that I was on the edge of Gorumna Island, but there seemed no way to check. The coastal features I could see were a recurring configuration along the entire coast. And besides, it didn't really matter; it was enough just to be on land; wet through and beginning to shiver, the important thing for the moment was to organise food and shelter. After hauling the kayak above the tidemark, I removed my dry clothes and camp gear from its hatches. Then, following a hedge of brambles laden with irresistible berries, over tumbled dykes and hollows, I found myself half-a-mile inland, in front of a rickety stone-built haybarn, such as the old books on Ireland used to call a 'cabin'. Like a prop from *Hansel and Gretel*, it seemed simply to have materialised from the mist. But it was sound and dry inside, and with the entire surrounding countryside smothered in a seeping cloud, it seemed the perfect place to doss down for the night.

Within an hour I was stripped, dried and snug in warm clothes. My sleeping bag was laid on a pile of dry sweet-smelling hay, and my wet gear dripped steadily from a drying line at the other end of the barn. The sodden efforts of the day were fast becoming a memory, banished for the moment beyond the solid walls of the little refuge. Outside the wind continued to push, and a dripping grey mist rolled in from the bay to engulf the building; but I read peacefully by the light of a candle, and felt sleep edge ever closer. I was in good spirits: infinitely happier than in a soggy tent at Doolin. I'd gained quite a few unexpected miles, and reached somewhere on the coast of county Galway, perhaps within striking distance of Connemara. It was progress, and to cap it all there was an improved forecast for the following day.

~ ~ ~

The morning light bled in by an east-facing window, diffusing through a dense golden smokescreen of haydust. Curled in the hay like a dormouse, I lay with one eye watching the day arrive, the other still reluctant to open. From a ball of straw and daub in a high corner of the rafters, came a steady plaintive cheep-cheeping as mother swift darted in and out of the light shafts with acrobatic brilliance, snatching drowsy insects to feed her nest of noisy youngsters. The heavy black clouds of the previous day had been replaced by a fine white mist, wet and swirling. A light breeze blew tiny particles of vapour in through gaps in the walls and windows, and all that they touched – including my jersey and longjohns – became quickly saturated. I rolled my sleeping bag, breakfasted on sausage sandwiches, and pulled on my wet gear. An early start would give me a chance to feel my way through the sea mist to Roundstone or Clifden in Connemara.

The little barn was completely shrouded in cotton-wool cloud, but I could hear the murmuring sea, and was able to retrace my bramble-lined route to the kayak's landing bay from the previous night. I could hardly believe my eyes when I climbed over the last stone wall and saw – no kayak! My gaze darted uneasily around the bay, then back to the shingle beach; and still no kayak. I was stunned. My familiar routine was so dependent on the kayak being there that I hardly knew where to turn. Was this the same bay? Yes, I was certain. Had I dragged the boat high enough? Of course – after seven weeks that had become almost instinctive. But perhaps there had been an unusually high tide? Yet all the signs were that the last tide had risen even less than the previous storm-driven one. How could a heavily laden kayak simply disappear? The gradual process of logical deduction began, and progressed to its almost incredible conclusion. The kayak had been taken; and surely by at least two people. But where had they come from, and where could they have taken it to?

Desperately, I searched the maze of low drystone walls –

wanting to believe that some well-wisher had just tucked the kayak away behind a dyke for extra safety – but there was no sign of it. There were no houses visible in either direction, but then I remembered some lights I'd seen further to the east just before coming ashore, and decided to head in that direction. For about an hour I scoured the rough countryside, clambering over low walls, losing my boots in boggy holes and tearing my clothes in tangles of bramble and dog rose. I hardly knew if I was even heading in the right direction. The first house I reached looked empty. No smoke came from its chimney, and its pebble-dashed gable was flaky and damp with neglect. But from beneath a pile of shore-salvaged timber, driftwood, plastic floats and wooden fishboxes, I caught a glimpse of a familiar yellow – *Sola*'s distinctive underbelly? Yes, there she was – stacked under a mound of stinking flotsam, the contents of her hatches strewn on the ground, and the paddle missing. There didn't seem to be any damage, and my relief at finding her at all was tremendous; but nonetheless I was furious, livid that someone would brazenly lift *Sola* from the shore and cart her away. I hammered on the door loudly enough to wake anyone unfortunate enough to be still sleeping inside; hammered again, but there was no reply. I jogged along to the next house and was puffing and hot in my paddling suit when the door opened slowly and a stout, middle-aged woman stood staring at me in puzzled silence.

'Do you know anything about a big canoe that's sitting beside the next house?' I said, trying to remain civil for just a moment longer.

'Oh the boat, indeed, yes,' she said. 'That came out of the sea. It belongs to my son Donal–'

'It certainly does not. It's mine!' I interrupted, beginning to lose my cool.

She looked me up and down – from the wetsuit boots to the hooded pink paddling jacket – then said: 'What do you mean, it's yours? It was washed up on our coast, you know, after the storm, and all the wreckage in the bay belongs to us.'

'Now, look here – it is *not* wreckage and it was *not* washed up – I *paddled* it up! And what's more it was well above the tideline. Where is your son now? Let me speak to him. He had a bloody cheek to move it at all,' I raved, wondering at the same time how to persuade a reluctant Irishman, who was probably twice my size, to carry the kayak back to the bay.

'Well, he is – oh, out hauling creels,' she said unconvincingly. 'But I daresay he might let you have the boat at a fair price, if you'll just–'

'Might what! I'll–'

'Now, now. You'll come in for some tea and breakfast?' she added, and I felt my indignation and anger give way to confusion, and even mild amusement at the bizarre situations I seemed regularly to end up in. I could cope with being tent-bound in a gale, or even kidnapped by Sherkin pirates, but to have the kayak taken as wreckage, then offered to me for sale, left me stuck for words. Not for the first time I thought the difficulty in kayaking around Ireland lay not so much in getting to a place, but in getting away from it. There are times when the flotsam analogy comes too close to the truth for comfort.

The woman shouted in Irish into the house, and a couple of doors slammed mysteriously before she led me into the warm kitchen. She sat me down beside the range, and seemed well-used to placating angry menfolk by filling their stomachs. Over several cups of tea, and a huge plate of ham and eggs with pancake and beans, and homemade soda bread, the picture became clearer. The rights of wreck and salvage along parts of the Irish coast – perhaps especially those where timber and other resources have traditionally been scarce – are extremely ancient and important, sometimes complicated, and often grimly defended. As in many parts of the British Isles, coastal people have looked on most forms of flotsam and jetsam as their legitimate property, a sort of Atlantic providence. Shipwrecks, especially during wars, have played an important part in the economy of Ireland's remoter coasts; even today houses and barns may be seen with mahogany mantelpieces, rafters riddled with shipworm boreholes, and ship's furniture recycled as kitchen units.

There are very subtle differences between wreck and wrack, flotsam and jetsam, smuggling and salvage, and many similar forms of coastal enterprise which have largely slipped through the net of written record-keeping. It is even harder to shed light on some of the shadier aspects of shore life, but it seems that in the past smuggling and deliberate wrecking have almost everywhere been regarded as more or less acceptable methods of obtaining food and supplementing a difficult living from the sea. Almost automatically, unwritten codes of practice have developed regarding aspects such as legitimate targets, division of shoreline, ownership and property, and rights of salvage. Generation after generation of coastal families has inherited rights to its own stretch of shoreline, perhaps demarcated by a stream on one boundary, and a cliff on the other.

In an area with no local woodland, bays that collect driftwood are the most jealously guarded of all. Every such bay has its own particular ideal wind, during which it reaps the optimum harvest from the sea; and wreck seekers keep as close an eye on wind and tide conditions as a Hawaiian surfer, for whatever the sea throws up on the land is theirs for the taking.

The woman pointed out of the kitchen window at stacks of driftwood, crates, baskets and creels, all of which had been found on 'her' shore. Enough new timber had come up last year to build a shed extension to the house; a hen-hut on the corner of her yard looked suspiciously like the wheelhouse of a Spanish trawler; and even the seat I was sitting on had come from a Norwegian whaler wrecked on Slyne Head. 'Timber doesn't grow on trees 'round here, you know,' she said.

Two days after a westerly storm, she explained, is the time when wreckage – either fresh, or old stuff stirred by the sea's movement – generally starts to float and drift onto her beaches. Her youngest son, eighteen-year-old Donal, had checked the beaches at about half-past eight the previous night. He had seen the kayak there and looked about in the mist for an owner, but as I was by then in the barn, he found no-one. By eleven o'clock he decided that the kayak was now not only legitimate wreck, but one of his best-ever finds, and enlisted his brother Michael to help carry it home.

Pouring me another cup of tea, and perhaps judging that I'd calmed down a little, she admitted that actually Donal was not at the lobsters, but in his room across the hall; but it was best to leave him there. 'He has a quick temper, and he wouldn't want you to be taking the boat.'

Smiling now, I calmly explained about my journey round Ireland, and that not only would I be taking the canoe away, but that the paddle was also missing, and I needed a hand to carry it all to the bay. 'I'll get Michael so,' she said.

Shouting in Irish, she opened the kitchen door and Michael, who had obviously been listening at the keyhole, almost fell into the room, sheepishly clutching the missing paddle. A big, stooping, quiet lad of about nineteen, with a neck like an ox, and hands almost as wide as the paddle blades, Michael exuded disappointment rather than temper, and agreed to help carry the kayak, just as soon as we'd finished the tea. All the way to the bay, except to answer me with a yes or no, Michael said nothing.

Then, on the water's edge: 'Will you write an' tell us how far you get to. Maybe you'll make it to Galway, God willing.'

'OK. Sure I will. And thanks for the lift,' I said, pushing off from the shore. 'What's this place called anyway?'

'This is Lettermullen. You'll pass Golam Head soon to the west,' he answered, and gave a gentle wave.

'Tell Donal I'm sorry about the canoe!' I shouted.

Michael mumbled a reply, which I didn't quite hear, but I felt sure any hard feelings had already vanished on the Iar Connaught breeze.

ROCKALL

Slyne Head to Benwee Head

75 miles

ROCKALL

The Stags of Broad Haven

Benwee Head

Portacloy

Broad Haven

Erris Head

Mullet Peninsula

Belmullet

MAYO

Inishkea Islands

Nephin Beg Mts.

Blacksod Bay

54°

Slievemore

Achill Sound

54°

Achill Head

Achill Island

Corraun Peninsula

Achillbeg Island

Clew Bay

Clare I.

Westport

Croagh Patrick

Inishturk

Atlantic Ocean

Inishbofin

Inishark

Killary Harbour

High Island

Connemara

Clifden

The Twelve Pins

N

Slyne Head

Croaghnakeela Sound

Ballyconneely Bay

ᴛonn dhuglass

| 0 | 5 | 10 | 15 | 20 | 25 miles |

10°

CHAPTER 14

In Search of the White Cow

Living on your western shore,
Saw summer sunsets, asked for more.
I stood by your Atlantic sea
And sang a song for Ireland.

'Song for Ireland', Phil Colclough

On the windward edge of the Atlantic seaboard, where so much of the Irish coastline is hacked and shattered by awesome winter storms and the constant peck-pecking of the waves, there is a slight softening at Connaught, ending in the sandy beaches, turquoise bays and the labyrinth of islets that make up Connemara. *Connemara.* Just as the name trips off the tongue, so the landscape seems to trip gently westward to the sea. From the solid mountainous backdrop of the Twelve Pins, over the lonely fringe-lands of peatbog and lily *lochan*, to the sand-dunes and rock pools of the coast, this rippling landscape blends with an equally rippling seascape, fading seamlessly into mist and echo.

One of Cromwell's generals, despairing of the lack of soil, trees or fresh water, and the predominance of bog and mountain, famously remarked of Connemara that 'there is not water enough to drown a man, wood enough to hang him, nor earth enough to bury him'. Many more recent writers have given the impression that the world ends somewhere in Connemara's wilderness; but it doesn't really end so much as just fade away. Three millennia of high rainfall on to impervious granite have provided conditions ideal for one thing only: the development of vast acreages of peatbog. Topped with moss and heather, cottongrass and carnivorous sundews, many of the Connemara boglands are several yards deep in accumulated peat or turf, and have been the region's main natural resource for many years. Before the rise of tourism, the export of peat-fuel to the Aran islands, the Burren and to Galway city – whose limestone plateaux and better-drained grounds could never produce peat – was the economic mainstay of Connemara and Iar Connaught.

A maze of sea inlets such as at Casla, Kilkeiran, Bertraghboy and Mannin, penetrating deep into the boglands, provided for easy sea transport of the dried peat. And largely because of the great trade in peat, there evolved, along the Connemara coast, a family of carvel-constructed wooden boats, robust and seaworthy, specialising in the transport of goods, people and livestock throughout Galway Bay. In addition to a carvel-built wooden currach, called *currach adhmaid*, which was used for sheep landing, seaweed collection and fishing around the inshore islands, there was the *púcán* – an eighteen-foot open boat with a keel – and the *gleoiteog* – a gaff-rigged yawl generally used as a half-decked fishing boat. But the queen of them all was the magnificent little galleon known as 'the Galway hooker'.

The largest of all the Connemara boats, the hooker was generally about thirty-six feet in length, half-decked and single-masted, gaff-rigged with a bowsprit, large mainsail and jib; and capable of carrying an enormous payload. For about two hundred years the distinctive, curvaceous hookers were the workhorses of Galway Bay, plying their trade endlessly back and forth from the Aran islands. On the outward journey they would generally be laden with peat for fuel, and turf cut from the coastal grasslands to be used as a thatch underlay. But Connemara's maze of inlets also made it perfect for hidden, illicit stills, and many a pot of rye *poteen* would have been carefully concealed among the hookers' heavier cargoes.

From Aran in turn came livestock, potatoes, sally-rods (willow) for basket weaving, and engraved limestone grave-markers. A hundred other minor trades were carried out on the back of the turf trade, with a hundred-and-fifty hookers working out of Greatman's Bay alone in the last century; but when coal and gas became prevalent, and the combination of lorry, train and steamer became more competitive, the Galway hooker was destined to become an anachronism, a relic of the Peat Ages. In recent years there has been a slight resurgence in the popularity of the hookers, mainly as a tourist attraction, or as a regular feature at the summer regattas of many towns along the west coast. But the most accessible of the Connemara peat stocks have long since been depleted. The outermost island, Lettermullen, was stripped bare over a hundred years ago, and its people had to carry fuel four miles from Gorumna. Now Gorumna itself is almost bare, as is Lettermore to the north of it. Placenames such as *Poll na Móna,* 'hole of the turf', and *Carraig na Móna,* 'rock of the turf', on both the Aran and south Connemara shores, are all that remain of the old trade, and the many loading places of the Galway hooker turf boats.

~ ~ ~

Dougie MacDonald, climber, gymnast and groundsman to the Scottish rugby squad, had the physique and athletic ability of a professional sportsman. Within two years of starting up, he had become one of the strongest sea-kayakers I knew, eskimo-rolling a kayak with ease, even without a paddle. When he'd suggested meeting me for two days paddling in Connemara, I'd been delighted to agree. His kayak, a shapely white *Fjord* design, had the MacDonald motto and coat of arms on the front deck, and a hand-painted cartoon strip along its bows, just below the waterline, warning Viking raiding parties against landing in Scotland. This cartoon was the last thing I saw before his kayak disappeared in one of the weirdest freak waves I've ever seen.

We were approaching Slyne Head, two sleek kayaks carving easily through a low swell, when the mist rolled in and we found ourselves close inshore, apparently trapped within the deep crescent of a bay. It was as sudden a mist as I'd ever experienced; or was it a fog? As a child I'd been intrigued by the enigmatic sounding 'Mr Fog' so often associated with radio forecast warnings of poor visibility; and of course there are as many incarnations of mist-or-fog as there are clouds in the sky. Some particularly dense mists are indeed nothing more exotic than sodden clouds which have dropped down to sea level to soak and muffle the coast and deprive navigators temporarily of their familiar bearings. Others are products of the sea itself, rising spookily from a glassy surface like alchemical steam or stagecraft ice vapour.

It takes complicated combinations of wind patterns, sea and land temperature, and atmospheric pressure to create the pea-soupers, the frets, hazes and boiling mists, and the great variety of maritime special effects that beset our coasts. Warm continental air masses tumble westwards over the North Sea, cooling rapidly on passage to form the thick rolling *haar* fogs which can settle for several days at a time along the east coasts of Scotland and Ireland; while temperature inversions, and water-level wind patterns conspire to create the sinister, rolling sea-frets with layers sometimes only a few feet thick, which are a relatively common phenomenon along the Irish coast.

But no amount of weather lore, of understanding how a mist is formed, what it is made of, or what name it is filed under at the Meteorological Office, can quite prepare you for the eerie experience of paddling a small boat through a white-out. In a fog at sea – whether it's a cloying, drenching cloud on which you feel you could lean your elbow, or a swirling ethereal mist which is at once everywhere and nowhere – 'fair is foul, and foul is fair'; and it seems at times as though an encounter with Macbeth's witches, or a glimpse of the genie-of-the-lamp would be no more fanciful than the belief that there is another boat, or indeed even a shoreline out there beyond the murk.

It was not the first mist Dougie and I had paddled in, indeed on one occasion we had spent a whole day weaving in and out of an almost sheer wall of mist which lay, like the cliff-girt edge of an

imaginary white continent, just half-a-mile offshore from
Edinburgh's Lothian coast. Within the mist itself all had been cold,
wet and silent, with visibility reduced to around ten feet; while mere
yards to our right was a world of sunshine, warmth, colour and all
the sounds of the coast. Paddling down the edge of that fog with
one ear in the cold and the other in sunshine, or weaving in and out
of the fog bank like dolphins leaping over the surface of a tilted sea
of steam, were amongst my finest and clearest kayaking memories.

The mist that descended on Connemara was of a different
order. Foul rather than fair, it was more in the manner of a shroud
than a veil and I found its almost tangible darkness a little
unsettling. The air thickened and filled in, and the land disappeared
as if down a funnel, leaving only wet rock, the smothered sea, and
the vaporous air. From a distance came the occasional hoarse
booming of waves bursting on skerries, and with visibility so poor,
we decided to hug the shore until we could get a bearing for Slyne
Head. I was a little behind Dougie, when suddenly a woman
appeared from the mist, presumably from a nearby cottage, and
shouted to me from the beach: 'You must turn back! Back, do you
hear me! Go back where you came from. This is a terrible place for a
boat!'

She had seal-grey hair, wet in the mist and tied in a scarf.
Muttering something in Irish, she gestured with her arms as though
cursing the sea, then shouted again, 'A man was drowned here in a
currach – only last week. Slyne Head; you must keep away from
Slyne Head. Go away back!' With that she turned and disappeared
almost immediately into the mist like a premonition of disaster
from an Irish folktale, leaving behind her a swirl of fog and a chill of
unreality. Over the years I had become used to people
under-estimating the seaworthiness of the kayak, and warning me
against the dangers of their local waters. But this seemed different;
both the intensity of her warning, and the way she had just
materialised out of the mist, had been quite disconcerting.

'What did she say?' asked Dougie, slowing down.

'She said – eh, to be careful at Slyne Head, that someone drowned there in a currach last week,' I said, paraphrasing and trying to look more composed than I felt.

'What's a currach when it's at home?' he asked.

'An open boat made of skins on a frame–'

'Not much wonder then!' he concluded, and we paddled on, looking for the exit to the bay.

Within minutes the worst of the mist had lifted, and we were looking at the broken series of islands that forms Slyne Head. Like Loop Head in county Clare, Slyne Head sticks out far enough west to be a notable exception to the generally weak tides which run off most headlands of the west coast. At Slyne a stream of up to four knots pours through between the islands, and can cause conditions dangerous to small boats in rough weather. Even on that day I expected some turbulence; but Slyne was still perhaps three miles off, and conditions for the moment looked fair and gentle. A long, low swell was running, with a stubborn power in it which was evident from the way the largest rollers rose up and dashed themselves down on shallow sub-surface skerries. To be caught in one of these sudden breaks – hundreds of tons of water dumping almost vertically onto hidden shelves of rock – could be fatal for a kayak, or indeed a currach; but their locations were generally obvious well in advance, and we habitually scanned the water ahead for the tell-tale sudden break, or white ring of foam which usually gave them away. But not all the sea's phenomena can be explained so easily. Just as the smallest crystal in a band of rock has behind it the full weight of all geology, sometimes a single coastal wave seems driven by all the force of the Seven Seas, and what happened next would have required an hydrographer's long and complicated equation. It defied all the conditions that we had so carefully been assessing in advance. It was what the old sailors called a 'widow-maker' – a rogue wave.

We both watched a series of swells advance and rear up as they approached a shallow submarine reef to seaward of the kayaks.

Each in turn shelved neatly, presented a smooth, angled front face, then folded forward in a long rush of gentle surf. The surf looked quite manageable, and as it ran for a long distance in our direction of travel, we decided to go for it, to hop onto one of those waves and hitch a free ride towards Slyne Head. There seemed nothing unusual or threatening in those waves at all.

In the still period between the passing of one swell and the arrival of the next, we paddled quickly into the area above the submerged reef where the wave-break would begin. But even before we could position the kayaks we began to feel that the next wave would be no ordinary one. All the angles suddenly changed. The reef lost its protective blanket of water, as all the sea around was sucked into one rapidly accumulating wave. Even as we turned and paddled for our lives, it seemed that the water on which we moved was being drawn into the body of the breaker, which continued to grow and build. Seconds later the wave was already towering above us. The angle of the face was so steep that we knew it must collapse like a damburst; at that moment it looked set to destroy us both. I glanced at Dougie, who was already sprinting towards the right shoulder of the curling monster, paddles spinning like rice flails; then I sped in the opposite direction, hoping to reach the smooth left shoulder before the wave-crest broke.

As soon as my bow gained the crest of the wave, I surged skyward at an almost vertical angle, then came crashing down like a pole vaulter, on the safe side of the freak breaker. But Dougie, fifteen yards away, was now hidden within the curling tube of the wave face, and I knew then he wouldn't make it. Just at the moment that his painted bow came clear, the wave crest broke in an avalanche of heavy water, and the whole kayak disappeared downwards and backwards into the body of the wave. With a sound like a block of flats collapsing, the main body of the wave erupted, and tumbling furiously, swept towards Slyne Head. Long seconds passed before I caught sight of Dougie's upturned hull. It was fifty yards away, surrounded by foaming white water and still moving at speed. As I headed towards it I saw Dougie attempt to roll, and fail. A second attempt also failed, and by the time I had reached the spot, he was out of the kayak and swimming. He grabbed the bow of his kayak in one hand, and the stern of mine in the other, and, while smaller waves continued to chop at us in the diminishing aftermath of the great breaker, I towed him quickly out of the main area of troubled water.

'Jesus! Have you ever seen the like of that before!' he gasped. 'I couldn't roll for the suction underwater – just seemed to pull me out of the boat!'

I glanced back at where the wave had been. 'It just came out of nowhere. And look now, it's almost flat bloody calm again!'

We were both stunned, and indeed during the time it took to pump Dougie's kayak dry, the area of broken water seemed to have just healed up completely. It was as if we'd been singled out by a completely maverick wave; perhaps a fourth Wave of Erin, *Tonn Dhuglass*, or Dougie's Wave, should have been added, there and then, to the ancient trio. But I couldn't help thinking back to the warning of the seal-grey woman in the mist.

It was Dougie who broke my superstitious gloom. From beneath his kayak he produced his paddle, snapped in half along one blade by his efforts to roll.

'Not your day really, is it?' I said, laughing loudly. 'There's a spare one on my back deck.'

'You may well laugh,' said Dougie, grinning, 'but that was one of *your* brand new paddles from Edinburgh!'

~ ~ ~

At Slyne Head we had an assisted passage from Shannon into Rockall. The breakers were hammering furiously at the rocks with the force of a four knot tide behind them, and the sea hurried and surged through the passages between the islands. Trails of deep foam and a haze of airborne water particles gave an unreal quality to the chain of broken land that culminates in Slyne Head itself. We pressed our way through Cromwell's Sound, just inside Chapel

Island, watching as idyllic beaches slid quickly past. It was a rough passage following the north-flowing tide, and I could immediately appreciate why so many people in the past few weeks had warned me about the dangers of this headland. With its combination of shallows, reefs and tides, it would take only a moderate wind from the wrong direction to render this area entirely unnavigable in a small boat, and equally treacherous for a larger one.

Beyond Slyne Head a sea-fret descended once more, although it was possible to see vague shapes occasionally amid the haze. We headed north along a coast fragmented with many small islands, taking regular bearings on the furthest, highest of these. From our left came the long Atlantic swell, heaving slowly out of the mist, then disappearing, wave after wave, towards the Connemara shore. To our right, one of Ireland's most beautiful seascapes, the Twelve Pins mountain range sweeping down to a fringe of islets, bays and beaches, lay tantalisingly hidden from view. Not far from here, in 1919, perhaps in very similar conditions, Alcock and Brown crash-landed triumphantly in an Irish bog at the end of the first ever transatlantic flight. Even with company, an hour in the mist, just paddling on a fixed bearing, seems an agonisingly long time; and it took over two hours to reach our marker, Cruagh Island, on which we'd promised ourselves a break. Then, finding nowhere to land on Cruagh, we had to paddle a further hour before stopping, for what seemed a very well-earned break, on the Cleggan peninsula.

The afternoon sun was now beginning to chase off the sea mist, and from a high point of land we could see our day's destination; floating lazily across four miles of sea was Inishbofin, 'the island of the white cow'. Many years ago, the island was enchanted, uninhabited, and perpetually hidden in a dense, cold mist. But one day two fishermen, lost in a fog at sea, came upon the island, landed their boat and made a fire to warm themselves. This fire broke the spell that had been on the island; the mist lifted, and they found themselves on a shingle beach near a little lake, on the north side of the island. After some time they became aware of an old woman driving a beautiful white cow down to the lake. When the cow reached the lake she struck it and it became a rock. The horrified fishermen, certain that she must be a witch, picked up sticks and tried to drive her away; and immediately they too became rocks. These rocks are still prominent on the island today, and it is from the large white one that the island takes its name. The story may be little more than a picturesque way of explaining some of the island's most prominent features, but when I first heard it I was immediately struck by the images of the island lost in the mist, and of the mysterious old woman, both of which had already found counterparts in my own brief experience of Connemara. The Irish coast seemed to have an uncanny ability to blur the distinction between reality and myth.

~ ~ ~

At early evening, having covered about sixteen miles since our morning mishap, we arrived at Inishbofin. Squeezing inside Port Island beneath the ruins of Bosco's Castle, superbly perched on the seaward promontory, we coasted into 'Bofin harbour, a peaceful natural inlet with a colourful and turbulent history. The little ferry from Cleggan was unhurriedly loading daytrippers for the journey back to the mainland. It bobbed at its mooring line and its reflection wobbled in ripples of its own making. A warm and languid calm had descended on 'Bofin harbour, and it was hard to imagine the very different scenes which had been enacted here in centuries past. In the fourteenth century the powerful O'Malley clan fortified the inlet, having captured the island from the O'Flahertys. Later it became a stronghold and hideaway for generations of smugglers and pirates. Bosco himself was a Spanish pirate of the seventeenth century who kept enemy ships from the inlet by stretching a strong chain across the harbour mouth. Later still his fortifications were used as a garrison for Cromwell's troops, and a grim prison for outlawed Irish priests and monks awaiting deportation.

We made camp on the beach beneath Bosco's Castle, swam in the harbour and, though the weather had turned drizzly, cooked kippers and potatoes on a driftwood fire. As darkness fell we paddled the kayaks across the harbour to the 'Bofin pub. One islander described how, as a child, he had lived on Inishshark, the small island next to Inishbofin. When he was evacuated to 'Bofin in 1960, it had seemed like moving to the mainland, what with the tracks, and the harbour, and the occasional ferry bringing visitors.

'What I remember best were the basking sharks,' he said. *'Muldoon,* we called them. They used to come in the summer months; some of them would be forty foot or more. Oh my! You had to be careful not to startle them if you were out in a currach!' he chuckled as the pictures became clearer. 'And there were the smells of autumn, and the ripe meadows ready for cutting, smelling of bees. The corncrake was noisy in those days: *crrk, crrk, crrk,* she went as the scythe went nearer to her nest.'

The corncrake, he said, had become scarce since tractors came to the islands. But I knew that, on a European scale, Inishbofin was still one of the corncrake's main strongholds. The hapless corncrake has suffered one of the most rapid and dramatic declines of any British bird. They were always furtive and elusive birds, but until relatively recently their distinctive rasping call was still a familiar feature of summer evenings all over the British Isles. Sadly, they failed to compete with modern, mechanised, intensive-farming developments, and are now found only on the remoter Hebridean isles of Scotland, and in parts of Ireland, where the mixture of hay, rushes and rough meadow boundaries, and the survival of less intensive harvesting methods, allow sanctuaries for this shy bird. Several of the Irish islands, still retaining traditional farming methods, and untouched by chemical sprays, have now become rare havens for wildflowers and bird species, such as the corncrake and the chough, which were once much more widespread, and it is with islands such as 'Bofin that hopes for the survival and eventual expansion of these species must lie.

Alone at the bar one man drank heavily, trembling violently, and ashen faced. He introduced himself as Leo, and told us how he had just that very evening had a terrible experience with his dog.

'He has the devil in him. I've known it for a long time now. That's why I had to drown him. Do you know how I did it?' he asked, knocking back another whisky. 'Well, I took a stone from the wall, beneath my bed, and tied it to his neck with a rope. Then at high tide there I put him off the pier. And wouldn't you think that would be the end of my troubles? But no ...' he paused for a sip, with all the dramatic art of the natural storyteller, '... I stopped in here for a drop – just the one – and when I got home the blasted dog was in front of the fire. But worse than that–' he rose to his feet with fear in his eyes, and said slowly, 'the stone was back in the wall!'

At midnight we left the little huddle of life and stories on the edge of the dark island, and fumbled in the black of night to find the kayaks. No sooner had we eased ourselves into the boats and pushed off from the shore than the water around us lit up with a green glow. Each paddle stroke brought a shower of phosphorescence, and the kayaks produced twin trails of fading ghostly green as we crossed the midnight water of the bay.

~ ~ ~

Over breakfast next morning we noticed on the map that Inishbofin, Inishturk, Clare Island and Achill are almost equally spaced out like stepping stones over which a giant could walk, dryshod, on a short-cut route between Connemara and county Mayo. A kayak following the same route would have a handy stopping point roughly every eight miles, thereby allowing a decent rest and snack every two hours. What's more, we realised, since each of the islands has its own little harbour and pub, we could have a pint of stout at each as an incentive to go on. What better way to spend Dougie's last day in Ireland in style. We had just devised the ultimate in direct-route, island-hopping, trans-county pub crawls!

After a brief bout of heavy rain we left the island of the white cow, coming out by Lyon Head and bearing north-northeast for the eastern corner of Inishturk. In contrast to the previous day a breeze kept the patchy cloud cover moving along at speed, dappling the water all around with alternate brightness and roving shadow. Oily colours spread over the shining surface of a sea which seemed to invite endless travel in a small boat. On the mainland coast the mountains and deep glens of Mweelrea and the Maumturks hinted at spectacular beauty, but remained shrouded in the more stubborn of the morning's clouds. The tide was running north with us, pushing up a swell which was not quite steep enough to surf on, but fast enough to make progress fairly rapid and easy. For the first time in days we were coasting. Well within two hours, we rounded Gabnagawny Point on the turtleback island of Inishturk, stopped to explore a long sea cave by torchlight, then paddled on into the sunny harbour at low tide. The pub on 'Turk was a small room in a house above the harbour, with its walls hung with recipes for champ, boxty and Irish stew. The barmaid had been out feeding some donkeys, but saw us coming up from the harbour, and already had two glasses of stout half-filled for us.

'Irish telepathy?' I asked.

'Well, you know, very few boats stop at the harbour that don't come up here. Besides, you looked very thirsty coming out of them canoes, I thought.'

'You're right there,' said Dougie. 'But how did you know we would drink Guinness?'

'Easy,' she laughed, topping up the glasses. 'It's all we've got, until the boat comes tomorrow anyway. You know, in the Republic of Cameroon they say it's an aphrodisiac, and the barmaids wear green plastic harps in their hair.'

'Might be a good place for the next trip,' said Dougie, grinning. *'Sláinte!'*

We signed the Inishturk visitor book with a cartoon sketch of two kayaks in a pint glass; then, among dogs playing and donkeys braying, we left 'Turk harbour bound for the distant double mound of Clare Island. A further two hours of paddling, during which the sun broke through the clouds and reflected strongly off the water, took us northeast until we could see the assortment of a hundred drowned drumlins deep down in Clew Bay. It was thirsty work, and the sea seemed to become sticky as we closed the final two miles towards the island. At last the beautiful harbour opened before us, washed in a range of paintbox blues, still and peaceful in the late afternoon sun. The island pubs are easy enough to locate by the mound of empty barrels, crates and bottles which accumulate outside the back door, waiting to be off-loaded, one far distant day, by boat. Dougie returned with two foaming pints and a couple of cheeseburgers, and we sat on the harbour sipping stout, absorbing the island scene. Twelve miles away on the mainland, across an inky blue sea, the peak of Mweelrea pushed its head above a thin layer of cloud and gazed down at the three islands at its foot. *'Sláinte!'*

At Clare pier the island ferry was loading up with mail, sheep, and backpackers. A small fishing boat chugged into the other side of the pier, and immediately, like a stretch limousine in a gangster movie, a black London taxi cab cruised down the winding island track and drew to a halt by the boat. Two fishermen piled armloads of nets, floats, bait baskets and two crates of fish into the back, and crammed themselves into the front seats. The driver then lifted the bonnet, hot-wired the engine, and they roared sedately back over the island and out of sight.

On the promontory by the harbour stands the ruined castle of Grace O'Malley, or *Granuaille*, the indomitable sixteenth-century pirate queen, scourge of the English fleet. As with so many of Ireland's historic characters, it is difficult to separate the facts from the legends that have grown up around her life. At the very least she was an unusually courageous woman, who largely personified the O'Malley motto 'Invincible on land and sea'. She rose above her male contemporaries to become chieftain of the O'Malleys, and commander of a powerful fleet of fighting and trading ships, with which she dominated the waters of western Ireland for many years. On land, she built, captured and defended castles throughout Connaught, and was even a feared cattle rustler.

Indomitable is the word invoked by the many stories of Grace

O'Malley of Clare Island. One popular account tells of how she gave birth to her son Tibbot-na-Long, 'Theobald of the Long Ships', on board one of her trading ships while at sea. The following day, as Grace rested and recovered below decks, the ship was attacked and almost overcome by Turkish pirates. Seeing that her men were losing badly and in need of leadership, Grace leapt half-clad from her maternity bed and burst on deck screaming at her crew to fight harder, and blasting bewildered Turks off the ship with a blunderbuss. Inspired by her spirit the crew fought with extra vigour and finally repelled the Turkish attack, while Granuaille shook off the role of warrior queen and returned below decks to nurse the baby.

Another story illustrated the strange mixture of tenderness and ruthlessness, nurse and Amazon, that seems to have existed in Granuaille. It was on a fierce and stormy St Brigid's Day, the first of February, that Grace and her followers abandoned their pilgrimage to a holy well on Clare in order to loot and salvage goods from a foreign ship which had been blown onto the rocks of nearby Achill Island. When they reached the wreck it seemed that all its crew had been drowned, and Grace's men busied themselves by filling their boats with loot. Suddenly Grace noticed a young man washed up on the rocks and barely alive. She rescued him, placed him in her boat and took him back to Clare where she nursed him gradually back to health. By the time he had fully recovered Grace and the young foreigner had fallen in love, and so he remained with her on the island.

However, while out hunting alone one day the young stranger was set upon and killed by members of the rival MacMahon clan. Although grief-stricken, Grace immediately vowed revenge on his murderers. She hunted them down, destroyed their boats so that they couldn't escape, and slaughtered the men responsible for the death of her beloved. Not content with that, she then set sail for the MacMahon stronghold, the castle of Doona in Blacksod Bay. She attacked the castle, expelled its occupants and replaced them with her own loyal O'Malleys, underlining her reputation as a woman not to be crossed, and earning for herself the name the 'Dark Lady of Doona'.

Granuaille lived in an age when Ireland, in the grip of great political and social changes, was both ripe for, and vulnerable to, piracy on a grand scale. The waters south of Connaught were the route taken by Spanish galleons carrying wine and other precious cargoes to the English-dominated merchant town of Galway; and throughout her reign, Granuaille's chief attacks were on the Elizabethan merchant ships, and the Spanish ships which supplied the strongholds of the colonial power. Despite the English government proclaiming her an outlaw, and offering the sum of five hundred pounds for her capture, she lived a full life, raised four children, and died in her seventies. It is even thought that in 1593 she managed to arrange an audience with Queen Elizabeth I in London, having travelled there by boat at the age of sixty-three, dodging the English patrol ships who would have dearly loved to capture the notorious pirate queen. Local legend says she is buried in an abbey on Clare Island, and that her influence is still felt in unusual ways. In recent years, for instance, a Scottish bone-collector, raiding the area for minor treasures, met with a strange death. He is said to have choked on one of Granuaille's molars, which was inside a turnip!

~ ~ ~

Well-fuelled by cheeseburgers and stout, we took to the water for a third time that day, pointing our bows northwards for Achill Island and the Corraun peninsula. Across five miles of open water, the evening scene was one of incredible peace and beauty. Achill, Ireland's largest island lies so close to the mainland that the appearance from the south was of an almost continuous west-running mountain ridge of over two thousand feet, dropping precipitously to the sea along most of its twenty-five mile length. From a vantage point a little further west we would have seen the distinct and separate peaks of Glennamong, Corraun, Knockmore,

Slievemore and the final Atlantic buttress of Croaghaun. From the south, were it not for the deck map, we would never have guessed the existence of Achill Sound at all. Its opening measures less than a fifth of a mile, is sandwiched between two steep hills, and is further blocked from view by the island of Achillbeg. There is no sign of the Sound until one is virtually upon it.

Through this narrow passage funnels a strong tide, running at up to five knots, doing its utmost to even the water pressure on either side of Achill Island. We knew we could not have paddled against the Achill tide, and had timed our arrival to coincide with the stream running up the Sound. Already, as we squeezed the kayaks between Achillbeg and Corraun, we could feel, and indeed see, the steady gathering and quickening of waters, bending powerfully and insistently around an S-bend, pouring like a river through the narrows, northward with the flood tide. The effect of adding paddle power to the strength of the tide was to increase our speed to about eight knots, and our passage up the narrow Achill Sound, emphasised by the shallow, sandy bottom was suddenly like cruising along a canal in a speedboat. Little clusters of houses lined the Sound on both sides, and the homely smell of turf fires, a boggish incense trapped between the mountains in the still of the evening, drifted over the water.

It took less than half-an-hour to reach the Achill bridge which spans the Sound at its narrowest point. Here the tides change, and beneath the bridge we had a head-on encounter with the south-flowing stream, filling the Sound from the north. We fought an angry meeting of eddies, past a mesh of scaffolding and under the bridge, to haul out beneath a scruffy warehouse building, just as a grey drizzle began to replace the evening light. *West Mayo Fisherman's Cooperative*, announced the building's signboard, significant in that it meant our stepping stone route was now complete; we had reached county Mayo. The trans-county island pub crawl, however, had not yet been fully consummated, and for a brief moment seemed in danger of failing at the last post. There were three weddings happening on Achill that evening, and the village of Achillbeg had all but closed down. Lavelles' pub had no food, and no barstaff, but kindly agreed to give us what they had left. So it was with a loaf of bread, a lump of cheddar, a pot of margarine and two final pints of stout that the day was saved. We retired to camp, content, in the dampness that was Achill, county Mayo. *'Sláinte!'*

CHAPTER 15

Friendly Fire

Let the images
go bright and fast
and the concepts be extravagant
(wild host to erratic guest)
that's the only way
to say the coast
all the irregular reality
of the rocky sea-washed west

from 'Scotia Deserta', Kenneth White

It was obvious from the strength of the tides in Achill Sound that progress through the narrower channels off the west Mayo coast would depend on careful timing of the flood and ebb streams. If I could just get out of Achill Sound on the last half of an ebb, for example, I could carve round Achill's northeast corner during slack water, then pick up the flood tide running north into Blacksod Bay towards Belmullet. On the other hand, if I timed it wrongly I was likely to waste a full day's effort on very little mileage at all.

While I waited for the tide to turn, Dougie unpacked his kayak, ready to head home to Edinburgh. It was like a scene from *Aladdin* as I swapped my rusty camp stove for Dougie's shiny new one, my leaky spraydeck for his tight neoprene version, and discarded my mouldy towel in favour of a fresh unused one. Between showers, I packed all the supplies the kayak could carry; it would be my last chance to stock up before the journey's end, perhaps three weeks away. At mid-ebb I was off, sliding quickly down Achill Sound with the assistance of both wind and tide. High above me the grey overcast morning was giving way to a bright afternoon of blue skies and fast, wind-rushed cloud. Four miles on I fired through the Bull's Mouth channel inside Inishbiggle like a racing kayak in a river rapid, and had to bank tightly out of the main flow to beach for a snack at Dooniver Strand. With my back propped against the kayak, I sat in weak sunshine for half-an-hour, eating chocolate and watching a large shaggy otter hunting and crunching crabs among the low ebb seaweeds of the channel.

Setting off again I took a direct bearing for Kinrovar Point, six miles north across the bay, and gradually pulled away from the Achill coast. Steadily the western islands of Duvillaun, and the abandoned whaling islands of Inishkea, came into view. All were white-fringed, with a strong swell breaking on their exposed western coasts, and I knew that my passage across and well into Blacksod Bay would lie exposed to the same westerly swell. The shelter afforded by Achill Island soon ran out, and the waves rolled into the great funnel of Blacksod Bay, giving *Sola* an unnerving lift on the port beam every few seconds.

Belmullet is a remote and curious peninsula. From Duvillaun in the south, to Erris Head in the north, it fronts the Atlantic over a distance of fifteen miles. Yet it is linked to the rest of the world across a tiny neck of land less than a quarter of a mile in width. Even this neck is severed by the Belmullet canal, which once gave access between Blacksod and Broadhaven bays for the coastal trading vessels of last century. Today commercial traffic goes mainly by road, and the Belmullet canal is used only by a few local inshore fishing boats.

As I entered Blacksod Bay, the flood tide had started, adding extra impetus to the Atlantic swells which continued to assault the west-facing mainland coast. Beaches high-banked with shingle suggested that this was a coast of frequent storms, and even in those relatively mild conditions I had to travel well out from the shore. Great rumbling leviathans of marine swell began their final break almost half-a-mile from shore, lifting steeply and gathering momentum as their crests gradually over-toppled their forward flanks, before collapsing in dramatic chaos on the shingle-banks, and sucking back with some of the most unnerving cases of undertow I've ever seen. Any small boat foolish enough to be surprised within the catchment of one of these waves, would very quickly have become an even smaller boat. I paddled carefully north, well beyond their reach until the protective western flank of Belmullet began to block the worst of the swell from Blacksod Bay.

Although I could have ridden the northgoing tide for a further two hours, I decided to beach at Kanfinalta, a promontory that reaches almost into the centre of Blacksod Bay, and to enjoy the evening from its dramatic position. South of Blacksod, the entire scene was dominated by the pure conical shape of Slievemore on Achill, which seemed to rise straight from the sea. Local people say that from its summit, on a clear day, 'you can damn near see the skyscrapers of New York'; but what was even more impressive on that August evening was the way the westering sun struck the mountain's wet screes of quartz and mica, making it shine with the brilliance of an iceberg, and lending a magical, mystical aura to the whole scene. These were the waters to which, according to legend, Fionnuala and her three brothers, children of the sea-god Lír, were banished by a jealous stepmother. They were turned into swans and condemned to live for three hundred years in the cold northern waters of Lake Derravaragh, three hundred years in the stormy Sea of Moyle between Ireland and Scotland, and three hundred years on Inishglora off Mayo on the Atlantic. The swans were cursed with voices so lovely that they would be constantly hunted as treasures for the sweetness of their songs. They would regain human shape and voices each year for only one day, when the light and darkness were equal. But on that day, if their feet should touch earth, they would instantly die. Fionnuala feared for the lives of herself and her brothers, but each year they were helped by a friendly whale, and miraculously they all survived. At the end of nine hundred years, the Children of Lír returned home, only to find that Lír had long since died, and not a stone was left of their homes. When they alighted on the ground, their feathers fell away and they regained human shape once more; not as the young children they had been, Fionnuala was an old, old woman and her brothers, three very frail old men. In the lee of shining Slievemore, nothing seemed too fantastic to believe.

I soon discovered the origin of the bay's curious name, for the greater part of the mainland which protrudes into its easterly waters is black bog. Cliffs and overhangs of rich dark peat, exposed where the sea has eaten into their soft flesh, extend for miles along this coast. After rain the streams flow rich and brown, but the outer crust of the black cliffs is wind-dried, hard as wood and superb for burning.

To me the concept of 'friendly fire' is something quite different from the term used by the British army. Fires of peat or driftwood were always an important morale boost; a focal point for a group travelling together, or a substitute for company on a solo journey. Fires were the scourge of the midge, the driers of clothes, burners of litter, savers of fuel. But also far more than that. Sometimes I almost felt that the entire logistical pantechnicon of setting out on an extended kayak expedition was little more than a vehicle for ensuring that I could have as many rip-roaring red-hearted fires as possible, on the remotest and most god-forsaken beaches of the world – a sort of sacred quest for the ultimate barbecue.

Simply by collecting the sods which had fallen most recently from a short stretch of bog-cliff, I soon had enough for a big fire on the shingle beach. Later, using an old biscuit tin from the beach, I made an oven by placing smouldering sods of turf around and on top of it, and cooked potatoes and ham, baked onions and honey-filled apples. The turf fire threw off a fierce but quiet heat, quite unlike the crackling of driftwood, and gave off an intoxicating distinctive smoke which was far from unpleasant. I read by its glow, then slept alongside the fire despite a light drizzle, and in the morning it was still hot enough to cook breakfast on.

I was up at six-thirty, kettle placed on the peat embers while I packed the kayak; then, after a coffee and crispbread breakfast, I caught the last of the early north-going flood tide, with a wind behind it, all the way to Belmullet. It was a fast and steady ride through the short canal and into Broad Haven, where I found a slipway and hauled out for a second breakfast. The tide was now at high slack, but by the time I had made some minor repairs to *Sola*'s rudder, and dodged beneath an upturned boat for the duration of a heavy rainstorm, the tide was beginning to ebb from Belmullet. Out through the snaking narrows off the north of Belmullet, it wound and washed, southeast, east and finally north, slowing as it emptied into the deeper, wider basin of Broad Haven. At Broad Haven the southwest wind had been waiting. Harsh and strong and with a sting of autumn cold, it whipped up large waves along its path, while grey swathes of rain belted across the bay in succession, temporarily obscuring everything from sight as they passed. I pulled on my hood and, keeping my back to the squalls, battled across the bay. It was a wild, and often blind, four mile crossing. But the heavy rain kept the swell at a manageable level, and the wind pushed at my back as if on a small sail.

Benwee Head, the exposed ocean corner of Mayo was dramatic. The Atlantic seemed bigger, deeper, greener and wetter where it touched this corner of county Mayo than I'd ever seen it before. The rugged coast – almost a thousand feet high in places, fell directly to the water, and in the absence of a shelving shore the Rockall Atlantic arrived unannounced on Mayo's threshold in pure, dark, unbroken swells. Around rock stacks and through narrow passages they surged and, still having felt no bottom, flung themselves in desperation against the cliffs. And still they remained unbroken. Green hills of sea surged up the cliff-face, hung briefly in freeze-frame stillness, then fell downward and outward with massive momentum. All along the rocky edge of Benwee Head, the great swells rose and dipped, easily covering twenty feet of cliff with their brief passage. *Sola* soared and dived on their heaving backs. One moment I'd be at eye level with clumps of thrift, brine dripping from their bowed pink heads; then, after a sudden fall, which often left me tingling and breathless, I would be wallowing in the dark troughs beneath the shadowy peaks of neighbouring swells.

Between Kid Island and 'the Stags of Broad Haven', this coast is guarded by an Atlantic equivalent of the Chinese Emperor's 'Terracotta Warriors'. Rock stacks, tall and towering, squat and sturdy, surreal and beautiful, litter the passage, making it impossible to paddle a straight inshore route. Between the stacks, the sea was an exploding mass of ever-changing levels, but there was plenty of sea-space, even for much larger boats than *Sola*. The stacks, like the cliffs, had very few reefs and skerries among them; they were true deepwater pillars, looking more like anchored oil-rigs than coastal rock towers, and I regretted being unable to spare a hand for photography during the most dramatic sections of the headland. I forged on around some tricky minor bluffs and stacks, gripping tightly on the paddle as an outrigger, expecting to capsize and roll at any minute. Lashed by showers of rain, and muffled up in full hood and rain gear, I thought briefly how insane my passage would look to any observer. Just then I came upon a lobsterman among the stacks. With his boat leaned right over and his steering fixed, the boat chugged steadily along while he hauled in a string of pots. Suddenly he saw me, see-sawing along through the rain and swell, and moved to the stern to get a better look. He returned my wave of reassurance with a flamboyant, friendly salute, but forgot to stop his engine, and almost ran directly into a rock stack. At the last possible moment instinct warned him; he lunged toward the wheelhouse and jammed the boat into reverse, avoiding the stack, but fowling a string of tangled lobsterpots with his propeller.

With my mind full of needles and pinnacles, and the incredible lumpy motion still ingrained in my body, I reached a final little promontory which the map called 'Doonvinalla'. Beyond it, in a rare dip between two mountains, lay the narrow sheltered haven of Portacloy. At the head of the long cove was a fine sandy beach, but the full force of the wind funnelling in from Broad Haven

concentrated itself between the mountains, and thundered out to
sea at well over gale force; I headed in for the first available landing
at a little slipway. Two fishermen, working from the most
magnificent old patched currach I'd seen yet, waved me over. At
first they seemed to be holding on to a floating wooden box to stop
the currach being blown out to sea. But they explained it was a *potaí
stóir*, a floating, anchored wooden case, in which they kept the
lobsters alive until they had a batch worth sending to market. In a
dampened sack on the bottom of the currach, trapped crustaceans
moved and clicked their pincers in a strange castanet; however, it
was not lobsters but live crabs that they began to pull from the sack.

'Do you like crabs' claw?' asked one fisherman, methodically
twisting and snapping off the pincers from a series of crabs, each
one about the size of a side plate. Thus disarmed, the crabs were
then dropped into the wooden case to feed the hungry lobsters,
which in turn would eventually grace tables in Paris and Madrid.

'Real jetsetters, the Mayo lobsters,' said the fisherman with
some pride.

'Do you ever keep any for yourself?' I asked.

'Oh now, I've never tried one,' he replied with a frown,
spitting over the side of the currach. 'I wouldn't fancy such a quare
insect as a lobster.'

It may have been the most barren corner of the poorest
county of Ireland's most impoverished province, but that night
there was a simple richness in the air. I cooked up some rice in a
billy of seawater, and sat beneath a clear sky, happily cracking and
munching my way through a small mountain of Crabs' Claws
Mayo-nnaise. Perched on a mat in the shelter of a seeping peat-bog
ledge, I threw the empty shells into a stream, brown as stout, which
tumbled in waterfalls to the sea, just about where Rockall gives way
to Malin.

MALIN

Benwee Head to Larne

314 miles

MALIN

tonn tuim

Atlantic Ocean

North Channel

Mull of Kintyre
Torr Head
Fair Head
Rathlin I.
Benbane Head
Giant's Causeway
Portrush
Coleraine
Downhill
Ballycastle
Bushmills
Dunluce
Ballintoy
Cushendun
Cushendall
Carnlough
Larne
Belfast
Red Bay

ANTRIM
DERRY

Lough Neagh

NORTHERN IRELAND

0 5 10 15 20 25 miles

Inishowen Head
Culdaff
Malin
Lough Foyle
Derry
Inishowen Peninsula

Inishtrahull
Inishtrahull Sound
Malin Head
Inewton Bay
Dunaff Head
Lough Swilly
Fanad Head

Dunfanaghy
Sheep Haven
Horn Head
Brinlack
Gola I.
Gweedore
Bunbeg
The Rosses
Aranmore I.
Croby Head
Gweebarra Bay
Dawros Head
Sturrall Pt.
Glen Bay
Rossan Pt.
Slieve League
Muckros Head
St. John's Point
Inishmurray I.
Mullaghmore
Sligo Bay
Easky
Lenadoon Point
Killala Bay
Lackan Bay
Downpatrick Head
Doon Briste
Bunatrahir
Belderg
Benwee Head
Portacloy
Slieve Fyagh

DONEGAL
Derryveagh Mts.
Blue Stack Mts.
Donegal
Bundoran
SLIGO
Sligo
The Ox Mountains

Errigal
Muckish
Tory I.
Bloody Foreland
Slieve Tooey
Glencolmcille
Killybegs
Donegal Bay
McSwyne's Bay

CHAPTER 16

Under the Blanket Bog

*Promontories, forelands, capes, headlands, breakers, and shoals
are veritable constructions. The geological changes of the earth are
trifling compared with the vast changes of the ocean.*

The Toilers of the Sea, Victor Hugo

Malin is a county of Atlantic excesses; a sector of superlative
sea-coast features, where salt air and ocean-breakers sweep the
desolate beaches and coastal ranges with an almost obsessive
scouring vigour, and where the sea itself is perhaps best sketched in
epithets of landscape. It is by far the largest of Ireland's sea areas,
stretching from Benwee Head on the cliff-girt coast of north Mayo,
round the bold mountains of Donegal and the rocky marvels of
Antrim, to the Ards peninsula of county Down.

Western Malin, where counties Mayo and Donegal meet the
Atlantic, is mountain and ocean with a mere wedge of land in
between them. That land is empty and beautiful; or rather it is a
beautiful land which has been emptied, for in the first half of the
nineteenth century, when Ireland's population stood at some nine
million, west Donegal was a crowded and congested region. Along
its narrow, continuous ribbon of available land, there were over
four hundred people to the square mile: more than in many modern
inner-city tenement estates. In fact there can scarcely ever have
been another area of western Europe in which such a density of
rural population has been able to survive in such a climate, and on
such meagre agricultural resources. But survive they did. In those
days both the mountains and coast were exploited in ways now
virtually forgotten even by rural people. Cattle were moved

seasonally between low and high ground, using both sorts of pasture to full capacity without over-grazing either of them. Shellfish, edible seaweeds, sea birds and eggs were harvested. Kelp, thatch and turf were gathered, and seaweed fertiliser was spread on the fields. One of the most striking features in the entire littoral landscape of west Donegal is the massive stone walls around the tiny fields, built not primarily for shelter or enclosure, but simply to clear the land itself of stones. A farmer here had to be first and foremost a quarrier – and a manual quarrier at that – and second, a stonemason.

One-and-a-half centuries later, the west Malin coast is one of Europe's most sparsely populated areas; crowded only by the ghostly absence of a recently departed people, whose ruins and remains speckle the islands and coasts, valleys and mountainsides. It was not just the so-called Great Famine of 1845-49 which cleared the land, but the floodgates of emigration, opened wide during those years, have never since then been closed. Today Ireland's population is less than half of its pre-famine peak; and although tourism and European grant-aid have brought relative prosperity to many rural regions in recent years, it is quite possible that the coastal wastelands of the Atlantic edge might never again know human communities. All along this beautiful empty coastland, walls have fallen, homes have crumbled, soils are washing away, and lazybeds are returning to the bog. The only things that are booming are the breaking waves which echo through the deserted *clachans*; as the sun dips west at the end of a day, it lays lengthening shadows alongside mounds and memories on the lonely ground. The people of the Malin coast have gone.

~ ~ ~

Between Benwee Head and Killala Bay, a distance of twenty-five sea miles east to west, the county of north Mayo meets the sea in a dramatic rampart of almost unbroken cliffs. Only at four small bays – Portacloy, Porturlin, Belderg and Bunatrahir – does Mayo let down its guard. These rare havens, where winding roads end in stone slipways, and black currachs lie at rest, are also where the high boggy plateau drains seaward down fast-flowing peat-stained burns. The great bog of Mayo is a vast saucer of peatland and *lochan*: a hundred square miles of it, trapped between the Nephin Beg mountains to the south and west, and the peaks of Slieve Fyagh, Benmore and Maumakeogh to the north. No major roads traverse this area, and there is no settlement larger than a small village. Nor is it tourist country; visitors here are either dedicated anglers, seekers of solitude, or are just passing through on the way to somewhere else. A walker on the Nephin Beg range, or on the lonely beaches of Mayo would have a solitude more assured than in many of the remotest valleys of the Himalaya.

This was one of the areas worst hit in the famine. Mayo people died in their thousands from disease and starvation, since they were largely isolated from the scant aid that was available by poor roads and inadequate housing. At least half the population fled to go to Britain or America, and youngsters are still leaving the area today. Indeed it is hard, even for the dreamer and optimist, to see what they could possibly find to stay for, other than the infinite peace and beauty of those bogs, that lonely coast, and those interminable cliffs.

From sea level the cliffs of north Mayo are seen at their most dramatic. Waterfalls tumble from their hunched shoulders, often vapourising in freefall, almost a thousand feet to the sea below. Sea-caves riddle the basements and lower storeys, where the Atlantic has split and widened the faults in the rock, patiently whittling away the foundations of the edifice above. Some of these caves are dark closed tunnels; others lead into greater caverns and vaults; yet others have skylight blowholes, ceiling vents which open far inland, and perhaps a stream pouring onto a land-locked shingle beach, briefly illuminated in a shaft of sunshine. All along the cliffs my kayak traced the architecture of decay; a process so slow, so constant, as to be almost imperceptible on the timescale of human observation; and yet so dramatic in its unfolding stages that I hardly noticed the miles sliding by. Gradually I became lost in a reverie of time, sea and stone.

As I passed through caves and tunnels, and behind arches which had collapsed to leave queer-shaped rock pinnacles, almost as high as the cliffs behind them, the rock seemed ever less of a permanent structure, and more of a brief static moment in a drama whose ultimate end was complete destruction. *Solid as a what?* The Atlantic is a restless sculptor, always working, constantly exhibiting, yet never satisfied. Even the sea itself, so often the symbol of change and inconstancy, seemed to have more of a claim to permanence than these great cliffs. In places massive blocks of shattered stone, recently toppled from the upper sectors of the undercut cliffs, temporarily protected the base of the cliff from the ocean's direct assault. But already these great blocks were being ground together, hammered by wave-borne debris, shattered and gradually swept aside by tide and weather. Soon the next swathe of cliff would be exposed, undercut and toppled in turn, the process repeating its cycle *ad infinitum*.

I paddled on, watching the fingers of the Atlantic teasing incessantly at faults in the rock walls, in exactly the same way as I'd watched nervous drinkers toying with beermats. The usual result was an-ever diminishing beermat, a pile of debris in an ashtray, and an angry barmaid. The only difference was in timescale. My mind, loosened by the meditative rhythm of the paddles, happily skipped over millennia, considering the odds and reckoning the outcome of the land-sea battle. For if no other disaster obliterates the world first, then of all the elements it is surely water which will endure longest. Waves gnaw endlessly at the feet of great cliffs; ice cleaves slabs from the mountain; rivers scrape and transport the fabric of the land down to the sea; and the wind carries soil-dust to fall to the ocean's floor. Sun, wind, ice and rain; all are allies of the sea in the erosion of rock. What chance, I wondered, watching a cormorant open its wings to dry in the bright breeze, has the land in the long-term?

The average height of land above sea level, I knew, was about half a mile; while the average depth of the oceans is more than five times greater. Even the distance between the earth's highest point, Mount Everest, to the sea's deepest, the Pacific's Philippine Trench, is only about twelve miles. Then at each end of the Atlantic are vast additional quantities of water held, for the moment, in reserve. The Greenland ice cap alone is greater in bulk than all the land of Europe; and if it melted it would raise the seas of the world by some twenty-five feet. And what of the rest of the ice at both poles? If the fight went the full distance, the sea would win on points. On a global average, ten square miles of land are lost to the sea each year. The process of levelling the land, of redressing the debt due to gravity, which began as soon as the land was heaved upward, must surely end with only the ocean surviving; one great ocean, spread over everything, only inches deep across a landless globe. *Panthalassa.*

In a brief sheltered corner, where the sun broke warmly through the inshore haze of ozone and sea-spray, my wandering thoughts, like a flight of homing pigeons, came tumbling back to Malin, and north Mayo at sea level. Groups of solemn shags crowded onto ledges above the spray like disorderly skittles, or dark wine bottles after a party. Rock-pipits darted daintily around, picking tiny titbits from the sheltered faces of tidewashed rocks, and oystercatchers, 'sea-pies', piped noisily in rapid fly-past circuits above the breaking waves. When the mind has not quite fully returned from previewing the end of the world and the absolute impermanence of rock, the lives of these colourful bundles of feathers suddenly seem quite incredibly short, frantic and touching.

My own life too, I reckoned, was about to become short and frantic if I didn't get a move on along the Mayo cliffs. With yet another gale forecast in operation, I sneaked what little progress I could. The wind came from the southwest, so that the kayak, close inshore beneath the mighty cliffs, travelled for the most part along a ribbon of sheltered water. Only the occasional squall, funnelling down the cliff valleys or raging, unannounced, from the clifftop itself, gave any cause for alarm. One particularly vicious downblast managed to catch me completely unawares, almost whisking my paddle away as it passed over the kayak with a force like a helicopter's rotor-blades. I spent a few shaken and unsteady moments while it lasted, then quickly tied the paddle to my wrist and paddled on, a little less complacent.

~ ~ ~

That evening I reached Belderg, unwilling to risk the next hop – seven miles without a landing – with the wind continuing to strengthen. I hauled the kayak out on a wide, steep shingle beach, and built a big fire of driftwood. Within minutes the smoke of my fire attracted a couple of visitors to my camp. The two girls, both in their early twenties, windswept and weatherbeaten, glowed with a kind of reckless and infectious enthusiasm which burst out all over in freckles, constant smiles and an inability to sit still. Their quick teasing banter was, to me, like suddenly hearing an old favourite tune, and soon they had me laughing at the slightest comment.

'Well, look here, it must be Robinson Crusoe!' said the one with 'Deirdre' written on a suncap placed backwards over an auburn ponytail.

'Or the Man from Atlantis,' said the other, dark-haired Niamh, brushing deposits of sea-salt off my forearm, then licking her fingers.

'And you must be the Belderg Banshees Express Meal Service,' I said, pointing to a large bag of juicy brambles they were carrying.

'Get away with you! If you hadn't spent so long making that smoky wee fire you could have picked some of your own.'

'Look at this, Dee,' said Niamh, picking up my food ration packet. 'He spends all day right out in the sea there, with all them fish and things, and here he's got Dehydrated Prawn Paella for his tay!'

They explained that they were archaeology students from a

Dublin University study group based in a cottage near the beach,
and had been out collecting the brambles for the evening meal.

'No!' said Dee, 'for the last time, you're not getting any!'

'Any *brambles*, she means!' added Niamh, collapsing with
giggles. 'But if you're house-trained you can join us all for the meal;
OK?'

'Up yonder at the cottage in about an hour. An' don't forget
your tie!' laughed Dee.

They didn't have to ask twice and, knotting a coloured
bandana round my neck as a token gesture, I quickly changed into
my cleanest dirty T-shirt for the occasion.

'Look what Dee found on the beach!' said Niamh, presenting
me like a piece of driftwood to the crowd of cheerful faces in the
cottage. 'This is Brian. He's been floating round Ireland in the sea;
he's collecting eyeballs, and he tastes of salt!'

The meal brought back countless memories of student flats
and conservation work-parties in Scotland. A mixed group of ten
students and one professor sat around a candlelit table, with huge
anonymous bowls of a vaguely curried mixture. The food itself was
a typical team production, a semi-intentional, semi-experimental
product of well-meaning individuals with widely divergent ideas, let
loose on a catering-sized jar of curry paste and a large box of
assorted vegetables. But it was warm, filling and plentiful; and
besides, everyone was more interested in discussing the progress of
their projects than in analysing the contents of their bowls. It was
like a meeting of the Peatbog Enthusiasts Club, and the dinner
conversation revolved entirely around bogs: *bog-bones, bog-stones,
bog-plants, big bogs, small bogs, bog-trotting, bog-swotting, a rare-bog, a
rattlin'-bog.*

Everyone had a dose of peat-fever, having been working for
days on the excavation of an ancient system of enclosed farmlands,
right there on the high boggy plateau of north Mayo, at a place
called the Céide Fields. Stone walls had been uncovered beneath
deep peat layers, initially by local people digging turf for fuel. Teams

of archaeologists had moved in, removing more peat to reveal full walls, ridges and field systems once used for growing cereal and fodder crops. Successive excavations had already found a house, a garden enclosure, and even Neolithic tombs, all preserved by the ubiquitous Céide blanket bog.

'So there were enclosed farms here before the bog formed?' I suggested.

'Well, yes, indeed,' said the professor. 'We think *well* before the bogs came. We know that the peat bogs began to form some three-and-a-half thousand years ago; so our farms are at least as old as that. But we now think that these walls represent the agriculture of the late Stone Age, perhaps around 3000BC, which makes them almost five thousand years old.' He leaned forward, and I could see why his enthusiasm had rubbed off on the students. 'It is just possible that the Irish were farming before anyone else in the *entire* world!'

'It must make life a bit difficult when a bog descends on your farm,' I said.

'Perhaps so, but at least the Neolithic farmers didn't have to put up with EC bureaucracy and this Common Agricultural Policy nonsense!' joked the professor.

'And why did the peat start to take over, anyway?' I asked.

'Good question; here, somebody fill this man's glass!' he said. 'Indeed nobody really knows why. And the thing is, it's still expanding. Now, Gerry here is a sedimentologist.'

Gerry, a big bruiser from Wicklow, looked like he'd be more at home playing rugby for Ireland than analysing the finer points of bog academics; nevertheless he quickly became lyrical about his own subject. 'It's the most amazing substance, you know – quite unique. A paradox. A sediment, right, which is made up of living plants growing on the accumulated remains of their dead ancestors. Imagine if, every time the people in a tenement flat died, another flat was just built up on top! Think about that; peat is at the same time both dead and alive; neither exactly geology nor botany, but both! Turf is the indigenous *solid* fuel of the Celtic nations; and yet in its natural state it's over ninety percent water by volume.'

'In Scotland', I told him, 'peat is supposed to warm you four times over: first when you cut it; secondly when you stack it; third when you transport and re-stack it; and fourth when you burn it.'

'Ha! that's a good one for sure. I should remember that. But sure in Ireland we even make *electricity* from the stuff. There's a power station at Bellacorick, just up the way there, and another at Ferbane, county Offaly, that are both fired up entirely by turf.'

Niamh came round the table and squeezed in between me and Gerry, lighting up a cigarette. Even livelier now after a couple of glasses of wine, she explained that her own special subject was mineral deposits from the sea. She suggested that she could probably write a whole project on the sea salt I'd gathered coming round the Irish coast. Seeing a peaty glow in her eye that was more than purely academic, I smiled and reminded her that I had a fair bit more salt to gather yet, and quickly moved the conversation onto a less intimate track. 'So where does all the salt come from in the first place?'

'Well, they used to think it came from rivers, you know, run-off from the land an' that. But that wouldn't account for a fraction of it. We think now that it comes from deep inside the earth, y'know? From volcanic upheavals beneath the sea. *Whooomph!*' she demonstrated, with a toss of black hair.

'Anyway,' she said, leaning back with a smile which seemed to take in the whole room, 'if all the oceans dried up, there would be enough salt, right, to build a wall one hundred yards high and one mile thick which would run right around the world at the equator! How's that for useless facts?' she giggled. At that point, to a large cheer, pudding arrived. A huge black steaming mound, it looked at first like something excavated from the Céide bog itself, but turned out to be an absolutely delicious baked alaska with wild bramble topping.

'Wow! There must be about five pounds of brambles on that,' I said, truly impressed.

'Well now,' said Niamh, winking, 'but there wouldn't have been if we'd let you get at Deirdre on the beach, would there!' And for once I was stumped for an answer.

~ ~ ~

Two lobstermen were on the beach at seven in the morning as I squeezed the last wayward items into *Sola*'s hatches and waited for the tide to creep up the shingle storm-beach.

'There's a bad forecast out,' said one. 'They're giving a force six to seven westerly, moving nor'west and strengthening to gale. You'd be right enough with the westerlies, I'd say, but this is the devil's coast in a nor'wester. There's nowhere for the sea to go, you see, and nowhere for a boat to land either; all cliffs and skerries it is 'til Bunatra'r, then the same again beyond.'

'And watch out for the *ground sea* below Downpatrick,' said the second man. 'By Christ I wouldn't even take a trawler round that one. Man, I remember one time ...'

Thanking them quickly for their advice, I took to the water before I got any more local horror stories. It would be so easy to collect everyone's worst experiences, and then spend the rest of the day fretting over them in the tent. For the moment the wind was strong, but still in the southwest. I'd have a little shelter from the high plateau for a short time yet, and it was important to make some progress while that shelter lasted.

Grey lumps of rolling cloud appeared from behind the high cliff-line, dropping heavy rain patterns on the water, flecking the sea with silver balls of rain which danced like mercury before merging with the brine. The whole surface would darken and flatten out as the rain shadows passed away off into the northwest. But far worse than either the general wind, or the rain showers, were the squalls. Travelling at more than forty knots, these could approach from almost any direction, at any time, and were always vigorously aggressive. From ahead they were announced by a distinctly ruffled patch of water, exactly like that beneath a helicopter, and moving just as fast. Usually I had time just to lean forward, clasp the paddle hard and sit tight until the squall passed, often losing ground backwards in the process. If they arrived from either side, I found that I could keep paddling as long as I threw my weight right over into the direction of the wind. But they arrived with most dramatic impact when coming unannounced from the rear. Like boisterous young bullocks they shunted the kayak suddenly forward, and would have carried off the paddles easily had I not strapped them to my wrists.

On the whole, despite the frequent squalls and showers, I was travelling fairly rapidly along another coast of dramatic cliffs and stacks, a paradise of a hundred rock forms. One of the great limitations of the Ordnance Survey maps was their inability to represent the superb cliffscapes that comprise so much of the Irish coast. Here was an intricate, pristine vertical landscape, unrepresented on plan-view maps, literally overlooked by aerial photography or satellite imaging, and seen by almost nobody other than a few lobster fishermen from one year's end to the next. Ireland's last resident sea eagle was shot along these cliffs in 1935, but the habitat itself remained, of all natural ecosystems, one of the least affected by man's activities over the years. An extensive sea eagle reintroduction programme has been underway among the neighbouring Scottish Hebrides for several years now, and it seemed possible that, given a little protection, and a lot of luck these magnificent birds might yet return of their own accord to the Mayo cliffs.

Between the squalls the day was warmer and brighter than recent days. After six spectacular miles I passed the first possible landing place, Bunatrahir, and turned my bow towards Downpatrick Head, which beckoned from four miles across the bay. As I closed in on the headland I could see Doon Briste, 'the broken fort', one of the tallest sea stacks in Europe, standing only a hundred yards from the main headland. Legend has it that a local farmer couldn't agree on how to divide his land between his two sons, only one of whom was a Christian; so St Patrick came along and, with a bolt of lightning, literally split the land for him, giving the isolated stack of Doon Briste to the unbeliever. Perhaps it was nothing more than a strange coincidence, but just as Downpatrick Head began to dominate my whole horizon, a shaft of jagged light, similar to a lightning bolt, but without the thunder, broke from the cloud-base and *zapped* the pinnacle of Doon Briste. This queer trick of the light made it very easy to see how a legend such as the St Patrick story could come about. For the moment, though, my attention was fully on the sea at the foot of the headland.

Beneath Downpatrick Head, between the stack of Doon Briste and the sheer towering wall of the headland, was the ground sea the lobsterman had been trying to warn me about. All along the coast the sea had been rough, wind-driven, but fairly regular and predictable in its movements. But a strange wind whirled around the base of the great stack, just as it does around the bottom of a high-rise block of flats. Between the sea stack and the cliff there was a cauldron of bucking, heaving freaky water, caused by the swell tripping and recirculating in a shallow space, confined on two sides by cliff walls, and sprayed constantly by a series of blowholes. Certainly it would have been hell in a trawler. In the kayak it proved to be much less of an ordeal. Rather than pitch and roll uncontrollably, the light boat simply rose and fell erratically, following the chaotic shapes and movements of the water itself, while I continued to propel her forward whenever I could. Several large waves broke across the decks, and I was soaked by waterspouts and blowholes, but *Sola* rose triumphantly each time, and within minutes I emerged from the corridor into what, in comparison, seemed a gentle, disciplined sea.

I paddled on, dodging beneath tumbling waterfalls, each of which gave the effect of an instant downpour, with a thundering drum roll along the kayak's decks for dramatic effect. Every mile of the Mayo coast seemed to offer new experiences and treasures. Suddenly, ahead of me I noticed a strange flurry in the water, extending over an area of perhaps ten square yards. Drawing closer,

I could see a cluster of six grey fins, each about the size of a cricket bat, slowly flapping, waving gently to and fro on the surface of the sea. *What on earth?* I wondered, questioning briefly the wisdom of going any closer. It bore no resemblance to any fish, shark or dolphin I'd ever seen, and my mind turned to tales of sea serpents and other 'monsters'. Cautiously I let the kayak drift towards the centre of the patch, ready to sprint away at the first sign of trouble. The long fins continued to wave, almost forlornly, as if to a departing ship. Looking down through the one patch of glare-free sea created by my own shadow I saw that I was among several large animals, rather than one monster. Then I realised exactly what they were; I had read about them in books about tropical oceans, but had never before seen one, and certainly hadn't expected to in Irish waters. I was sitting virtually on top of a group of *sunfish*.

Each sunfish was about eight feet in diameter, shaped like a large puffy disc, and wallowed horizontally just beneath the water's surface. Mottled grey in colour and, I guessed, about four hundred pounds in weight, they appeared to swim aimlessly, if cautiously, conserving energy. The face had the slightly bovine look of the village idiot in a rural farce: soft-featured, with a broad forehead and a small, prim, thick-lipped mouth. There was no real tail, only two big lateral fins, one projecting down into the sea, the other reaching skyward and beckoning constantly. With one large, staring eye, placed near the sea's surface, each fish seemed to be watching my movements for the slightest sign of danger, but I sat still, just looking. As the name would suggest, sunfish are not common in the cold northern Atlantic, being more at home off the coast of Africa. However the warmer waters of the Gulf Stream, that great global radiator, do pass close to the Irish coast in several places and it is not unknown for species from more balmy climes, such as loggerhead turtles or man-o'-war jellyfish, to turn up occasionally along these shores. Six loggerheads had been caught in fishing nets off the Irish coast that very year. I dipped a paddle respectfully among the sedate little group of tropical wanderers, wishing I could at least have given them an encouraging weather forecast, and pushed *Sola* clear on her way.

Just around Creevagh Head, several creel-boats were fishing under power in the lee of the headland. Suddenly, as if at the drop of a hat, they all simultaneously left what they were doing and charged straight towards me. *Sola*, it turned out, had been featured that very day on the front page of the local paper, the *Western People*, and the kayak journey had become the subject of great speculation within the strange network of sea gossip that passes from boat to boat along radio links and at the small ports around the Irish coast. The six boats that now jostled around *Sola* had, just minutes earlier, been in the radio-controlled process of taking bets as to when – if ever – I would reach Killala Bay, when someone spotted the kayak. Not one of them, apparently, had expected any sign of me yet because of the strong winds.

'Would she tip over?' said one skipper, giving me a hefty poke on the shoulder with his boat hook. He tried again, and almost fell overboard himself when I parried the hook and tugged sharply.

'Not so easily,' I said.

'Nice one yourself, so!' he laughed, and took a volley of jokes from his colleagues. One of the other skippers explained that a very bad forecast was still in force, and that a severe gale force nine had been announced for 'later'. I assured them that I didn't intend to go very far today.

Then, from the forward cabin of one boat came the crackle of a VHF radio, and in the twanging nasal accent of the north, the coastguard announcement: 'All ships, all ships, all ships. This is Malin Head radio. Gale warnings are *now* in force for all coasts.'

'I'd say you'd better be off the bay as soon as you can,' shouted someone. 'Good luck to you now!' The chorus was echoed from all the boats as they revved their engines and eased away to finish their own hauls quickly before the gale blew in.

I wondered if I might yet make it across Killala Bay, taking advantage of the continuing westerlies, and still manage to be off

the water before it got too strong. Ten miles on, at Easky there
would be a pier, a safe landing and, hopefully, a sheltered pitch for
the tent.

At Lackan Bay, shielded from the west wind by a steep beach,
backed by mountainous sand-dunes thickly matted in waving
marram, I stopped for lunch and a rest. But, damp through from the
morning's paddle, even the light breeze in the lee of the dunes soon
had me shivering, and my teeth were chattering almost hard enough
to dislodge a few fillings. Besides, the tide was ebbing fast, and
about to leave me stranded by revealing a huge sandbar across the
bay, fifty yards from the kayak. It was not a day for hanging about
on land, and suddenly I understood William Pitt's verse from the
'Sailor's Consolation':

> *A strong nor'wester's blowing Bill*
> *Hark don't ye hear it roar now!*
> *Lord help 'em, how I pities them*
> *Unhappy folks on shore now!*

On a cold Irish day, when the body is already damp, and the wind
has an edge like a scythe, it is a great comfort to pull on the extra
warmth of the spraydeck and padded lifejacket, and to squeeze
oneself into the kayak cockpit. Once sealed below decks, one's legs
are completely cocooned and warm, and the upper body soon
generates its own warmth in the process of paddling. So I let the
offshore wind from Lackan blow me to the first headland. Through
binoculars I studied the swell, five miles offshore in the middle of
Killala Bay, where it might have shown signs of getting out of hand.
For the moment, I decided, it looked manageable. With the wind
still behind me it would take less than two hours to reach the next
possible landing at Easky; after that the wind could do what it liked.
I decided to go for the dash across the bay, and within a few paddle
strokes I was among grey and churning wind-generated waves.

The wind remained firmly behind me, and extremely strong,
perhaps force seven. I knew I could never have paddled *against* such
a wind – it would probably have been difficult even to breathe in it

directly – but was content for the moment to travel with it, hardly paddling except to keep the kayak upright and pointing in the right direction, due east. Regular squalls, and occasional black downpours scudded past me, exploding on all sides, and similarly travelling due east. It was essential to hold strictly to the course, for fear of being blown right out to sea, unable to turn against the wind. However, despite poor visibility in the squalls, I found that I could almost have dispensed with the compass. I was navigating on an entirely new system: not GPS but a system based on DET, Differential Ear Temperature. With my ears constantly wet from the squalls, and the wind blowing strongly onto them from the west behind me, it was easy to tell, even with eyes closed, when I deviated from the course. If I deviated left, I got more direct wind on my left ear and it grew immediately chilled; if I deviated right, my right ear became similarly chilled. By holding a true course, each ear felt at the same temperature. And within the short hour it took to master this renaissance technique, I had blown clean across the bay, and was bearing down quickly on the surf at Lenadoon Point.

Clochanaffrin, Carrickadda. All the way from Lenadoon Point, three miles east to Easky, and again beyond Easky, a series of great shelving shingle-banks curve out from the rocky shore, their scimitar shapes hidden by the sea at all but the lowest of tides. *Carrownabina, Lackavarna, Belturlin.* The fact that they have names at all is a mark of the respect with which inshore fishermen have traditionally regarded these thinly veiled horrors. This is a bad place for a small boat at any time; but when large ocean wave-trains run in from anywhere north of due west, the massive surf which then breaks on the submarine banks would put most Hawaiian beaches to shame. Off the banks of Clochanaffrin and Carrickadda, the swell rolling in from the northwest first began to feel the bottom about half-a-mile from shore. The forward part of each broad swell-wave slowed down, while the sea behind it continued to forge onward, to heap up on top of it. Gradually, but still travelling at speed, the front face would begin to steepen, grow and form; the mass of ocean at its back seemed to reach its summit, hover for a moment, then throw itself over the long curling crest like a battalion charging from the trenches. '*Right lads, over the top! Charge!*' The wind whipped plumes of spray shoreward from the steaming crests, while each smooth forward flank rolled itself into an oval tube, rifled with spirals of foam, and collapsed in a massive forward surge with a booming roar of escaping air. These waves might quite possibly have covered several thousand miles in their journey across the Atlantic, but the final half-mile which each travelled in the path of its own breaking was surely the most furious of all.

I thought of Holna, forerunner of modern surfers, the legendary Hawaiian who made the first, the longest and the wildest surf ride ever. When a series of seismic ocean waves swept across Big Island, Hawaii, destroying his house and village in their path, he is said to have survived by grabbing a plank and riding for his life on a hundred foot wave, which carried him all the way to the shore of the next island. Now the rolling swell from deepest Rockall was tumbling into Malin, each broad rank becoming a devastating series of classic surf waves, any one of which would have offered the ride of a lifetime – half a mile of clean fast surf to the Mayo shore. In the right conditions these breaks to the west of Easky, beautifully profiled, king-sized and reliable, attract surfers from all over Europe; and the old names of the banks on which the best breaks occur have become part of the coastal vocabulary once more. But in these conditions the breaks were just too big; I decided to keep well clear of them in the kayak, and paddled on for the final wind-assisted mile to Easky. It was then five o'clock; I'd been on the water for nine hours, with only a half-hour break. I was famished, sleepy and desperate for a pee; and with a force nine gale right on my tail, it was definitely time to be ashore.

~ ~ ~

In anxious anticipation of the gale, I had camped on the lee side of the best shelter I could find: the tall, but crumbling, ruined tower of the former McDonnel of Roselee Castle. The kayak and paddle were securely lashed and pegged down, and my tent was anchored amid a protective debris of fridge-sized stone blocks, fallen from the tower's battlement thirty feet above. The wind howled fiercely all night, reached gale force and continued to strengthen towards dawn. Sheer exhaustion allowed me to sleep for a couple of hours, but by morning the wind had topped the predicted force nine. It was as if I'd pitched the tent in a war zone, such a deafening roar was coming up from the sea. But at the height of the gale, I began to worry less about the state of the sea than the condition of the castle tower itself. It suddenly occurred to me that some of the fallen masonry blocks – many of them several hundredweight in mass – seemed relatively recent. My Log from the thirtieth of August reads:

> *End of second month draws near – and I'm stormbound again! The sea is marbled grey & white, and HUGE – pounding over Easky pier in crazy starbursts of white water. But it may turn out that the sea is the least of my worries. Some fresh pieces of masonry on the grass overnight. I can already picture the next headline in the* **Western People:** *OCEAN VOYAGER KILLED BY CRUMBLING CASTLE.*

The final day of August began with another cocktail of wind and rain, grey waves and green swell. The sea slopped and piled over the pier, where the fishing boats still huddled, weather-bound. But a little of the former regularity had returned to the Easky breaks, the swell was less maverick, and the southwesterly wind had dropped to a force five. Briefly, very briefly, the massive sea cliff of Slieve League was visible, thirty miles north across Donegal Bay; it seemed at that moment a very distant target indeed.

At mid-morning, for the second consecutive day, a van was parked at the Easky pier, and two sea-dreaming electricians sat staring out, between the beats of the windscreen wipers, at the wind-tormented wastes of Donegal Bay. They explained listlessly that they'd had a bit of a late start anyway, encountered a few problems on the job, and now as it was nearly lunchtime it was hardly worth getting properly started until afternoon. Then with much greater enthusiasm they lit the gas kettle in the back of the van, opened a packet of biscuits, and talked about Donegal Bay.

'Did you hear the rescue on the radio yesterday?' they asked, as though it was a football match. On the van's VHF set they had been able to tune in to the cliff-hanger drama of a Sea King helicopter searching for two men drifting in a small boat for eighteen hours in the gale-tossed sea.

'It was just ten miles out there,' said one of them. 'But you couldn't see a thing from the shore. No flares; nothing. *Eighteen hours!* Jesus, I'd like to have seen the look on those fellas' faces when the chopper found them, eh? Needle in a haystack really, but he found them, so he did. 'nother cup of tea?'

After several cups of tea, the rain on the windscreen began to ease, and the two electricians gave me a hand to carry *Sola* to the slipway for what turned out to be an erratic and action-packed launch. Even in the lee of the big pier, the sea was swirling in with tremendous force. Immediately, a big wave dumped onto the middle of the kayak, sucked me off the slipway with its backwash, then a second heavy breaker slammed me against the side of the pier. I slapped wildly at the water for support, trying desperately to protect the fragile rudder from damage on the concrete. A third big wave broke behind me, and on its backwash I hurried clear of danger. The two boys cheered, perhaps thinking that was my normal start to the day.

'We'll be listening on the radio!' they shouted, and went back to the van.

Leaving Easky, I had to head directly out to sea for over a mile to escape the region of surf which continued to drive solidly towards the shore. Then the southwest wind began to assist me towards Aughris Head and the mouth of Sligo Bay. Once I had gauged the condition of the sea, and settled into a rhythm, I took compass bearings from Benbulben and King's Mountain, and set off across Sligo Bay at its widest point.

Three hours later, cold and hungry, I pulled the kayak ashore near Roskeeragh Point. In heavy rain I sat among lobster creels and outboard motors and cooked up some beef hash and hot chocolate, followed by Kit-Kats, peanuts and then brambles from a well-loaded bush. Standing on a knoll, between showers, I could see Inishmurray Island. The grey sea broke heavily on the exposed side of the island, and on Sligo's rocky coastline fading away into the northeast. It was already half-past five, and the Mullaghmore peninsula on the southern fringe of Donegal Bay still lay twelve miles away. Darkness would fall at about nine o'clock on a cloudy night; with a determined push, and the wind behind me all the way, I decided, I might just reach Mullaghmore by nightfall.

I knew it had to be a strenuous and single-minded three-hour battle, and that a detour to Inishmurray would have to be missed. When the showers hit, I pulled up my hood and paddled cautiously; in between I paddled hard and fast, anxious not to let the dampness turn to chill. I drew level with Inishmurray, then slowly edged past its rainy shadow low on the western horizon. So low in the water is Inishmurray, that on a dark night during the last war, a destroyer mistook it for a German submarine and discharged a torpedo at it, terrifying the islanders. It is today, though not necessarily for that reason, uninhabited.

Many of the small headlands made for rougher, wetter passages, but *Sola* ploughed boldly through all that the Sligo shore could put in her way, shedding water in every direction as her bow forged onward and the paddle blades dug deeply into the grey waves. The final battle was one of judgement and timing as I squeezed the kayak between surging and breaking waves at the tip of the peninsula, through the shelter of Darby's Hole, then into the last sprint towards Mullaghmore. I coasted into the harbour at eight o'clock with steam rising from the backs of my hands and the neck of my rainjacket, entirely exhausted, but elated to have finished August on a defiant twenty-eight mile hop.

CHAPTER 17

Lair of Whirlwinds

This morning
the coast is transparent
and the highest reaches
of the mind
are in their element.

from 'Cape Breton Uplight', Kenneth White

September blew in on a force five westerly and with it the rain strengthened. Between showers I repacked the kayak, studied a new map and, over coffee in the pub above the Mullaghmore slipway, allowed my gaze to drift out across the inshore waters of Donegal Bay where, in 1979, the IRA had blown up Lord Mountbatten in his yacht. The waters in mid-bay still looked terrorised and agitated, the Donegal shore was but a distant blur, and it was with some reluctance that I began to think about a crossing to county Donegal. I had made a vague arrangement to meet an old friend for breakfast. But Iain lived well inland, in county Fermanagh, and I was just beginning to suspect he wouldn't be able to make it when Basil, his patch-faced collie, jumped onto the windowsill of the pub and sat staring in at me. Seconds later Iain walked through the door, simultaneously cheering me up, postponing the kayak launch, and giving me the perfect excuse for a second breakfast. Eventually, after several coffees, and a worrying forecast for strengthening winds, we scanned the maps once more and decided I should perhaps set off, agreeing to attempt a rendezvous at Muckros Head, twelve miles across Donegal Bay, on the southern shore of Ireland's most mountainous peninsula.

On a choppy, disturbed sea, with a short, tight swell hitting beam-on from the left, I bore first for the lighthouse at St John's Point, but soon changed to a more direct bearing for Muckros itself, setting into a measured rhythm for what would likely be yet another three hour crossing. Far away on my right, McSwynes Bay opened up, and the lighthouse at Rotten Island marked the entrance to Killybegs harbour, Ireland's largest remaining fishing port. Then, above the cauldron of torn sea which frothed around the Inishduff skerries, the sweep of sand at Fintragh Bay was occasionally visible. But ahead, already dominating the scene beyond the kayak's pointed bow was the high rocky rampart of Slieve League.

From Bundoran in the south, to the northern claw of Malin Head, Donegal rebuffs the gale-driven surges of the Atlantic with a crust of wild mountains. The granite mounds of the Bluestacks, the Rosses and Fanad Head in the north have an air of permanence and solidity. But perhaps more impressive are the spectacular quartzite peaks of Errigal, Muckish and the Slieves, for here the frontier between land and sea, the timeless struggle of rock against wave, is graphically illustrated in sheer crumbling cliffs and broken stone. Slieve League, 'the mountain of flags', and its sister peak, Slieve Leahan, form the Atlantic tip of the northern rim of Donegal Bay. But of the original Slieve League only half a mountain remains; the Atlantic has eaten into its very core, exposing a giddy spectacular sea-cliff. Measuring two thousand feet from the mountain's head in the clouds to its foot in the western ocean, the sea-cliff of Slieve League is the tallest in Europe.

Fierce katabatic winds plunge from the mountain summit down the ragged face of the cliff like avalanches. There they meet and mix with the harsh breath of the Atlantic, swirling and dancing together like dervishes over the surface of the sea, and sending broken renegade lumps of Atlantic chaos into angry motion. At one particular sharp bend in the cliff-face, beneath a corrie called the Eagle's Nest and facing due west, are spawned some of the most vicious squalls in the entire Atlantic realm. It is known locally as 'the lair of whirlwinds', and although I was soon to pass below that very spot, it would not be until the following day that I would encounter the dreaded whirlwinds of Donegal Bay.

Almost exactly three hours later I closed in below Muckros Head, and was just beginning to wonder where to land when I spotted Basil, the dog, high above on the cliff. Iain, jumping up and down, a tiny distant figure swinging a red jacket, waved and guided me round the headland to Muckros Bay, where I was able to make a surf-landing onto a wide beach of sand and shingle, and stop for a much-needed lunch. Iain seemed to be concerned about my nutrition. Apparently under the impression that everyone exposed to seawater for lengthy periods was likely to get scurvy, he had taken the trouble to bring with him a huge bag of assorted groceries. From the contents of the bag he proceeded to concoct an unrivalled lunch for two of sardines and spring onions, smoked mackerel, peanut butter and bananas, dried apricots, fruit cake and coffee. And when I went to throw a stick for Basil, I saw Iain hastily stowing a bag of fresh oranges in the kayak's cockpit as if they were some contraband substance.

~ ~ ~

The westerly wind increased to force six, and progress directly into it became ever more laborious; but I found that with an extra hard punch in each paddle stroke, I could still make steady headway against the wind. After an hour I rounded Carrigan Head, confirming that I was travelling at around my normal four knots. Energy levels had been magnificently boosted by the therapeutic anti-scurvy lunch, but I was well aware that I was burning off massive amounts of energy to sustain my present pace. Beyond Carrigan Head stretched the full length of the Slieve League sea-cliff. While the summits of most of the other mountains were visible, Slieve League disappeared dizzily into the cloud. I struggled with the sheer scale, grew sick and unsteady looking up past a half-mile of brightly variegated rock, and paddled on, feeling incredibly small. 'It's a long, *long* way from Clare to here,' I hummed, and thought of Clare's lofty Cliffs of Moher, which are in fact only one-third of the height of Slieve League. Two thousand feet below the summit, as the boulder flies, a tiny piece of green and yellow plastic moved steadily westward against the wind, feeling like an ant on the pavement beneath a tower block.

One hour later the headwind became a *left-ear-wind* as I began to skirt the lesser slopes of Leahan mountain, and eventually Rossarell Point. Ahead lay the island of Rathlin O'Byrne, and a maze of minor headlands and skerries, bathed in the foam and spray which told me that the next six miles to Glen Bay, where I had arranged to meet Iain, would be very exposed. Having used a lot of energy on the Slieve League stretch, I was now reluctant to finish the day with yet another battle. Besides, I could see through the binoculars that the cove at Rossarell Point was as idyllic a landing point as I could hope for. It was south-facing, surrounded by cliffs, its entrance protected by an island, it even had a broad sandy beach. Then I saw the distinctive man-and-dog profile on the very next headland, gesticulating wildly towards the cove. With great relief I headed in to run the kayak up on the luxury of soft sand; and after pitching the tents in a sheltered cliff alcove and swimming off the aches of the day, there was time left for a couple of pints down at the nearest village.

~ ~ ~

A day which begins in drizzle and wind, with a sticky struggle into rain-sodden clothes, and with the departure of some much appreciated company, ought by rights only to improve. However, things didn't seem to work that way in Donegal. A hefty goodbye push from Iain sent me out into the bay, from which viewing point it was still difficult to assess conditions on the open sea beyond the bay's mouth. The weather pattern, much as in recent days, was for winds to increase from the southwest, then move into the northwest and strengthen further, bringing rain and poor visibility. With the first six miles of coast too exposed to risk a landing, my initial target had to be Glen Bay. The wind, constant all night at force five, had created a furious sea, and I had to stay well offshore to avoid a series of very nasty-looking skerry breaks. Even offshore the waves were large and steep, and broke frequently across my decks. *Sola* seemed less buoyant than usual, wallowing sluggishly, and hiding her plimsoll-line in the troughs, while squalls and showers lashed continuously across the water. By far the worst stretch of water was below the towering ominous cliffs at Rossan Point. Just when I'd expected conditions to ease, the wind increased from the southwest, sending lumps of confused sea all over the little kayak; but worse still was the unnerving crosswind that swooped down from the hill and removed any pattern or predictability from the water. All around me was a mess of heaving random blackness.

Visibility dropped at times to mere yards, and I had to check the compass regularly to ensure that I was still heading for Glen Bay. I knew already that I had to get off the water as soon as possible, yet the next half-hour passed in a blur of bracing and surfing through a brutal sea beneath a ceiling of slate-grey sky. I had several frights and near tumbles as waves, larger than expected, slammed at me or spun the kayak broadsides. If there had been a single shred of decency in those waves they'd have been torn, frayed, or at least dented, by the pounding and battering they gave both to me and to the shore. But it was entirely a one-way relationship; untiring, unwavering, undamaged, the waves just kept on coming, as though neither I, nor even Ireland, were worthy of a second glance. These were boat-tossing, rock-crushing, sand-shifting mavericks from the deep Atlantic; invading bays, gobbling cliffs, defying foghorns and rattling men. Glen Bay itself, at least, proved to be reasonably sheltered, and after a graceless landing in a dumping surf, I rolled the boat up a steep shingle-bank, desperate to turn my back on the sea.

For the first time on the journey I felt a real need to be with people, *any* people; to seek out some new faces and to listen to some lighthearted chatter. Glencolmcille village, revived in recent years through the imaginative and persistent work of the late Father Dwyer, with its combination of cooperative farming, craftwork and tourist accommodation in traditional-style thatched houses, seemed at least likely to offer the prospect of some company. Strangely, on that day, the whole place was entirely morose and deserted. The café was closed, and there seemed to be hardly a scrap of colour, a hint of activity or a cheerful face in the whole village. I climbed the road to one of the village pubs, from which I hoped to get some information about the coast beyond Glen Bay, and perhaps to meet a couple of fellow travellers.

As I made my way up the street, a red-faced man, who looked as if he'd been drinking, suddenly appeared out of nowhere and came charging towards me, roaring and shouting angrily, 'Get the fuck out of here! We don't need the likes of you! I've known your sort before! I'll fucking show you!' He was a big man, bullishly built, with a heavy stomach, and he was moving fast. Before I could answer, or even fully register that it was me he was shouting at, he was upon me, shoving me roughly towards the road and punching viciously at the back of my head.

There was little time for rationalising. As soon as I had regained my balance, I planted my feet and swung an elbow back sharply, catching him just between ribs and stomach, winding him briefly. 'Look, mate, hold on! I think you've got the wrong person. You'd better calm down,' I said. 'I've just come from a canoe at the bay.'

By this time we were well down the road. He had recovered and, looking just as menacing as before, was advancing again. 'I know fine well who you are,' he growled. 'Get the fuck away from me, you dirty bastard!'

One of my earliest memories is of wrestling in the garden with my dad, who is a judo black belt. As a teenager I began training and competing myself, also gaining a black belt. Judo uses the momentum of an opponent's attack to his disadvantage, at which point he comes crashing heavily to the ground. The bigger he is, the faster he moves, the harder he falls. While judo is primarily a sport, it is usually practised on slightly padded mats, with partners who know how to fall safely. Used as a form of self-defence on an opponent who is unused to falling heavily, it can be quite devastating, and can make a quick and decisive difference to what might otherwise turn out to be a messy and prolonged outdoor scuffle; and, as with riding a bike, once learned, you never really forget the basic moves.

With surprising speed, the big man swung round to kick me. As he did so I found myself moving into a routine move that I must have rehearsed a hundred times in years gone by. Instinctively, I moved aside, caught his leg under my arm, knocked his chin upward with the heel of my hand, and swept away his other leg. He went down like a rotten tree; crashed heavily to the ground and, thankfully, remained there, hurling stones and verbal abuse as I turned and slowly walked away.

My heart was beating like a steam engine, and I felt very close to tears as I returned to the beach bewildered and sickened. I wanted no explanation from that madman, no further involvement. My brief search for company had drawn a dismal blank, and I felt hollow and tired because of it. I thought perhaps I might never fully understand what had happened there in that strange village; but a passage in Synge's *Riders to the Sea,* which I had initially thought melodramatic and exaggerated, now seemed to sum up my gloomy impression of Glencolmcille:

> *This peculiar climate, acting on a population that is already lonely and dwindling, has caused or increased a tendency to nervous depression among the people, and every degree of sadness, from that of the man who is merely mournful, to the man who has spent half his life in the madhouse, is common among the hills.*

Whatever the reason behind the strange outburst, whatever the cause of the black gloom which had descended on Glencolmcille, I wanted only to get away from it, to crawl back into the kayak and move on north, alone. My desire for company had passed.

~ ~ ~

At first there seemed to be a lightening of the cloud, and a slight improvement in the sea state in Glen Bay. However, both my sense of where I was heading and my natural fear of a wild sea, were dulled by an aching fatalistic weariness, and a combination of careworn emotions. Beyond the slight shelter of the bay itself it soon became obvious that any improvement was a mere illusion. These were marginal conditions. Consistent with the tone of the day, the next two hours were about to present one of the most terrifying experiences of my entire life.

The kayak was handling superbly, leaning and carving well into turns; spinning accurately to change course on the crest of a wave; rising buoyantly after being deluged in a trough. Even my technique seemed accurate and fluent. Every motion of the sea met its counterpart in an adjustment of my balance. I was reaching almost subconsciously to power or brace the kayak, finding paddle-purchase amongst the ever-changing, increasingly unpredictable shapes of an ungovernable sea. For about a mile, the combination of a fine boat and fluent handling remained equal to the savage contortions of the sea. Then, off Sturrall Point I began to lose it. The tangled intimacy of wave and paddle began to dissolve. I felt a tenseness develop in my arms, and became slowly aware that the waves were getting steeper, cramming closer together, and appearing from every direction in weird tortured forms. Then came the katabatic winds, fierce, downward sweeping squalls from the mountain, between force six and eight in strength, hammering down on the sea's surface from any and every direction, and lasting up to three minutes at a time. The screaming roar of mountain squalls and crashing sea filled my head until I knew nothing outside that terrifying world of water.

Just around Sturrall, I found myself surrounded by towering, jagged rock pinnacles, trapped in a cauldron of wind-crazed sea which was endlessly crashing between the towers, perpetually recycling its own clapotis until the water could jump no higher. The kayak seemed to shy back, like a horse before an impossible jump, then throw herself forward until I felt we were sure to somersault. Seconds later the bow would be rising at speed, while simultaneously a wave was breaking over my head from behind. The sea was utter mayhem. I had never been amongst anything like it. I didn't know what I had to do to survive, or for how long I could fight it. And whilst I had no sense of my life flashing before me, I clearly remember feeling, in a strangely objective way, that while I remained in that arena, death was a distinct possibility.

The pinnacles! I told myself. *Must get clear of the pinnacles!* I powered my way desperately through that cauldron, knowing that I had to get off the water soon or all would be lost. Then I saw the first whirlwind. It charged out from behind a bend in the rock-face, and stampeded down between the kayak and the cliff like a rogue elephant. Along its narrow, erratic wake, the sea went berserk, as though the waves themselves were in agony. A second whirlwind launched itself from among the cliffs, this time raising a top-heavy waterspout which, travelling at speed, passed about ten yards to seaward of me. As I drew level with the bend in the cliff which was generating the whirlwinds, a third one formed, separated, and sent two identical waterspouts spinning past my bows and out to sea. They passed within yards of *Sola*, each one a screaming mist of white-spray particles, five feet high, with a hollow vortex widening towards the top.

Oh shit! I thought, if one of these hits me I'm finished. I had no idea how to handle a whirlwind in a kayak, or even a kayak in a whirlwind. It's not something that ever cropped up in training on Edinburgh's Union Canal, nor a subject dealt with in the Canoe Association Handbook. I had a brief cartoon-style vision of a whirlwind passing over the kayak, whipping off all my clothes, and leaving me paddling along unharmed but stark naked. But it seemed a desperately optimistic caricature. On the whole I was petrified. If that miscreant sea had been a form of torture designed in order to wheedle secrets from me, I'd have willingly given in; anything to get airlifted out of those horrors there and then. Suddenly I caught a glimpse of a distant indentation in the coast, and the shingle beach at Port Bay. If I could only reach that beach ...

With every last shred of strength, every drop of adrenalin, I fought the kayak forward over the sea's folded surface. For ten intense minutes I channelled the fear and near panic into strong paddle strokes; and gradually I began to pull clear of the path of the whirlwinds. Beyond Sturrall the coast presented a more acute angle to the swell, the cliff winds tumbled from less of a height, and the sea became ever more manageable as I drew towards Port. Perhaps further on it might have become easier; but I knew I was done. With knees trembling and knuckles aching I reached the inshore waters at Port, gratefully aware that I had looked something wild in the eye – and survived.

~ ~ ~

At Port, within the relative shelter of a crumbling stone breakwater, I landed roughly and hauled the kayak up the timbers of an ancient slipway. High above the steep shelving beach of storm-graded cobblestones were the deserted remains of a settlement; a damp valley refuge on the edge of the sodden Donegal peatland. A whole community had once lived in this valley, now wiped clean as if by some pestilence or plague. Among the stone ruins of once-thatched homes, now roofless and derelict, there was camp space and fresh water in abundance; and soon I'd pitched the tent on a patch of sward immediately behind the storm-beach. The coastguard forecast made it perfectly plain that I'd be on that site for a further day at least. Gale warnings were repeated several times, and I lost no time in collecting driftwood, building a fire and rigging a drying line. After a quick wash in a prune-juice stream of peatwater, and a change into dry clothes, I settled in for the evening. As night wore on the wind continued to increase, driving rain and spray against the little tent.

I woke next morning to the sound of sheep stomping over loose shingle beyond the tent, and looked out on a bright and boisterous Atlantic scene. Shining cushions of moss campion, dancing pink heads of thrift and mosaic-lichened rocks sprang into life in intermittent sunshine, drawing the sleepy eye seaward. Great billowing cumulus cloud masses – bright whipped on top, but leaden shadowed below, like boulders topped with fresh snow, tumbled over the bay at speed. It would be a day of stampeding fronts, Atlantic rain and squalls with glimpses of sun between them; a boatman's dread of a day at sea, but one of the finest sort to spend on the coast. The mild warmth of late summer was gone, and I spent the day wearing all my spare clothes, wandering the broken coast and coves, and the peat-stripped lands of a bygone era. It was the boisterous best of Donegal days, filling the head and inflating the chest with bright and noisy air.

Heavy, often violent, showers of hail and rain scudded across the Atlantic, constantly recharging the sea's frenzy and assaulting the coast with vigour undiminished. But between these came a light of incredible, almost disturbing intensity; a light from the outer edges of sanity. It was as though the heavens were spotlighting Donegal through a magnifying lens, purifying the coast and arc-welding the senses simultaneously until the two began to merge into one. The frenetic sea, so recently grime-grey and white-capped, would suddenly flush to the far horizon with a silver sheen so bright that it burned the eye. And the reflected glow, catching in suspended curtains of spume and spray, gave the whole coast a hazy otherworldly beauty. Rainbow fragments formed and hovered above crashing waves and rock stacks until it was impossible to understand how anyone could possibly expect to continue with the mundane practical concerns of daily life. All day long I walked the coast, collecting driftwood, gazing over precipices, lying in sheltered hollows, entranced by scene after shining scene. Sometimes I would be high on a clifftop, looking over the wild ocean and the foam-catching rock stacks; other times picking carefully over ankle-twisting cobble-beaches, almost deafened by the sea's constant roar. Through my whole body I could feel the rumbling shock of the breaking waves as they reverberated up the shingle beaches. *Boooomm! .... hssshhhh....boooomm!....hssshhhh!*

I was entirely alone, but without the slightest sense of

loneliness; *suaimhneas gan uaigneas* – enjoying an immense solitude yet without isolation. There is no *remoteness* unless you are anxious to get back; and no *loneliness* for one who no longer craves company. To feel isolation one has to be conscious of oneself in an uncomfortable way. But the edges of my self were already dissolving into the roaring ocean and bright haze of Donegal. I had hardly any sense of my own body, and seemed to exist simply in the intensity of the cries and calls of the sea birds, the smells of kelp and ozone, and the thundering closeness of the waves. There was no past, and no future; and I felt, in those moments, that had I looked in a mirror I might have had no reflection.

There followed a night of fierce gales and slashing bouts of rain, interspersed with velvet-dark clear spells in which a whole cruel-looking moon slid from behind a cloud and shone bright enough to read by. By morning the inshore wind seemed noticeably weaker. The forecast gave force four to five for the day, but with another gale warning for the evening and beyond, which meant I had only a short weather-window in which to consider moving on. The problem was that the sea itself remained restless and vindictive, topping and lashing with spume all the same rock stacks as it had during the gales of previous days, producing deep accumulations of foam, much noise, and generally offering very little encouragement. Poised between waiting for the sea to settle – which could take several days – and pushing for some distance north before the next gale came in, a decision had to be made.

Despite the wild beauty of the place and the spectacular changing seascapes, I was becoming restless for movement; for progress towards the journey's end. Besides, resources were getting low. With no bread or biscuits left, I had a stomach-turning powdered egg for breakfast, whittled away the morning trying to will the sea to settle, then followed it with a dehydrated beef hash lunch. Somewhere, north along this desolate coast, there must be a shop with fresh bread, milk, fruit – even *chocolate!* But what fuelled my decision in the end was neither the thought of fresh food supplies, nor any actual improvement in sea conditions, but the fear of becoming trapped by further deteriorating conditions to come.

In a brief patch of sunshine I packed the boat and slid it down into the bay at low tide. Sheltered at first by the dog-leg skeleton of the stone breakwater, I was able to tighten clothing and adjust the rudder ready for the fray beyond. The sea reigned in hellcat fury – a jostling rabble of swell roused by the anarchy of the gales of the day before and of this day's continuing westerlies. The rock stacks and pinnacles to the south, among which I'd dodged the whirlwinds of two days ago, were now almost obscured by swirling spray and foam. Very carefully, with adrenalin coursing through trembling arms, and jittering calf muscles pressing on the foot-rests, I picked my way directly out to sea, giving a wide berth to the frothing cauldrons which surrounded the Toralaydon Island stacks. The swell was breaking not only around these stacks, but on unseen reefs beneath the sea's surface, and only now, from close quarters, could I properly judge the size of those breaks. Some of the rises reached more than twenty feet before curling and crashing down. And despite the horrendous weight of water which must have been in them, they frequently took over a second in freefall!

It is particularly difficult to negotiate a passage through the breaks when so much of the sea room between them forms part of the catchment area of yet another breaker, when most of the time I was wallowing down in deep, uneven troughs, or tottering precariously on ragged edges of advancing broken swells. On the rises I could occasionally see the dangerous succession of breaking traps extending like a minefield for about a half-mile seaward of the Toralaydon group and looking an almost suicidal prospect. Did I dare go out *that* far to avoid them? Or must I turn back and abort the journey. To turn back would probably have been dangerous in itself, but ahead lay a sea that gave every indication of being bigger and more unruly than I'd ever survived before. Perhaps it would only be for that half-mile stretch, but one thing was certain – there'd be no short cut: to try to cut through the Toralaydon breakers would have meant certain destruction.

At one point I had to thread a tight passage between two serious crushing breaks. Beyond these, an extra large set of swells revealed that I had stumbled into the catchment area of the next major break. What's more it seemed I was being sucked steadily in towards the business end of the wave – certain doom! Quickly, and I suppose in slight panic, I altered course radically and grabbed several strokes of distance, just as a massive wave-mound collected, steepened its slope, curled forward over its face and then erupted like a quarry blast. I came clear, feeling the rush of air that was forced from the wave-tube, but I was now heading southwest, almost one-hundred-and-eighty degrees off course! My heart pumped terror and tension through my body. It was too late to turn back now, if only because I'd never find the safe passage back between those last two mashers. Besides, I really believed that I could get beyond the worst area and begin again to head northeast.

I pushed on for perhaps a further half-hour, during which time the waves were breaking less fiercely. *Sola* would rise to them as if going up in a lift, hang unsteadily on their crests, and then tumble away into their troughs with a sickening burst of speed. Sometimes the next wave towering up behind would douse her as she lay there, but mostly she was up and over ... up and over again ... and again. Immediately around me there was still nothing but a waste of sea, a living slate colour, whipped up here and there to buff foam; but beyond, like a barrier of darkness, I could see my target – an almost black sea of swell, irregular and reaching about fifteen feet from trough to crest, but only very rarely breaking. I felt a glorious release of pressure, and gradually began to sing under my heaving breath: *'There is a house in New Orleans'* – I'd made it! – *'they call the rising sun.'*

For much of the next few miles I felt as though I was beneath sea level as, glancing up between dark walls of moving water, I could see the dramatic stacks and tortured pinnacles of the

Slievetooey coast stretching away northeast. As I paddled on ... and on ... it became obvious that the inshore passage – with the sea breaking on reefs, skerries and stacks, and with the danger of mountain squalls – was a false psychological safeguard; that a far better course would be to leave the shore behind; to head out across dark, heaving Loughros Bay. I wondered if, after the exertions of the escape from Port, I could sustain the effort for what would most likely be a two hour crossing, and whether the gale would hold off for that long. A shifting field of light suddenly illuminated distant Dawros Head, eight miles across the forbidding sea, just long enough to make it look like an attractive option, and so I turned the bow towards it and began a measured, rhythmic stroke:

'*–And it's been the ruin of many a poor boy; Dear Lord, I know, I'm one.*'

What followed was a hard slog in a big sea, sometimes foundering along with waves breaking right over me from behind. The wind remained strong, but the size of the swell itself sheltered the little kayak from the worst of the blasts. By four o'clock I was level with Dawros, having covered about twelve miles from Port in under three hours. In such marginal conditions it was good progress indeed. Looking back south, the serrated Slievetooey coastline was still impressive and grim – but now unmistakeably and triumphantly *distant!*

The desire to make up for the previous day's lack, and the adrenalin of the exit from Port must still have been with me – or perhaps it was the influence of the full moon – but I found myself again forsaking the possibility of heading inshore for a landing within Gweebarra Bay, and striking out instead for Crohy Head, a further eight mile commitment. With the sea and wind behind me, and my mind on many matters, ranging from passing Roaninish island to whether I might find fresh food and chocolate at Maghery, the far shore drew steadily nearer. In fact it was little over an hour before, with a half-gale at my back, I beached among the broken kelp logs and purple weed of high-tide at Maghery.

Maghery shop was the first call, to stock up on basic stores and to boost flagging blood-sugar levels. Walking back to the shore, with a bag of groceries and a bellyful of chocolate bars, apples and milk, I found that energy levels were surprisingly quickly restored, and began to suspect that the day's paddling was not yet over. Now I was almost certain the full moon was responsible. Spurred on by the ever-impending storm, I decided to put in a final hour's trip, six miles northwest to Aranmore Island:

'My mother was a tailor; Sewed my new blue jeans. My father was a gamblin' man; Way down in New Orleans.'

For most of the crossing Aranmore disappeared, and I wove past Ternon, Inishfree and Rutland islands in a dense band of rain that obliterated the entire area. Despite the downpour and a chaotic wave-pattern, there was none of the mortal threat which I'd felt earlier in the day, and I found myself enjoying the crossing immensely. A compass bearing took me past Hook Point and eventually to Aranmore's main bay where I hauled the boat and pitched tent under a constant drizzle. Sitting outside the tent in full paddling gear, the constant gentle rain flushed away the salt, sweat and stress of a long and very full afternoon. I felt a smug glow of defiance at having outpaced the gale, and at snatching twenty-six miles under severe sea conditions. Best of all, there would be no powdered egg tonight: tinned ravioli, rice pudding and strawberries, were followed by biscuits and cheese, fresh bread and coffee with real milk – the spoils of my raid on the Maghery shop – while *Sola* lay among the marram like a faithful horse. Then I leaned back on the wet sand with a distended stomach and waited for the Malin gale.

CHAPTER 18

Doineann

*Of all natural phenomena, there are, perhaps, none which
civilised man feels himself more powerless to influence than
the wind.*

The Golden Bough, Sir James Frazier

From among the Aranmore dunes it was impossible to gauge the
day's wind. The radio, my link with the world outside, forecast
'Gales from the south, moving northwesterly and strengthening',
giving no great encouragement to get up and venture out. In fact I
was almost resigned to being storm-bound yet again, and perhaps
the following day too. But there's a limit to how many mugs of tea
you can consume before having to step outside for a leak. What I
met was a grey morning of continuous rain, with swirls of
beach-sand bowling up the faces of the low Aranmore dunes.
Through binoculars I watched waves smashing off the exposed
edge of Owey Island, and also occasionally off skerries in the
Rosses Sound. But gradually it dawned on me that the bulk of
Aranmore itself – a mountain of seven-hundred-and-fifty feet – was
giving some protection from the southwest wind to the sea passage
which lay northeast and therefore downwind of it. Of course the
wind might strengthen again, or veer northward as forecast, but *if* I
could cross quickly in the lee to Eighter Island, then to Lahon
Island, or even to Inishinny – all in a northeasterly direction – I'd be
able to reassess the passage north from there.

In a bright spell between showers, on the rapid ebbing of a
spring tide, I launched the kayak northeast from Aranmore into the
Sound. Almost immediately a squall scudded over, blocking the

light and greywashing the sea and sky; but when it had passed I was already in mid-channel. The southwesterly at my back helped offset the effects of the strong ebb, whose power could be seen forging south around rocks and skerries in the channel. The sea work was tricky at times, but not threatening, and very soon I had crossed the Sound. Between blanking showers there were brief bright glimpses of a myriad of beaches, island settlements and *machair*-land – the gentle tangle of land and water known as 'the Rosses'. The seductive beauty of this area, which extends into the sea in a scatter of islands off the Donegal coast, hides a dangerous reality, for the sea passages that wind around and between the islands are the conduits of treacherous tides that can render any of the islands inaccessible for days on end during adverse weather. A local story tells of a mainland priest confronting several islandmen for not having crossed to the mainland for Mass or even confession for some weeks.

'Well, Father,' said one of the men, 'it's the Sound, you see, it can be getting terrible rough, and it's many a day a currach might be lost out there.'

'The way we see it,' continued another, 'it's too far to travel for a venial sin, and far too risky for a mortal sin!'

Crossing from Inishinny to Cruit Island conditions began to change. As I lost the shelter of Aranmore the sea became more boisterous, and the tide continued to ebb against me. But the southwest wind was stronger – forcing and funnelling the sea powerfully northwards, even against the tide – and it looked as though it might just escort me onward to the gap between Owey and Cruit. By now I was surfing north on small, determined ripple-waves, twisting and leaning into adjustments to keep the kayak on course, struggling a little at times, but if I could only reach the gap there would be shelter on the far side. Speed picked up rapidly as the gap loomed. The flood tide was with me now, and after a sluice run through the narrows I reached a sheltered haven. The wind throttled back slightly and the swell was damped by the island barrier. The scenery changed too. Now four miles to the northeast lay Gola, the largest of the Gweedore islands, and a tempting target if only the full gale would delay just a little longer.

Two surf-fringed islets named Allagh, a curiously Islamic-sounding enclave in the Catholic west, guarded the approach to the slipway at Gola. I had looked forward to getting here for rest and shelter, however brief. But Gola, I now found, had an eerie, ghost-town atmosphere. Abandoned houses gazed like stunned animals out over the islands of Gweedore. Ashore, debris filled the ditches; fields and former gardens lay derelict, and the skeletons of rotting wooden fishing boats littered the pier and shingle shore. A scattering of solid, two-storey houses towered impotently above the Sound, looking from a low angle like the redundant monoliths of Easter Island. I was no stranger to abandoned houses, neglected land and the remains of long departed communities. The Irish coast, like the highlands and islands of Scotland, is littered with ruined crofthouses, ancient field patterns, abandoned piers and moorings, the recurring evidence of economic and social decay. And at one level Gola was just another abandoned island on the edge of one of Europe's most remote and economically backward regions. But what struck me most was the atmosphere of abandonment without decay. The houses could not yet be called ruins; one felt as though, like faithful dogs, they were just waiting for their owners to return. More than that, it was as if the island itself was still waiting. Whatever had happened here had happened relatively recently.

From the main track, which runs from the slipway to the north side of the island, countless shades of green made up the island palette. White specks of bog-cotton waved in the wind, lapwings wheeled and piped above the moorland, and the potent scent of the sea was on the breeze. In the dazzling freshness of the landscape, and the beauty of its setting it was almost possible, for a short time, to overlook its ghosts, but all around stood poignant reminders of a recently vanished population. Discarded peatbanks still had spades sticking out proud, as though their owners had merely taken a short tea-break. I could still imagine the playground laughter as I passed the island school: a school which had a roll of sixty laughing children in 1930, and was still open in 1966, the year I had started school myself.

From close-up the houses, like giant severed heads with gaping mouths and pecked-out eyes, seemed to peer sightlessly out over the islands of Gweedore. Spacious, two-storey structures, sturdily built of local granite, they must have been fine, comfortable homes in their time. Everything useful or valuable had been stripped from them, but many still had sound roofs and dry interiors. What memories had they of peat-warmed rooms and busy families? Inside the highest house on the island I climbed a wooden staircase and looked out of a top floor window. Patiently in the distance the sea breathed and sighed, and the changing lights of its surface shone through the frameless window onto the pitch-pine panelling of the room. Despite that, the house remained heavy around me; the presence of the recent past filled the rooms like an odourless gas, and the day was full of questions. What had Gola been like as a living island? Where were its people, and why had they left? Would human communities ever return to these islands?

During the eighteenth and nineteenth centuries most of the Gweedore islands, were used for seasonal cattle grazing and a little fishing. But by the mid-nineteenth century fishing had begun to change from a supplementary activity to a dominant one. The population of the area, as in much of Ireland, was rising more rapidly than anywhere else in Europe, and the sea was one of the few resources able to supply local needs. And, as the economy of west Donegal shifted from a subsistence to a commercial basis, fishing assumed additional prominence as a source of cash income. The people of Gola became fishermen first and foremost, and the use of the land was relegated to second place.

Throughout the world the history of fishing has been dominated by the increasing centralisation, mechanisation, and indeed industrialisation, of fishing activities, with bigger boats based at larger ports able to travel and fish ever farther afield. Donegal was no exception. Outlying islands and small ports, with their small-scale, low capital fishing fleets, became unable to compete with the sophistication of the equipment and the scale of operations at the big ports. By the early part of this century fishermen in areas such as the Aran and Blasket islands and west Donegal began to feel the effects of competition with larger and better equipped boats from Scotland and England – especially the fleets of powerful steam drifters. Gola was unusual in that, despite these problems, despite growing transport costs and 'the Troubles', for a short time at least, fishing actually grew in importance. The main pier, built at the end of the nineteenth century by the Congested Districts Board, is large and well sited. Protected by an outcrop of rock from the north and northeast, and by the curve of the island from the west, it freed fishermen from dependence on any particular tide. Gola fishermen were able to continue to work throughout the year, and the island even became a summer base for fishermen from the mainland.

It seems that it was the growing pattern of seasonal labour migration, rather than the direct effects of the mechanisation of fishing, which eventually led to the decline and ultimate fall of Gola. Seasonal human migration from the glens, coasts and islands of the Rosses and Gweedore to Scotland and England for paid work, increased in importance during the nineteenth century. Being the only source, other than fishing, of bringing hard cash into local families, it quickly became the outstanding feature of this area's economic and social life. In some areas almost all the able-bodied men, girls and even children would leave their homes for six months of the year in order to find seasonal farm, construction or domestic work, mainly in rural Scotland. Increasingly in the twentieth century the migrant workers were drawn to the cities where building sites and factories offered more year-round employment, and they became permanent emigrants. The social impact of the cities on the migrant workers, who returned home to the glens and the islands, soon began to show in their lives. Because of the seasonal opportunities offered by the fishing, Gola was affected relatively late by the inevitable crisis of changing values, but the onset of population decline, though belated, was rapid and dramatic.

When the first few families leave an island community, the reallocation of available resources, such as land or peatbanks, may initially mean a partial rise in living standards for those who stay behind. However, this is usually not adequate to compensate for the deterioration of local social conditions, or to compete with the imagined standards of living available elsewhere. As the population dwindles, certain communal activities such as track repairs, ditch maintenance or peat gathering become more difficult; services – such as buses, shops, schools, pubs and ferries – eventually become uneconomic to run, and each family increasingly has to provide for its own needs. When the last family with children leaves an already ailing island, that island ceases to be a self-perpetuating community; almost every aspect of island life is from that moment caught in an accelerating fatal spiral. It took less than a century for Gola, once a thriving community of two hundred people, to become an island of ghosts.

All the clearer for being an island, more poignant for being so recent, Gola is as powerful an illustration as you could hope to find, of what had happened along much of Ireland's Atlantic edge. Somewhere in its desolate salt-fringed loneliness there is an important lesson in human transience; a reminder of the fragile impermanence of men, families, even whole human communities in the face of the great or gradual tide-like sweeps which we call economics.

Halfway along the Gola pier a little shrine and effigy of 'Our Lady' had been carefully built into the rock, where fishermen would once have stood and prayed before and after trips to sea. The fishermen were now gone, but 'Our Lady' was still there and I wished I could have asked her: to what extent was it sheer necessity and survival, and to what extent was it the seductive images of mainland and city life, that drove the people from Gola? And did they really find the grass greener, or were those images eventually to prove as far removed from reality as the ones many of us now hold of island life?

The last thing I wanted was to get storm-bound among the ghosts of Gola; and from high on the Gola wasteland I could see that a further, relatively sheltered, area of sea existed beyond: that another couple of miles might yet be snatched before the impending gale. So I relaunched the kayak, skirted Gola and headed northeast past the final two islands of the Gweedore archipelago. Four miles away across open water the great corner of land called *Cnoc Fola*, or Bloody Foreland, made a tempting target. But as my shelter receded and the wind continued to freshen, a nasty swell built and broke on the skerries, and Bloody Foreland seemed an increasingly foolhardy goal. There would be no landing place for at least a further five miles around the headland, so I decided to call it a day and headed into a bay at Brinlack, thirteen opportunistic miles after leaving Aranmore.

~ ~ ~

If there are fifty words for 'snow' and 'ice' in the language of the Greenland Innuit, then the Irish language should be peppered with names and expressions for wind. Next to the sea itself, wind is the single most all-pervading, life-and-death force in the coastal counties. Squeezed between a huge continental landmass and the vast Atlantic Ocean, and set in a stormy frontal region where polar and tropical air masses meet and mix, Ireland is meteorologically challenged in the extreme; winds are an inescapable fact of Irish daily life. And yet, strangely, in Ireland the winds remain unnamed.

All over the windy world, particularly in coastal and desert regions, rather than simply referring to them by the points of the compass, people have given beautiful, expressive, even poetic names to their winds. The Japanese, for example, have many winds:

from *Enbata*, the sea-breeze and *Hegochuria*, the warm southerly wind, to *Iphara*, the cold northerly, *Yama-arashi*, the mountain squall, and *Idaki-haizea*, the wind of the sun. It is as if by labelling these uncontrollable forces that blow through their lives, people somehow stake a claim on the maverick breezes and thereby diminish their own impotence. Naming is, after all, a form of power. Fear of the unknown, or unnamed, is always worse than facing that which has a name and can, by virtue of that name, be cursed or blessed, banished or summoned. Un-named is un-claimed is un-tamed. Perhaps the Irish winds are so much harder to bear simply because they are nebulous and unidentified.

The Norse sagas talked of the *Vind's-gnyr*; *Koshava* is the snowy wind of the Slavic plains; the *Pittarak* roars down from the Greenland icefields, and the *Purgas, Crivetz* and *Vingas* winds ensure that Siberia never gets too warm and stuffy. The Nova Scotians fear the *Blaast*, the *Blue Norther* and the *Landlash*; and the Alaskans have their *Williwaw*. Of the world's warm winds, there are the *Bora* of the Adriatic, the whirling *Notus* of the Cyclades, and the *Autan* of France, Corsica and the Balearic Isles. The chillier *Mistral* blows down through France and over the Mediterranean; while the northerly *Meltemi*, the 'bad-tempered one', scours the Aegean in summer. The powerful southwesterly wind, known as *Rebojo* in Buenos Aires, and *Pampero* in Chile, fills the wings of the great Condor high above the Andean plains. Sailors of the Channel islands were wary of the northwesterly *Galerno*; and so evocative of speed and power are names like *Zephyr* and *Sirocco*, that they have been hijacked in modern language by the advertising agents of the motor industry. Even the lonely prospectors of the Californian goldrush had a name for the wind. Thinking of her as a cold, fickle woman, haunting their dreams and never letting them forget her, they called the wind *Maria*. I feel sure she left several un-named sisters back home in Ireland.

The softest, most poetic names are those of the short-lived, helpful, pleasant winds such as the sea-breezes, among which are the *Datoo*, which fans cool Atlantic air over sweaty Gibraltar, the *Virazon* which tempers the Atacama desert of Chile, the *Imbat* of Tunisia, and the *Medina* of Cadiz. *Laawan*, 'the helper', is the winnowing breeze of the Moroccan Atlas mountains, while *Mezzer-ifoullousen* is the delightful Berber name for the cool southeasterly, meaning 'the one which plucks the fowls'!

To any global conference of winds, Ireland could send heroic delegates of international calibre, rank and authority; but they would have no titles to wear on a lapel-badge, and could be distinguished only by direction and strength. *Doineann* is the word used in the Irish Gaeltacht for foul and stormy weather, including a restless gale building up for a storm; and *creithleag* is the gentle Irish term for a light breeze. But of the prevailing southwesterlies which scour the Atlantic coast; the chill easterlies which stir the Irish Sea into madness; or even the great equinoctial gales which build up massive seas, and may also rearrange the coastline a little, not one has ever had the honour of a proper name. Ireland, it seems, is content to be squall-raddled and breeze-blasted by an unmentionable legion of anonymous winds.

For the first time in the entire journey I was about to be hit by a wind that I could name; a wind to which I had been formally introduced by the BBC forecasters, and with which I could now form a direct and personal relationship. *Hurricane Gusta* was at that very moment scouring her way across the north Atlantic. Her passage had already ensured that winds, during the ten days I had been travelling through Malin, had averaged force seven, and often been above gale force. Tonight, according to the warning from Malin Head radio, the tail end of *Hurricane Gusta* was due to lash the northwest coast of Ireland, before spinning off north towards the Arctic circle. Choice of camp site would be crucial. All the initial options of sites sheltered from the sector of the forecast gale were either sloping or extremely boggy. And I eventually plumped for a napkin of turf which I hoped would be shielded slightly by the steep rise of the shingle beach itself. I pitched the tent rear into the northwest, lined the flysheet fringe with boulders and logs to block the ground-travelling of the gale, hauled the kayak itself up for an extra windbreak, and weighed it down with stone slabs. I removed any upwind debris that could be blown towards the tent, and left nothing loose around the camp. Then, satisfied that I could do no more, I retreated into the little tent to wait. The dramatic sky showed, not only that a severe blasting was on its way, but that it wouldn't be long in coming.

The first squalls, rattling the panels of the tent, were like frantic *bodhran* solos on a taut goatskin drum drowning out the full volume of my little radio. Vibrating guy ropes hummed like tuning forks. The wind-backed tide had been unable to ebb from the bay, so that the breakers crashed in noisy frustration at the foot of my shingle-bank. By midnight the wind was straight out of the west. Then came the almost unreal, film-effect howling of the gale itself, as the first lashings of wind-whipped spray came from the bay below. When the wind reached force nine I began to fear for the safety of the little tent. Lying alone in a gale-ravaged tent is like being the frayed nerve-centre of a tooth in agony. Each violent, panel-flapping squall sends volts of panic through raw nerve-endings as you strain and listen for tearing guy-ropes and the ripping of fabric. Sleep becomes impossible, and much of that night was spent playing the human pit-prop, bracing my body against tent panels which threatened to flatten and collapse. Daylight arrived without a lowering of the wind, and the six o'clock forecast told that a force nine northwesterly severe gale warning was still in force. But the tent was intact. The long-awaited rip never came. And somehow the daylight seemed to make the situation less threatening.

By now the sea was awesome; stirred huge as far as the eye could see, and over-ridden constantly by massive billowing clouds. Occasionally the whole scene was blanked out by dense sky-swells of rain. But in an Atlantic force nine nothing hangs around in one place for long, and soon the sun broke through, illuminating ranks of waves, which pushed steadily between the islands, and some appalling explosions of swell upon the inshore rocks. Half a mile out, where the sea was dark and sticky-looking, flecked untidily with white-caps, grey combers seemed to heave suddenly skyward and come tumbling in towards the shore – massive, menacing and unstoppable. Row upon row they came. Stripped by the wind of their white cloaks of foam, they seemed even more nightmarish, and I flinched reflexively as each broke. Towards Bloody Foreland was a further scene of terror – the sea a tattered shroud of white and blue, and the spray spinning out above the headland in a great swirling cloud. All along the coast lobstermen had winched their boats high up on the shore for fear of losing them to the sea, and many of these were now buried under deep foam. The foam collected in Brinlack Bay in long straight rows, two feet deep along the line of the wind, then tumbled off inland in great flying gobbets. I could hardly stand up against the wind, and each squall sent me stumbling to keep balance; so most of the day was spent in the tent reading, sleeping and worrying; especially the latter.

At about nine o'clock on my second evening at Brinlack, the shingle-bank began to reverberate and rumble like a waking monster. The waves, on a high and storm-backed spring tide, had reached halfway up the steep beach and were dumping so fiercely that I could feel the bass tremor of each one along my stomach as I lay reading. This unsettling phenomenon was to continue for most of the night. Following the weather pattern of the previous week, the gale abated to force four by morning. The storm had passed, and my little carnival tent had once more somehow survived unscathed. The sea remained tense and angry, showing no sign of abating; but in buoyant confident mood I decided to allow it a short calming period, then to launch at midday for a twenty-five mile hop around Bloody Foreland. It was to prove a rash and sorry mistake.

At midday the tide was fully out, so that launching required a massive man-hauling effort with the kayak and roller; down the steep shingle-banks, and a hundred yards across wet sand. At the sea's edge everything seemed to assume a grander scale. The wind-blown streaks of storm-stacked foam were eye-deep as I sat in the kayak; and the waves, piling up on the skerries that fringed the bay and breaking wildly for about a half-mile seaward, seemed much more daunting than they had from camp. For about half-an-hour I headed northwest into a force five wind, carefully timing and avoiding the most dangerous breaking waves, then I began to turn gradually northward. Heavy industrial-scale breakers could now be seen, fringing Bloody Foreland in a priestly collar of white. There was also a heavy break along the shingle-banks leading north, and at Altawinny Bay which would otherwise have offered a possible sanctuary or bolt hole. The only alternative seemed to be to head well out to sea; but there the water still seethed with the anger of the previous day's severe gale. It was irregular, broken and very large, and each towering wave-ridge seemed to exude a very persuasive death threat.

My escapes of recent days – from Port and from Aranmore – had perhaps been more in the mould of calculated risks than pure gambles. But the more I calculated and weighed up this particular risk, the more it now seemed like Russian roulette – and intuition told me that the bullet was in the very next chamber! The sea just wasn't ready to be ridden yet – especially round a place like Bloody Foreland. Suddenly I found myself in an area where the wave shoulders were reaching twenty feet, with faces steepening far too quickly and easily for my liking. It was a sure sign that I was over a shallow reef; the kind of place where massive breaks can rear up and collapse with virtually no warning and with lethal consequences. That was the final straw. I decided I had to get out. Spin around. Turn back. *And quick!*

Well, that was something I hadn't done on this trip, and only ever chose to do once before, for the simple reason that it's not necessarily an easy option. The kayak is at its most stable when being propelled forward, and the whole balance regime is repeatedly challenged as you attempt to spin the kayak around one-hundred-and-eighty degrees. Nervously, I let the crests lift me, shifting position gradually at the top of each, while the kayak had most of its length out of the water. At last, when I could feel the momentum of each wave forging from behind me I began to pick a careful route back, paddling like hell on the safe stretches, surfing through the venomous breaks on the inshore skerries and once more into Brinlack Bay.

It was a strange mixture of emotions I felt at that moment: relief and righteous caution, were soon replaced by frustration, dejection, even anger; and whether the anger was with myself or with the sea it was hard to know, and didn't matter. I glowered at Bloody Foreland and knew in that moment that it was named, not for the way the evening sun lights its rocks to a reddish hue, but because it's such a damned difficult place to get round in a kayak! The marks in the sand where I'd launched were still visible, and there followed the long haul back over the sand, up the steep shingle-bank to my original campsite (like re-winding a home video). I was suddenly glad that there was no-one watching, for the whole point of the exercise would have been far from obvious; it would have seemed to any observer that kayaking was more a strange sport of hauling over land than travelling over sea. I'd launched at one o'clock. It was now only a quarter past two, but already three cows and a goat had shat over my campsite in derision. I cleared the turf with my paddle, built a fire, and boiled a pot of tea as a consolation. Finally, what scunnered me more than anything else was that I'd no milk left for my tea, having poured out a half-pint on that very spot only an hour before!

For all its apparent anger and frenzy, the sea itself is patient and persistent in its message. Each wave is a unique expression of complex natural laws; of moon, of wind, of tide, of atmospheric pressure. Among its many voices, and many messages, the sea is constantly reminding us that it will not be conquered; that we can only work *with* it, not against it, and that even the land itself must eventually submit. Many people hear it; but very few listen, and fewer still take the trouble to understand. I had just demonstrated to myself that I still hadn't understood; that I was still able to make the wrong decisions, at the wrong times and for the wrong reasons. Decisions fuelled not by knowledge and assessment of the moods and patterns of the sea and its weather ways, but by haste and bravado. I'd launched in spite of my awareness of the sea's state; not because of it, and had almost suffered the consequences. I'd been given yet another chance to listen, and perhaps next time to understand.

~ ~ ~

That afternoon I wandered for miles along the fractile coastline of the Rosses, watching the waves break in upon those bays and islands, pacing the beaches, and wondering if anything other than myself had been washed up out of the west. Down in one small, curved, west-facing bay, formed of rounded cobbles banked steeply by storm-tides, and almost entirely enclosed by roughly built stone walls, an old man was bent double, pulling thick stems of seaweed from the strand line. Another younger man, perhaps his son, followed behind him making little piles of these stems. *Yaark! Keeeah-Keeeah!* Three herring gulls flapped and shrieked around behind, picking titbits from the debris, and oystercatchers piped in exaggerated alarm as the men moved slowly along the tight arc of the beach. It was a timeless, archaic scene. They were gathering sea-tangle rods, known as *slata-mara* in Irish; the thick, tough, four-foot stems of *laminaria* seaweed that are often washed up after a storm. Whenever he had an armful, the younger man would march up the steep beach to a low dyke of cobbles and arrange the sea-rods across it to dry in the sea air. Soon the little dyke was entirely hidden in tangle which hung down on both sides and looked like an elongated shaggy animal.

I had noticed these little dykes before, in small bays all along the Gaeltacht, from the Aran islands to Donegal, and also seen their Scottish counterparts on the Uist beaches of the Outer Hebrides. I knew what they were for, but had never before watched one being stacked. I knew also that this apparently ancient, insular activity was actually the unlikely first stage in what is in fact a modern industrial process of chemical engineering, an unlikely link between the Atlantic Gaeltacht and the world of international consumerism. The rods would be air-dried and bundled on the beaches, then driven to a small factory, perhaps in Connemara, where they would be burned down into an ash known as kelp. The kelp would be sold to the alginates industry in Scotland and England, and made into an inert thickening agent which is used in literally hundreds of everyday products, from paints and cosmetics to medicines, ice-cream and jelly. To this day there is no commercial synthetic substitute for good quality seaweed-derived alginates, nor any easy industrial means of harvesting the weed.

Suddenly the two men stopped working. Both sat down and lit pipes, avoiding looking in my direction and acting as guilty as schoolboys caught up an apple tree. I went over to introduce myself.

'By Jesus, we thought you might be a *gauger*, you know, from the social security. You had us worried there, right enough. We don't get many out walking in these parts.'

We had a good laugh over that. The son, about my own age, was an exact replica of the father. Both were dark-haired and swarthy – the type of Irishmen that popular culture claims to be descended from shipwrecked sailors of the Spanish Armada.

'Sure, this is just a wee sideline,' said the son. 'Not much money in it at all.'

'What else do you find to do round here?' I asked.

'Oh, fook all really.' But he went on to list so many 'wee sidelines' that I wondered how he ever found time to go and cash his social security cheques.

'At the low tide, specially in the winter, like, we'd be gatherin' the whelks. Or sometimes we'd be findin' pots, or ould buoys, washed up, like, an' sell them to the fishermen. Then there's the carrageen. It's like – a kind of thin seaweed. Da there dries it out and sells it in the town. And there's always the driftwood an' wreck. Some nice timber if you can get at it.'

He told me about one huge mahogany beam, measuring thirty feet with a two foot diameter, that he reckoned had come up on the Gulf Stream, and should be worth several hundred pounds if only he could figure out a way to get it off the rocks.

The old man claimed, as old men do, that it wasn't like the old days. He said that instead of relying on the storms to throw up seaweed they used to harvest it, standing in the water at low tide and hacking it off at the base. Good stretches of shore were carefully allotted and jealously guarded, as were the underwater kelp 'fields'. The types of seaweed that could be gathered at different times of the year, and where it could be dried were also carefully controlled; and there were about thirty different types that would be used for different purposes, from the black wracks of the middle and upper shores, to the red-weeds – including the tangle – which only showed themselves once a month at the lowest tides. He thought that the number of sea-rods being washed up had declined over recent years, and felt the lobster fishing might be to blame. Perhaps he was right too; if too many lobsters were being caught, their prey species, including urchins would increase, leading to increased grazing of the young seaweeds. Perhaps urchins themselves will be the next boom crop for the beachcombers of the Rosses.

They wished me luck on my way; I picked up a bundle of rods, climbed the beach and laid them on the dyke, and followed my footsteps back to the tent.

~ ~ ~

I slept in my canoe shirt, with my pink over-trousers as a salty, fishy pillow, and woke early for the RTE forecast of westerly force four to five. True to pattern the sea had at last lost its murderous edge and seemed more manageable. I had packed and breakfasted, and was steaming out of the bay by eight. It was by no means calm yet. A stiff breeze was in my face as I headed out through the wave layers and the persistent breaking swell. Again it proved necessary to go well clear of the bay before heading north, and to stay well abreast of several areas where swell was rising from far out to sea and breaking savagely on inshore reefs. On *Cnoc Fola* the cloud hung stolidly at half-mast, though it was blowing hard at its summit. Occasional showers passed over greying all, wetting all, and painting Malin with a dull palette.

At Bloody Foreland I was almost a mile out to sea, avoiding an area of heavy, travelling surf on the inshore shoals. On several salient points where fingers of land continued seaward as coastal reefs, the sea broke in stylish, arched, successive rushes – very impressive, but not to be played with or under-estimated. Some of these, reaching twenty feet before creaming forward in a fully committing run that would end in an abandonment of jagged destruction, required careful control and judgement, and confirmed that, in conditions such as those of the day before, Bloody Foreland would have been quite unmanageable. Just as I had thought, there was no possible landing point before Curran's Port, four miles beyond the Foreland itself.

Tidal streams, largely absent off most of the headlands of the west coast, begin to feature again from Bloody Foreland northwards, as the Atlantic swings round to fill the Irish Sea. But with the wind behind me, cancelling the slight effects of the adverse tide around the point, I reached Innis Bo Finne, or Inishbofin (yes, another one!), quickly and easily, having covered twelve miles in under three hours. This was more like it; the old rhythm was returning. The sun showed briefly here, although the wind picked up, and heavy cloud ranked itself above Tory Island before blowing over in a further succession of heavy grey showers during the afternoon. In the shallow Inishbofin Sound it became obvious that the tide was indeed against me, ebbing westward towards Foreland with the strength of springs, which made the island a good place to stop for a snack, and a preview of Malin's next hurdle.

From the island, Horn Head, eight miles across the bay, looked mean and prominent. The 'horn' in the name comes from an animal rather than a musical analogy; the headland is a great undercut promontory, with what looks like the nasal spike of a giant rhino grafted out to seaward. With the tide rapidly ebbing from Inishbofin Sound and threatening to leave me high and dry, I lost little time in striking out for the headland, the first of several along the mountain-fringed sea route to Malin Head. At first the crossing was sheltered, both from the wind, and from much of the swell which was being broken by the island line, from 'Bofin to Tory. But I knew that Horn Head itself would be fully exposed to the northwest wind, and would have a strong contra-tide rushing around it. This I began to feel as soon as I closed in under the head itself. Clapotis extending from the cliffs too far seaward to avoid, made for a choppy exciting inshore passage along a stunning seascape surely seen by very few people; great crumbling cliffs, largely undercut by storm and wave, with a maze of spouting blowholes and caves in banded multicoloured rock.

The hardest battle for the little kayak was with the tide flowing north off the east side of the Horn, which was opposed by the strong breeze. This required stiff paddling in some very rough and technical water, where every rest brought some loss of ground as the tide swept me back towards the Horn. A half-hour of hard work and concentration brought me safely through this short section and at last into an area where relatively calm water invited the inevitable decision on *where next?* The options were: to cross the next bay, the famous Sheep Haven to the Rosguill peninsula; to head further round the Horn to the fleshpots of Dunfanaghy village; or to pull out for a quick lunch. 'There is no love sincerer than the love of food,' wrote Shaw, and I had little hesitation in choosing the lunch option. I squeezed through a gap in the swell breaking off two shallow rocks, to reach a boulder beach in a small cove tucked beneath the six-hundred-foot cliffs of the Horn, and within sight of the tide race that seemed to protect the Haven like a ring-fence. Here I demolished a fittingly fine lunch of cheese, biscuits, Mars Bars, potato and veg hotpot, and two cups of hot chocolate. And as

I sat quietly rolling a cigarette, a lone seal cruised in, a sleek youngster, timidly sniffing the rudder of the kayak with a whiskery snout raised high out of the water.

The two hour crossing of Sheep Haven Bay to the Rosguill peninsula was protected by Horn Head until I reached the surf breaking on shallow reefs at its far shore. In a squall of visionless grey, like a TV breakdown, I squeezed the kayak behind the islet groups lying offshore from stunning Tranarossan Bay, and headed northeast, by way of Melmore Head to Ballyhoorisky Point. It was now just a matter of deciding how much farther to go before stopping for the night. The ideal would be somewhere perfectly sheltered from rain, wind and tide, with freshwater, a phonebox and a friendly little pub, all within striking distance of the ever more imminent Malin Head. Ballyhoorisky Point was far from ideal, open to the wind and swell, and predictably rough as a result. But it wasn't too difficult to dodge out of the tide race, surfing a few waves to find the shelter of the bay beyond. A final mile-and-a-half, brought me to Rinboy Point. There was no shortage of sandy sheltered bays there, but many were open to the swell, and therefore hammered by surf. The area of heavy break on shallow skerries looked fairly impenetrable, and a bit daunting at first; but from close in I found a safe channel, and beyond the surf barrier lay a peaceful, gently profiled landing beach. It was about five o'clock; time for a sand-dune camp and a well-earned rest.

~ ~ ~

Somewhere in the wilds of the Fanad peninsula, I found a little pub where the sight of a stranger, coming in from the dark night, was enough to stop the pool players in their tracks. A row of gloomy drinkers turned on their barstools, and the barman himself just stood and stared! There was such an oppressive hush that no-one spoke, neither to return my hello, nor even to converse among themselves. Four elderly men in grey jackets and caps, and two young lads in leather jackets, huddled at the cold bar, as if worried that the cosy peat fire at the other end of the room might melt their stony faces. They muttered angrily to each other in clipped northern accents; all poured bottled Guinness with shaky hands, and looked at my draught pint as though it was hemlock. The contrast with the bustling, warm, welcoming atmosphere of the pubs of Cork and Kerry could hardly have been more pronounced.

It wasn't exactly a scene from 'Cheers', but it was at least a warm place to sit, write up my log and take stock. I'd done thirty miles that day, cape-hopping from Fola to Fanad, a good day by any standards. The next day's forecast was no worse, putting Malin Head within reach. It would be a long haul, with Fanad Head to tackle first, but if I did manage Malin Head, and if the weather turned good, then I was probably within three days of reaching Larne, and the journey's end. It was a strange realisation. I'd felt a growing anxiety and determination to get done during recent weeks. But to be suddenly – in spite of recent difficulties – within striking distance was almost a cause of anxiety in itself.

CHAPTER 19

'Ducksqueezer'

> *... It was what I'd always lived for*
> *what I always will live for*
> *till they throw me*
> *into the trough of the waves*
> *I was used to dance over ...*

'Labrador', Kenneth White

One of the most ironic aspects of the division and apportionment of the Irish island is that Malin Head, the remotest extremity of what is sometimes referred to as Southern Ireland, is in fact Ireland's most northerly point. Reaching far into the streaming tides that forge back and forward between Ireland, Scotland and the open Atlantic, and exposed to all the weather systems of the north and west, Malin Head has earned – many times over – its starring role in the national shipping forecasts and coastal warnings. I tried to reassure myself that just because it was the site of a tidal gauge, a coastguard station and one of the most infamous weather stations in Europe, didn't necessarily mean that Malin Head was *always* subject to dramatic tide and weather conditions. But as I launched on that morning with a forecast of strong sea breezes for later in the day, I was ready for anything, in what might well turn out to be the hardest battle of the journey so far.

It seemed a long haul across Ballyhiernan Bay, but within the hour I found myself below the Fanad lighthouse point, with five miles already under the belt. Pulling east of Fanad, the great fjord of Lough Swilly opened to the south of me, cutting a gash almost thirty miles deep into the heart of Donegal. The morning light revealed hazy blue lines of mountains stretching towards the southern and eastern horizons, like sleeping camels in a purple desert-train. Fronted by bright sweeping beaches, the Donegal seaboard had a morning skyline the equal of any in the world. I twisted in my seat and looked back to the west. Tory Island was still visible, while the six-hundred-foot cliffs of Horn Head had begun to shrink back to a more manageable scale. It was a stunning coast; hundreds of miles of the loneliest, wildest land in Europe, arranged dramatically on the edge of the western ocean; the epitome of a mountain-fringed Atlantic seascape.

Five miles east across Lough Swilly, morning cloud still congregated around the spectacular sea-cliff and stacks of Dunaff Head. A further eight miles away to the northeast, like the outstretched head of a monster blowing froth at the nostrils, lay Malin Head itself. Several shower fronts overtook me on the long crossing, whipping up a fairly large and boisterous sea as the wind climbed to a respectable force five. This required extra vigilance in paddling, but was on the whole a fine problem to have, raising my speed to around six knots and bringing me so much sooner towards Malin Head. It made sense to tackle Malin as soon as possible, for the wind would continue to increase, and a strong wind in conjunction with the five knot tide race could quickly lead to unmanageable conditions.

Almost three hours later, as Malin Head loomed large, I began to feel a dramatic increase in the size of the sea. Some very large wave builds and breakers were in progress close under the Inishowen peninsula, and already I could see the line of a boisterous tide race spinning out west of Malin Head itself. Close inshore, within the relative shelter of Ineuran bay, I spied a lone lobster boat, brightly bobbing about its business, and headed towards it hoping for a cheerful word of reassurance. It was too choppy to get right alongside, but I shouted 'Hi' from a few yards away.

'Jesus! What a scare. Where the heck did you come from?'

'Back that way,' I shouted, pointing west over my shoulder with a thumb.

'Aye, but ... *where* from?' he persisted, looking over miles of open sea. 'How far have ye come in that thing?'

'Well, from Larne actually; the long way. About a thousand miles, I suppose.'

He considered, for a moment, whether I was taking the mickey; but decided to give me the benefit of the doubt.

'Ye'd have the arms for it, I'd say,' he pondered, carefully looping a coil of rope. 'And where would ye be heading for now?'

'Back to Larne.' I pointed eastward with the paddle, while his puzzled gaze anticipated my route past the race at Malin Head.

'Through *that!*' he barked, shaking his head. 'I hope you're fucking well insured!'

Hardly reassured by the brief exchange, I began to feel the nerves that always gripped my stomach before a major obstacle, and was aware of the blood pumping hard in the veins of my arms, strapped beneath the buoyancy aid. But it was midday, and I'd already done twenty miles in about five hours. I was as well warmed-up as I could possibly be for any confrontation that lay ahead. From close quarters I could see the race for what it was, a fierce ebb belting westward and roughened by the stiff westerly breeze; a set of mad-looking white-capped waves were running out to seaward at about five knots like a river rapid, much too fast to fight against. It seemed also that the race was still strengthening, but I wondered if it might just be possible to sneak a passage inshore of it. Among the stacks and pillars – the ancient gneisses and schists of Inishowen – the sea boiled as in a witches' wash-tub. I started off in superb form by taking a dead-end route into a *cul-de-sac* of frothing horror, backed by sheer cliffs, and had to backtrack sheepishly out to find an open sea route. The most daunting aspect of the inshore passage was the horrendous din of the main race itself, roaring by on my left, especially as I now had to creep along eastward on its very edge. It was like being too near the front of a railway platform when a long fast train surges past: safe where you are, but only feet away from certain destruction. Squeezed between the cliffs and the tide race was a narrow, marginal area of clapotis, where the swell was violently reflected by the cliffs, but it was an area where it was just possible to make some progress. Off minor outcrops the kayak would hit the strong flow of the adverse tide momentarily before regaining the eddy stream. The whole passage was quite terrifying, and etched a stream of consciousness on my memory, that I still recall in fevered moments today:

> *I watch the compass going SW, W, NW and eventually, but so slowly, round to NE, and I know that I'm getting somewhere. Glancing shoreward I see the cliffs moving by at snail pace. The roar of the race is deadly. If I stop paddling, or have to pull two or three strokes for support or balance – which I do frequently! – I lose ground. Don't look at the race – the noise alone is almost unnerving. Gradual progress though. Almost an hour gone. Fighting constantly. Almost over now. Just one final promontory – looks unusually rough but I can see quieter water beyond.*

It was then that I hit the true fray. Everything suddenly seemed to happen at breakneck speed – surfing over standing waves and dodging clapotis. Realising I was reacting quickly and accurately I began to feel quite exhilarated, until I glanced at the cliff and discovered that I wasn't moving at all! Then *Wham!* I almost lost it. I braced off a wave, surfed the next one and struggled to regain control. Almost before I could shake the water from my eyes I was being carried backwards into the main race. I 'changed gear' instantly, beefed up the paddling and began slowly to pull clear; then again *Wham!* A fast powerful wave knocked me clean over. Some defensive strokes and a sweeping brace brought me upright, but I had lost more ground and was caught in a tide pulling back at about four knots through broken water. Everything seemed to be in motion. I knew I couldn't keep this up for long, but there was no place where I could possibly pull out for a rest. I'd either have to get through it, or turn and follow the sucking rapids back to Ineuran Bay. So top gear it was; hard race-paddling; full power, incorporating adjustments and support strokes into forward motion, pulling hard through the full stroke and minimising the

air-time of the paddle. Sweat poured from my face; chest, arm and
stomach muscles strained and burned; but slowly and surely I
pulled clear of Malin Head. As the race relaxed its grip I felt all the
relief of a hedgehog which has just crossed a six-lane motorway at
rush hour. The battle was over, and the retreat from the Atlantic
had begun.

~ ~ ~

It was the first peaceful, windless, dry evening in the whole of the
past fortnight. Beside a small, flickering fire of driftwood and dead
heather I lay at the tent's mouth listening to the wine-dark sea
sucking in and out on the rattling shingle below. Darkness was slow
in coming; I watched the sunset, then the moonrise, and the regular
blinking rhythm of the lighthouse on the Inishtrahull islets.
Digesting a feed of brambles, which had exploded into ripeness and
hung plump, gourd-like and dog-snout black on all the hedgerows, I
was in no doubt that autumn had now fully replaced summer on the
Malin coast. Nor was I now in any doubt that I could complete my
journey. With Malin Head behind me, tomorrow would be my last
day in the Republic. The coast of county Antrim, and my final run
towards Larne, began just across the Lough Foyle border.

It was a particularly early dew that I had shaken from my
sleeping bag that morning. Sunrise through the Inishtrahull Sound
made me squint into the glare, but I was fairly zipping along. In two
hours I'd covered twelve miles, reaching the little town of Culdaff,
my last port of call in the Irish Republic, in time for breakfast. I
pulled out at Bunawee pier and walked yet another brambled lane
into Culdaff, hoping to find a grocery for some supplies. As fate
would have it all the stores were closed because of an important
local funeral. However, one hospitable shopkeeper took pity on me
and invited me behind the counter, into her house for coffee and
breakfast with the kids by the TV. Accepting a second cup of
coffee, I sat subdued by the unaccustomed warmth of a house, and
mesmerised by the antics of the 'Pink Panther', one of my favourite
cartoons.

'You're just like the Pink Panther, so ye are!' said one little girl, referring to my cerise WildWater suit, and causing hilarity in the back shop kitchen. 'You even *walk* like the Pink Panther.'

I suppose she was right; I had been walking oddly, trying to keep my salt-starched trousers and shorts from rubbing against the sores on my bum, which were becoming ever more painful; and it was, after all, an unusual outfit in which to be walking through town – a lesson I was very soon to learn.

As I retraced my panther steps down the main street, I became conscious of a terrible hush. All the shops were boarded, and not a single car stirred. Crowds of solemn black-clad mourners lined the pavements on both sides of the street, and I walked briskly down the centre, anxious to get clear of the town as soon as possible. Gradually I became aware of their glaring, muttering, even pointing angrily as I passed. Not just a stranger, but a stranger dressed in shocking *pink!* Running a gauntlet of Catholic black solemnity, I speeded my steps down the long main street until I reached midway. Suddenly I noticed some activity at the street's far end, and cringed, realising that the pall bearers and black cars were gathering in readiness to head this way! This was the kind of tide you just don't oppose. I wished there had been a manhole to climb down, as the real Pink Panther would probably have done, but had to make do with ducking away through the crowd to find the first available refuge. For the next ten minutes, as the coffin passed, followed by a swarm of angry-looking mourners, and a seemingly endless dirge of black cars, I huddled like a sore pink thumb in a phonebox with neither door nor windows, which at least half the procession must have known had been out of order for years. Give me Malin Head anytime, I thought as I made my clumsy pink way back to Bunawee pier.

~ ~ ~

And a LONG sort of SIGH seemed to RISE from us ALL,
As the WAVES hid the LAST bit of OULD DoneGAL.

John de Jean Frazer's poignant rhyme from *The Emigrant's Letter* made an appropriate paddling mantra, which quickly developed into a rap rhythm as I jogged the kayak along the final cliffs of the Inishowen peninsula, around craggy Inishowen Head and the last few coastal miles of the Irish Republic. Somewhere off the mouth of Lough Foyle I let the kayak drift, chewing a chocolate snack, with my mind in neutral as I crossed the invisible watery border into the 'six counties'. I could already see Benbane Head and Rathlin Island twenty-five miles away on the north Antrim coast, and 'ould Donegal' was receding quickly behind me. I had opened my final deck map, spreading before me the last of the coastal counties. Three miles south was the green coast of county Derry, and a little town which the map called Downhill. Surely it was all 'downhill' from here, I pondered, turning the bows eastward and heading for the Antrim town of Portrush.

It was a long, wide crossing, sometimes painful, sometimes peaceful, helped along by plenty of singing and shouting; and by the time I reached Portrush I had covered thirty-five sea miles since morning. Although only seven o'clock, it was beginning to turn dark and cloudy; and at the Portrush skerries the tide had turned strongly against me in the form of some offshore races. I had little choice but to head ashore to camp at the town itself. Within the space of a single day wild Ireland had slipped from my grasp. Portrush was a reminder that from now on civilisation would never be far away. The Antrim coast, although starkly beautiful in its own way, washed by strong tidal streams and occasionally subject to extremes of weather, is no Atlantic wilderness.

Portrush itself was a pretty holiday town, at what I imagined must be the tail end of its high season: a mecca of arcades and take-aways, hotels and guesthouses, souvenir shops and postcard parlours. I camped, quite illegally, on soft council-mown grass beside the promenade, adding an unusual element to the otherwise idyllic seaview advertised by the row of waterfront hotels. Streetlights illuminated my notepads. Kids on mountain bikes leapt over the inverted kayak, and dog-walkers passed by nodding

'How're ya', as Portrush defied the autumn chill and Malin breeze with an almost continental burst of late-evening vitality. At ten o'clock, when I would normally have been curling up in my sleeping bag with hot chocolate and a book, the arcades and cafés, cinemas, bingo halls and night clubs of Portrush were touting for trade with loud music and flashing neon lights. A fire engine whizzed by within feet of my tent in a valiant rush to quench a blaze at a waterfront guesthouse. As I had discovered many weeks before at Dunmore East, it's hard to be a hermit on the edge of an Irish holiday village in full flow.

I soon gave up trying to sleep, and went instead in search of a snack and a pint. After two months around the coast of the Republic, the red postboxes and British phone kiosks seemed quaintly foreign; and I soon realised that I had no British money. I tried to cash a cheque in a few pubs without success. Then I tried a desperate form of foreign exchange by gambling my Irish tenpence coins on the arcade machines. At one point I had almost won enough to buy a Guinness, but went on to lose the lot within five minutes. At last I found a baked potato shop which took Irish *punts*, and a friendly waitress, taking pity on me, gave me some spare bread and butter for my breakfast, and my change in sterling.

~ ~ ~

I launched *Sola* in a misty stillness through which the morning light filtered, blending the colours of sea and sky until the whole scene looked like the swirling water in which an aquarelle painter has rinsed his brushes. In this dreamy half-world I passed the Portrush skerries, dormant in the absence of both wind and tide, and the crumbling ruins of Dunluce Castle, perched high above me on the Antrim cliffs. In 1584, a strong brave Irishman hauled his comrades up that same sheer cliff-face in a basket so that 'Sorley Boy' MacDonnell could capture the castle from the occupying English garrison. Four years later Sorley Boy (*Somhairle Bhuidhe* – the 'yellow-haired summer warrior') became a wealthy man overnight when the Spanish treasure ship *Girona* was wrecked in a storm near the Giant's Causeway. He used the salvaged wealth to upgrade and modernise Dunluce Castle, but there was nothing he could do to halt the course of nature. In 1639 the cliff crumbled and the castle's kitchen crumbled with it, pitching a roomful of cooks and servants into the sea below. Sorley Boy himself survived, and today his descendants are still the earls of Antrim, and the remains of the castle, defying the inevitability of geological decay, still stand proudly on the slowly crumbling cliff at Dunluce.

Geologically, Antrim is a marvel; a crazy *mélange* of volcanic, sedimentary and metamorphic rocks, shaped and scraped by glaciation, continuously sanded and polished by the weather, and cleverly exhibited by the sea along an unrivalled coastal gallery. The Antrim coast is at once both a textbook illustration on the history of the earth, and one of the most visually spectacular shorelines in all Europe. The combinations of white limestone, black basalt and red sandstone are, in places, quite dazzling. I had only once before seen such a wealth of geology in a comparably small area. That was among the southern Inner Hebrides of Scotland, at islands such as Jura, Mull and Staffa, where although a similar range of features can be seen from the sea, they are not grouped or displayed with the compact artistry of Antrim.

The links between the Antrim coast and Scotland have always been strong, and the folk history and coastal mythology of times past have their modern counterparts in scientifically tested geological explanations. At Culdaff, for example, I had seen a large coastal boulder known as St Boden's Boat, in which the saint is supposed to have sailed miraculously from Scotland. Indeed, saints apart, the boulder may well have come from Scotland; not on the waves, but on the back of a glacier at the end of the last Ice Age. And then of course there's the Giant's Causeway, that stair-stepped spectacle of columnar basalt. Perhaps the only natural feature in all Ireland that is famous thoughout the world, it was explained in times past as a result of a feud between an Irish and a Scottish giant. In one version the Scottish giant, *Fionn Gall* (Fingal), had been taunting and baiting the Irish hero *Fionn MacCumhaill* (Finn McCool), but carefully avoiding an actual confrontation. He had been boasting about his fighting prowess, and what he would do to the Irish giant whenever he got a hold of him; but claimed that he didn't want to get his feet wet and risk catching a cold just to come to Ireland. So Fionn Mac Cumhaill piled up the distinctive basalt columns and called his bluff by building a causeway that stretched over to the Scottish coast; and the big-mouthed Scottish giant was no doubt quickly made to eat his words. Indeed the causeway does stretch all the way to Scotland, albeit beneath the present sea surface, and traces of the same bizarre column-shapes of rapidly cooled basalt can be seen on southwest Mull, and of course at the famous Fingal's Cave on the island of Staffa.

From my lunch stop amid the basalt columns of the Giant's Causeway I could clearly see the hills of Islay and Jura, and had I climbed the cliff I would have seen the Scottish mainland. Indeed from the Antrim coast to the Mull of Kintyre is a distance of only twelve sea miles. Until the relatively recent advent of a good road network in northern Ireland, much of coastal Antrim, Derry and Donegal had closer trade, and even family links with these southwesterly regions of Scotland than with much of the rest of Ireland. The very name 'Scotland' derives from the name of an Irish warrior-tribe, the *Scotti*, who invaded and won land in *Dalriada*, the kingdom across the water. Sea was the common highway. On the tidal straits of Malin bobbed the currachs of the Celtic saints; through these channels coursed the longboats of the Norse invaders; and over these horizons rowed the great birlinns and galleys of the Macdonalds of Clanranald, Lords of the Isles. Dr Johnson, never one to feign unnecessary enthusiasm, said that the Giant's Causeway was 'worth seeing, though not worth going to see'. I found that it was at least worth landing on in passing, but that its display of interlocking hexagonal basalt blocks, sweeping down to sea level, were more like an amphitheatre than the start of a causeway. If nothing else, it provided a fantastic assortment of sheltered, natural lunch tables and level stools on which to sit for a while in the sun. Later, looking back from the kayak as I bobbed restlessly off Benbane Head, the infamous Giant's Causeway, wonder of the natural world, resembled nothing more than an untidy pile of children's building blocks, although I'm not sure that I would like to say so to Mr Fionn MacCumhaill!

On the first flush of a strong spring tide I paddled round Benbane Head, watching the cliffs slide quickly by and the coast of Antrim reel off like a film loop in front of me. It was a bright afternoon. Not too hot, and with a westerly sea breeze at my back. The kayak, carrying only the final dregs of its initial payload of food, stove-fuel, maps and books, now bounced along like a young puppy in sunshine; and I was paddling with the accumulated fitness of almost ten weeks, and over a thousand miles, on the water. This was as fast and fluent as it was ever likely to get: small boat travel at its most arrogant and exhilarating, and I was loving every minute of it.

By early afternoon I was passing between Sheep Island and bright Ballintoy, which, in the sunshine, looked more like a Mediterranean fishing port than a breezy autumn village on the North Channel of the Irish Sea. The afternoon tide, now at full strength, ripped between a maze of reefs and made for a tricky inshore passage, full of whitewater and quick thinking. Legend has it that these reefs, parts of which are above water at low tide, are the last visible remains of an ancient city, razed to the ground by God, its inhabitants turned to stone for their evil practices. It is thought that perhaps this area was associated with serpent worship or some form of pagan snake cult, although no evidence or record of actual snakes has ever been found in Ireland. St Patrick, of course, is commonly credited with ridding Ireland of snakes in the fifth century, by dumping them all in the sea. But if there *never were* any snakes, then perhaps this was simply a picturesque way of recording the fact that Patrick's charismatic influence eventually helped Christianity to succeed the more naturalistic pagan belief systems, including snake cults, which the Celtic tribes may have collected on their long migrations through Europe.

Rathlin Island lies in the North Channel, between Scotland and Ireland, surrounded by some of the strongest tidal streams, overfalls and whirlpools known in either country. It was perhaps inevitable that the ownership of Rathlin would at some time have been in dispute between Ireland and Scotland. And it was desirable also that these two largely neighbourly countries should have found a peaceful means of establishing its ownership once and for all. One of the few major differences between Scotland and Ireland is that Scotland has snakes. In fact vipers, or adders, are actually relatively common on some of the Scottish islands quite close to the Irish coast. It was decided therefore that if a snake could be found on Rathlin then the island would be declared Scottish. The fact that, after a thorough search, no snakes were found, resulted in Rathlin being declared unambiguously Irish, and it remains so to this day. If only the territorial disputes of present day Ireland could be resolved so easily, I thought, as Rathlin's odd boomerang shape slid slowly over, dominating the northern horizon and gathering the tidewaters into an ever-decreasing bottleneck at Fair Head.

Fighting to keep the kayak straight and upright in the reflected waves of an even more constricted tidal channel, I squeezed from Larrybane Bay, between Carrick-a-rede Island and the mainland coast. Eighty feet above me, like a deliberately flimsy prop from an *Indiana Jones* film, a nightmarish bridge of rope and narrow boards, about sixty feet in span, was swinging in the wind: the famous Carrick-a-rede rope bridge. The sea surged through the wave-choked tideway, making it difficult for me to look up, but I saw a fisherman jog nimbly across to the mainland, using the oscillation of the swinging bridge to his advantage and, despite the lethal drop, holding on with only one hand. Two tourists then attempted to cross to the island, clutching stiffly onto both ropes and shuffling their feet forward on the boards. The whole bridge swung wildly in the breeze, and tried to adjust itself to the changing weight burden. At the centre point, where the flowing structure both wobbled and swung with maximum energy, the tourists paused, unsure whether to continue over to the island, or to turn tail back to their car. They looked down from their precarious perch at the thrashing sea far below, and I could imagine their horror as they pointed out my tiny bobbing shape among the waves; but the feeling was more than reciprocated: I would not have swapped places with them for the world.

~ ~ ~

Fair Head dominates the whole of the northeast coast, standing over six hundred feet above the waves. Its bottom half consists of broken rock, crumbling screes and the precarious paths of sheep and feral goats, much as any other section of high rocky coast. But its upper section is a soaring, spectacular, inaccessible cliff formed from rows of basalt columns. From the sea at its foot it looked like a massive church organ, and I found myself wondering whether the pugilistic Fionn MacCumhaill had secretly enjoyed singing hymns and oratorios between conquests. Had I been walking I might have stood and stared at the great organ-pipes for much longer, and would almost certainly have taken a photograph; but on a spring tide around Fair Head, with millions of salty gallons pouring between Rathlin and the mainland to refill the Irish Sea, nothing hangs about for long.

Very soon there was a southerly element in my easterly compass bearing. The tide dragged me on across Murlough Bay, where the ancient kings of Dalriada had their summer residence. It was the oldest example of an Irish holiday home I had ever heard of, and with its hospitable looking tree-fringed, cliff-backed beach, it looked as fine a site for it as any. After Torr Head the tide began to slacken, and the kayak's course went ever more southerly until, by the time I had reached Cushendun, the Irish Sea was full and resting, and the kayak was heading due south. It had been a long and satisfying day of beauty, variety and physical progress, and I pitched tent that evening on the beach, well outside the village, fully aware that it would most likely be the last camp of my journey.

~ ~ ~

There was frost on the ground on that September morning as I rolled the tent and prepared to set off on the final paddle, completing the great circle, returning to the Irish Sea ferryport of Larne. Past Cushendall, Garron Point, Carnlough and Glenarm I paddled, beneath the beautiful winding corniche route of the Antrim coast road. Although determined to enjoy every remaining mile of the journey, I found it increasingly difficult to focus my mind on the present. It flew off on wild tangents, reviewing and collating, collecting, reflecting and abstracting from the ten magical weeks of adventure which had brought me full circle around Ireland. In the seventy days since I left Larne the wind had averaged force five to six, and on fifteen days it had been gale force or above. But despite being land-bound during the strongest of the winds, and tent-bound with flu on the Great Blasket, I had been able to travel by kayak on six days in every seven, averaging twenty miles on each day. At a peak of fitness, with the help of some gentler weather and spring tides, I had covered over two hundred miles in the last five days alone, making a journey total of almost twelve hundred miles; and now the end was literally in sight. Over the phone I had learned that the Eyebank had raised over £30,000, and that Sola Lenses staff were running a sweepstake on my finish date and time.

In that same frame of mind I might have gone on to calculate how many paddle strokes had been taken; how much money each stroke had helped raise for the Eyebank; what weight of dehydrated stew, or how many Kit-Kat biscuits I'd consumed; or even how many gallons of stout had been needed to lubricate the travelling kayak. But a journey is so much more than the mundane sums of its statistical figures, I mused, as I pulled in at a tiny stone harbour only two miles north of Larne. The outcomes of travel and adventure, or of a voyage, cannot be calculated in the same terms as Gross National Product or a quarterly VAT return. They require an entirely different currency. Distances, times, costs and quantities may be interesting for certain purposes, but they fade into irrelevance in the longer term. Nor are first ascents, fastest descents or longest marathons necessarily all they are flagged up to be. There is a much fuller picture to be painted. It is a picture of extended immersion in, and movement through the natural world; appreciating and accepting the extremes of terror and peace, beauty and balance within that world. A basic meal taken when desperately hungry; a warm dry sleep at the end of a chilling sodden sea-battle; a chance meeting or adventure in a magical setting, are each worth far more than any first or fastest claim. And often the lasting values of a journey only become apparent much later. I was already aware that my Irish journey had been a chain of paradoxes; a blend of many opposites. I had been able to reaffirm my own need for creative solitude; and yet had become aware, perhaps more than ever before, of the timeless virtue of genuine hospitality and friendships, offered unconditionally and accepted without embarrassment. The basic realities of places, people and events encountered or experienced during the course of the journey had at times been overlaid with mythological dimensions in a way that I had come to accept as normal. Perhaps at certain times within a life or a journey, myth and reality are not the opposite poles which we more often than not assume them to be. Towards the end of the journey I had been touched with a growing sense of completeness. An idea, for which much had been sacrificed, and towards which so many people had contributed in so many ways, had been successfully carried out. Some of that success was due to training, preparation and ongoing commitment, but much of it had of course been due to that most mysterious and elusive of natural resources, luck.

The little stone harbour was thickly full of nature's flotsam; leathery, dried-up aurelia jellyfish, creatures entirely at the mercy of wind and tide, whose luck had run out. When I thought of the flotsam element in my own journey: of the illusory nature of any real control; of the potential disasters which didn't happen; and of the many people and events which seemed to find their own places and purposes in the journey, I knew that a strong tide of assistance had flowed favourably right through it. If I was a piece of flotsam, then I was a piece of *lucky* flotsam. My hand, rummaging in my lifejacket pocket for a last piece of chocolate, suddenly felt a small, metallic disc. It didn't feel like a coin, and in curiosity I fished out the lucky silver angel, pressed on me by Joe 'the martyr' before I'd reached Cork city. Perhaps in some unknown ways its magic had also helped.

'So you made it then, by Jesus! Sure, and I knew you would, so I did. Good on ye now, that fairly makes my day!' Hammy Robertson, skipper of the little Island Magee ferry which uses the same Larne slipway as I had launched from at the start of my Irish journey, shook my hand much more firmly than he had done on my departure ten weeks previously.

'*Jees!* Look at the arms on ye now; but there was days I was fair worried for ye, I'll tell ye!' A fanatical boatman and model-boat builder himself, he had once held the distinction of crossing the Irish Sea in the smallest boat ever. Nowadays he is master of a much shorter crossing, in a much larger boat. His Island Magee ferry crosses back and fore, many times a day, most days of most weeks in the year, like a little orange shuttle weaving a pattern of salt and wave onto a constantly changing coastal tapestry.

The unmistakable figure of Brian Fryer-Kelsey, the Irish giant who had helped haul me ashore three weeks before at Dunquin, came striding across the dockside and, unworried about getting sea-salt stains on his smart suit, locked me in a great bear-hug. The personification of Irish hospitality, he had been determined to be there to welcome me ashore.

'Welcome back, and congratulations!' he bellowed, with all the energy I remembered from our chance meeting in county Kerry. 'It seems like a long time ago!'

'It certainly does! Great to see you, Brian,' I returned, glancing a little anxiously at the two uniformed Harbour Police hovering right behind him.

'Oh yes,' said Brian, understating his obvious efforts to

smooth my path in advance. 'These two gentlemen have agreed to look after your boat; I'm making you an honorary member of the Donegal Ducksqueezers Canoe Club, and I thought you and I should go into Belfast to celebrate!'

After a couple of delicious dark pints at Belfast's inimitable Crown Bar – the beer drinkers equivalent of a cathedral, right down to the stained-glass windows and hushed confessional snugs – I reminded Brian that I had to get a train to Dublin for a final reception with my sponsors.

'Right you are,' he said, 'wait here. There's a fella over there who might like to help.' Within minutes, Brian had fought his way back to the bar, accosted the Controller of Railways for Northern Ireland, who had been in the Scouts with him, and was back with a return ticket to Dublin, stamped *Courtesy of British Rail. FIRST CLASS*.

The southbound train was rattling through Lisburn before I discovered that, in fact, there were no First Class carriages on it at all. It had stopped briefly at Portadown before I could ease the painful sores on my bottom down onto the padded seats. But I think it was not until the train was running alongside Dundalk Bay, and I was watching the long crescent-shaped waves crowding in towards the Irish shore, bright, timeless and undiminished, that I remembered that *Sola* was under lock and key at Larne harbour.

For a moment it seemed I was back down among the fingers of those waves, crouching on the damp sand where they pooled around my feet, inhaling the salt breaths of them. In the distance an old man in dark clothes was walking by the water's edge, hands behind his back, watching the sand at his feet. He bent down, collected a stick and threw it far into the sea. His dog leapt over the lower waves, breasted into the larger ones, fixed his jaws on to the stick and returned triumphant, shaking a bright arc of spray from his coat. Slowly the old man bent down, picked up the stick and threw it once more. It spiralled through the air, a metaphor for time itself.

The evening was dwindling softly towards a blue darkness,

while off Ireland's other coast, I knew the sun would be tipping embers over a damp horizon. I seemed to hear again the measured regular huffing of wave after wave on to the shore, but no; as the train at last pulled away from Dundalk Bay I realised that the dominant rhythms were no longer those of wave or paddle, but those of the train itself, and I finally accepted that my kayak journey round Ireland was over.

Expedition Information

The following details are given as a pool of reference material for readers interested in specific sponsorship, charitable or technical aspects of the journey:

~ The Round Ireland Solo Kayak Expedition set off on 1 July 1990 from the port of Larne on the Antrim coast, on a journey that was to measure approximately 1200 miles and take ten weeks to complete.

~ The main expedition sponsors, Sola Lenses of Wexford, Ireland, provided the financial support, publicity and general friendly back-up which helped to make the expedition such a success.

~ One of the aims of the expedition was to provide a fundraising and publicity generating opportunity for the recently established national optical charity Eyebank Ireland – set up in 1990 to collect, test and supply corneas for transplants throughout the whole of Ireland, north and south – for which it helped raise over £30,000.

~ The kayak used was an Alaskean Expedition sea kayak by McNulty Seaglass of South Shields, England. It measures eighteen feet (length) by twenty-three inches (beam) and weighs thirty-four kilogrammes unladen. Features included waterproof storage hatches fore and aft, a foot-operated rudder and bilge pump, and a deck-mounted Suunto K158 compass.

~ Safety equipment carried included a VHF hand-held radio: Sea Lab SL9 00G for coastguard forecasts and emergency contact, and an assortment of marine distress flares.

~ The tent used was a Vango Force 10 Featherweight MK1 (1.45kg).

~ All photos were taken using a Ricoh KR-10 Super with Tokina 28-85mm zoom and polarising filter, and a Minolta Weathermatic 35DL, with Fujichrome 100 and Kodachrome 64 films.

Also by Brian Wilson

BLAZING PADDLES

A Scottish Coastal Odyssey

The riveting tale of Brian Wilson's first solo kayak voyage, 1,800 miles around the fearsome sea passages, grand cliffscapes and Hebridean islands of Scotland. Brim-full with whirlpools and whales, nautical disasters, haunted bothies and the exploits of Celtic saints, Viking raiders and mermaids. This colourfully written account will appeal to all lovers of the coast.

'As good a maritime saga as has come out of the Scottish seas'
SCOTSMAN

'A quite exceptionally gifted writer ... This is an outstanding travel book'
JERSEY EVENING POST

'... One of the classic pieces of canoe writing. This is without doubt the best sea canoeing travel book I have ever read'
CANOEIST Magazine

BLAZING PADDLES is published by The Wildland Press, £7.99stg pb
ISBN 0 9532768 0 5

ORDER FORM

Please supply ..... Copies of BLAZING PADDLES @ £7.99stg each + £1.00 p & p each
I enclose cheque/PO for the full amount, £.............

Name _____

Address _____

_____

Telephone _____

Please send orders to: The Wildland Press,
Achlunachan, Inverbroom, Ullapool, Ross-shire, IV23 2SA, Scotland.